CW01095144

Cutting Point

CHRISTER HOLMGREN

CUTTING POINT

*Solving the Jack the Ripper and the
Thames Torso Murders*

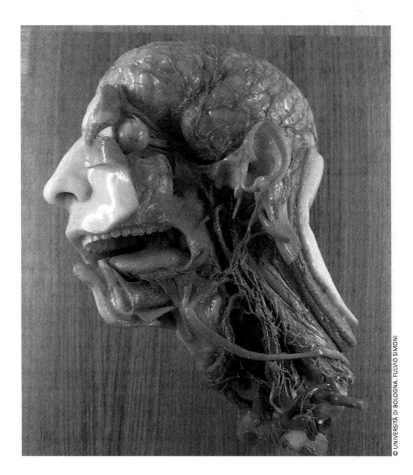

EDITOR:
Rickard Berghorn
Author, literary historian, publisher, and
student of history of science
and ideas.

COVER:
Nicolas Krizan
Swedish illustrator, cartoonist, book designer, and author.
The back cover photo is on the anatomical model
La Venerina, same picture as on p. 135.
Photo © Università di Bologna.
Fulvio Simoni.

Timaios Press, Sweden
www.timaiospress.com
Imprint of Aleph Bokförlag

This is the first edition (hardcover) from Timaios Press, February 2021
The second edition (paperback), February 2021

ISBN 978-91-87611-37-7

CONTENTS

La Venerina, an example of an Anatomical Venus, a popular wax model used in museums for purposes of education in Victorian times. The model, on display at Palazzo Poggi in Bologna, Italy, was sculpted by Clemente Susini around 1870. Photo courtesy of Sistema Museale di Ateneo—Museo di Palazzo Poggi. © Università di Bologna. Fulvio Simoni.

Introduction

The East End carman Charles Allen Lechmere was not only Jack the Ripper but also the dismemberment murderer who became known as the Thames Torso killer. That is what this book sets out to establish.

It is in many ways an easy task, because there is ample evidence to support the suggestion. There always has been, although it has been curiously overlooked by most people researching the two murder series.

From another angle, the task of making the identification of Charles Lechmere as the combined Ripper and Torso killer is a truly daunting and difficult one. This is because there was always going to be a massive resistance toward any suggestion claiming to present solutions to these old cases. Much as so-called Ripperology has always been as skilled when it comes to taking apart suspect theories as the Torso killer was with his bodies, it has had little or no training when it comes to acknowledging good, solid theories. This is not strange in any way; in the Ripper case, more than three hundred suspects have been put forward, some better than others, many ridiculous—but there has never really been any factually strong contender.

A common conception among many sober students of the case is that there have only ever been bad and slightly less bad suspects. It is a view I subscribed to myself for more than thirty years as a student of the Ripper case. Once I was pointed to Charles Lechmere and started delving into the material concerning him, that all changed. In my view, he is the one suspect who changes the Ripper hunt from parlor game to police investigation.

Just as there has been a steady growing pile of suspects over the years, we have also seen a mountain of Ripper books taking shape. It goes without saying that the quality of the literature has varied drastically. What cannot be denied is that numerous excellent and deep-probing books have been written. The amount of detail they go into is often quite staggering, and I find I am neither able nor inclined to compete with them. Instead, my aim is to be as short and succinct as possible, and to that end I will leave out a whole array of topics that are normally discussed in great depth in the Ripper literature. One example would be the Goulston Street graffito. It does not in any way impact the theory I am going to put forward, and so I find it would only detract from the clarity and simplicity I strive for. Similarly, I will not in detail bring up all the murders that may or may not be involved in the two series, although I will touch very briefly on a number of the ones I leave out.

Another matter that I will touch upon only marginally is the biographical material linked to Charles Lechmere and his family. One reason for this is that I am simply not the best source for presenting it. I have over the years worked a great deal together with Edward Stow, and he is the true go-to source for anybody who wants to know anything about the biography of the East End carman. Edward is also the reason that I have taken an interest in Charles Lechmere at all. Edward Stow and I first met in London back in 2011, and he generously shared his views on the murders with me. After that, we did a fundraiser for the Stairway to Heaven foundation based on the case, and in 2014 we worked together on the Blink Film documentary *The Missing Evidence—Jack the Ripper*, in which a Queens counsel stated that there is a prima facie case against Charles Lechmere, suggesting that he was the killer. Much of what is known today about Charles Lechmere has been unearthed by Edward Stow, and vital parts of this book lean against his research.

Having made it clear that I will leave out a lot of the material that is traditionally presented in Ripper books, I should add that I will instead present material that is normally not included. The simple reason for this is that the material in question is essential to make my case. Consequently, the various aspects of the two cases of serial murder I do bring up should fill a good many pages. Those interested in laying their hands on a practical and comprehensive book about how the three topics—Charles Lechmere, the Ripper murders, and the Thames Torso murders—are linked to one another should hopefully be in for an interesting read.

The case of Charles Lechmere, and that case only, allows for a truly practical approach. We can actually take part in what he did and said on the morning of the Polly Nichols murder on the 31st of August, 1888, in much detail. It is a case that is largely built on chronological comparisons, measuring distances, blood flow timings, and so on—all the things a sound investigation should build on, and all the things that no other hitherto named suspect allows for checking.

Otherwise, it would be squandering the only truly good case there ever was against anybody in these two Victorian murder series.

This is not the typical suspect book, with little or no evidence and a lot of footnotes at the end. The reason is simple: Charles Lechmere is not a suspect like any other suspect. He does not offer the kind of material that is normally used to elevate somebody to a suspect in the Ripper case. He had no police

A carman based at the Broad Street Station. The cart would much resemble the kind of cart Charles Lechmere drove. They were normally manned by two carmen.

record that we are aware of. There is no record of him having been a violent man. There is nothing to tell us that he threatened to do harm to others. He is not known to have been part of any organization that planned to throw Britain into anarchy. We have no evidence that he was treated for any venereal disease. These are the kind of things that lie behind why a huge amount of men have been awarded suspect status in the case.

In police investigations, this is the group of people who are sought after when no viable suspect with a factual link to a series of violent murders can be identified. It is a group of people who substitute for the ones who are recorded as being physically connected to the murder series, if none of the latter are likely to have been part of the murders themselves.

It is only when the police have satisfied themselves that those who were at or in close vicinity to the murder sites, or who had personal relations to the victims, are not likely to have been their culprit that they move on to searching for people who have antecedents that may turn them into suspects.

Charles Lechmere instead belongs to the first group of people whom the police need to look at, those who actually have a factual link to the crime that is being investigated. His suspect status is not built upon what he may have done or planned or claimed. It is instead built on what he actually did and said, the paths he chose, the timings involved, and so on.

With the carman, the investigation into those we can place at a Ripper crime site can be reopened, and we find ourselves with a prime suspect who seems to have been inexplicably overlooked. Once we scrutinize the way the Victorians looked at crime and criminals, however, an explanation for why Lechmere was never investigated in depth emerges.

Edward Stow was not the first one to suggest Charles Lechmere as the killer. Derek Osborne and Michael Connor threw the suggestion forward in the early stages of the twenty-first century. Sadly, they found themselves in the unrewarding situation of dealing with a man who could not be found in the records because he had called himself Charles Cross back in 1888. It took more than a hundred years to find out his real name, and it is only thereafter that the research concerning him has produced what I firmly believe is and will remain the prime suspect. In Lechmere's case, the hunt is still very much on; more material surrounding him may very well surface in the near future, as it has for the past decade.

When it comes to the Thames Torso murders, there has always been another go-to source, namely Debra Arif. Her insights into the case have been instrumental for my understanding of it. It is a well-known fact that anybody who has a genuine interest in the criminology of late Victorian London never goes to bed without praying for a book on the subject by her hand.

Until that happens, however, I must make do on my own. Personally, I am quite satisfied that I have the solution to Victorian London's two great murder mysteries. It is in no way a complex or far-fetched solution. Once Charles Lechmere became accessible for research purposes, the case against him proved to be very simple, very obvious, and totally straightforward. Whether the readers of this book will agree is of course another matter. Accordingly, the following pages are offered for those with a genuine interest in the history of Jack the Ripper and the Thames Torso killer to decide for themselves how strong the case against the East End carman is.

—CHRISTER HOLMGREN
Helsingborg, October 2020

SETTING THE STAGE

The Victorian View of Crime and Criminals

1888. The year of the Ripper and the autumn of terror. The suggested death toll of five victims in ten weeks is considered remarkable, but there were others around in this period of time who were also prolific killers. Take Thomas de Grey, for example, the sixth Baron Walsingham, a politician and an entomologist. The day before the first canonical Ripper victim died in Whitechapel, Walsingham managed to kill 1070 grouse between 5:12 A.M. and 6:45 P.M., during a hunt on Blubberhouses Moore in Yorkshire.

Contrary to the Ripper deeds, Walsingham's effort was regarded as a true accomplishment and he was applauded by his fellow Victorians. He even managed to shoot a further fourteen grouse on his walk home from the hunt.

We have come a long way from those days. Today, the carnage Baron Walsingham engaged in would have been booed by an outraged public. The times change and new values replace old ones, in the same way new scientific findings and achievements replace old beliefs.

In December of 1888, Henry Morton Stanley's expedition in search for David Livingstone reached Fort Bodo in East Africa. Back then, it was considered a remarkable thing and an example of heroism. Today, it reeks of stale colonialism. Three months prior to Stanley's exploits, Queen Victoria had granted William MacKinnon's British East Africa Company political and economical rights. The rights of the indigenous East Africans were never considered in the context.

1888 was a year of development optimism: the Victorians were constantly extending the boundaries of their empire, while people were living in absolute squalor a mere five miles from Buckingham Palace. Abroad, British troops were battling the Tibetans in the Sikkim region of India. At home, they had already racked up a number of subdued and killed protesting Eastenders in Trafalgar Square.

In July, the month preceding the first canonical Ripper murder, 200 workers, most of them teenage girls, went on strike following the dismissal of three of their colleagues from the Bryant and May match factory, led on by an article revealing the working conditions there. As a result of the strike, the workers formed a union on the 27th of July.

Four months later, a New York jeweler by the name of William Bundy would patent the first timecard clock.

As the year drew to its close, a depressed Vincent Van Gogh cut off one of his ears in Arles. It happened in the same month of December that also saw the completion of the first building stage of the Edinburgh Museum of Science and Art. This was a time when the term science encompassed a good many things that we have long since found out are completely unscientific. Some decades earlier, a monkey head and torso sewn onto a fishtail caused sensation when it was presented as a Fiji mermaid, and two and a half decades afterwards a concoction of a human skull, an orangutan jawbone, and some chimpanzee teeth were passed off and hailed as «the Piltdown man,» the missing link between humans and apes, a belief that was not dispelled until in the 1940s.

It was a time of newfound insights and bottomless ignorance, a time of great prosperity and utter poverty, a time of science and sideshows. And in the sideshow galleries, the wax figures of the body snatchers Burke and Hare were soon to be replaced by effigies of the victims of the even more sinister figure of Jack the Ripper. To the Victorians, this killer was a ghoul, a demon, an unholy merging of beast and man, much like the horrifying conflation of Dr. Jekyll and Mr. Hyde that had people fainting in the Lyceum Theatre of London in the autumn of 1888.

It was not a society well suited to track down a typical sexual serial killer. In actual fact, even today that kind of task can prove extremely difficult, although we now know indefinitely more about the psychology of these elusive creatures. It is always the case that before we can draw upon this superior knowledge and insight of our modern world, we must apply it to the correct suspect. If we fail to do so, we will not come up with the identification we are seeking.

This leads us to the East End carman Charles Allen Lechmere. If he is the solution to the riddle of Jack the Ripper, then why is it that this solution has taken so long to surface? The question is justified: after all, not only was there a huge police investigation back in 1888 and the following years, but there have also been innumerable people researching the case ever since. So why was the carman not revealed for what he did a long time ago, if he so obviously was the perpetrator?

Writing down this question here in Helsingborg, Sweden, I think a lot about how the Swedish investigation into the murder of prime minister Olof Palme back in 1986 has recently been cancelled after decades of hard work by hundreds of devoted detectives. The prosecutor general has disclosed the name of the man he reasons must have been the killer, and lo and behold: a case that in many ways mirrors the case I make against Charles Lechmere has been presented.

It turns out that a man who injected himself into the investigation as a witness and who seemingly lied about his participation in what took place on the murder night is now officially accepted as the killer of Olof Palme.

It was quite easy from the outset to see that his testimony did not jibe with what the other witnesses said, and the police had all the time in the world to check him out; but instead they wrote him off, leaving him by and large totally uninvestigated.

The cost of the Palme police investigation rose to around 50 million British pounds over the years; hundreds and hundreds of books were written, suggesting suspect after suspect—and nothing came from it. And all the while, the obvious solution was there for anybody to see.

The police were definitely at fault for not investigating each and every person they knew had been at the murder site. That must always be priority one and taken care of before more lofty speculations about foreign organizations and political assassins are brought to the table. The failure to perform this the most basic of duties was seemingly what caused the total fiasco we Swedes were left with.

But what about those who took it upon themselves to do the job the police failed to manage properly? The amateur sleuths, the criminologists, the historians? Why did it take thirty years plus for them to reach the goal, although there was always such an obvious suspect right in front of them?

Did it have something to do with the enormity of the material involved?

Did prejudiced thinking play a role?

Did many of the researchers simply—but wrongly—assume that the police had already checked out all the people from the murder site in depth?

Or were there other parameters involved in the collective failure?

Regardless of what applies here, it is totally absorbing for me, as a proponent of Charles Lechmere being the combined Ripper and Thames Torso killer, to see how even the simplest of solutions can be overlooked by the police as well as by hordes of researchers of the case. To me, it totally deflates the traditional stance among many researchers of the Victorian double-drama. It is a stance claiming that such an old case cannot be solved today, since a huge police effort back then has subsequently been accompanied by generations of dedicated students of the case, amateurs and professionals alike. It is reasoned that this should guarantee that all angles have been covered.

The plain truth is that even apparently simple solutions may well be over-

The Italian mutilator and eviscerator Vincenz Verzeni.

looked. It saddens me that it took an incompetent investigation of the Swedish police into the Palme murder in combination with endless efforts on behalf of Swedish researchers to prove that point. Wouldn't it be appropriate, then, if a Swedish author could—at least to a degree—contribute to the clearing up of the two greatest serial murder cases of Victorian London?

In order to try and fulfill that task, I am going to begin by pointing out two factors that I believe have been instrumental in the failure to couple and solve the Ripper and Thames Torso cases. The first one is how Charles Lechmere hid the name he was registered by from the world, resulting in how he could not be effectively researched until well into our own century. For the longest time and to no avail, researchers looked for «Charles Cross» in the registers. However, when the name Lechmere was revealed as his real, official name, the hunt was on.

The second and perhaps more important factor has to do with how the

Victorians looked upon crime and criminals. Not least interesting is their view of the criminal psyche and how it is expressed in criminals. This in its turn means that we will not yet venture out onto the London streets and start the search for our killer.

We will get there soon enough, but before we do so, we need to take a long hard look at criminal anthropology, which was the order of the day back in 1888. It was a «science» that is very hard for many people to comprehend today. However, once we realize that we have to travel more than 130 years back in time to reach the days of the Ripper scare, the gap between criminal anthropology and our own understanding of the underlying mechanisms of crime becomes easier to understand.

When presenting what criminal anthropology was, a useful starting point is to take a look at another case of multiple murder, but from 1872. It is the case of the twenty-two-year-old Italian killer Vincenz Verzeni. In some ways, he is a useful parallel to the Ripper. He was jailed in January of 1872 in Lombardy, accused and—correctly—convicted of two cases of murder and four cases of attempted murder.

In both of the murder cases the victims, one of them a girl of fourteen years and the other a woman of twice that age, were suffocated. In both cases, the abdomens had been sliced open. In the case of the girl, the intestines and genitalia had been cut from the body, and a piece of the right calf was found some distance from it. Verzeni had cut it out so that he could later cook and consume it, but forgot to bring it with himself as he left the murder site. In the other case, the victim was left at the murder scene with her abdomen cut open and the intestines protruding from the wound.

Verzeni had no problem attracting women, and he had had a couple of girlfriends at the time of the murders. When associating with these girlfriends, however, he felt nothing of the excitement he experienced when attacking his victims. Once he was caught, he professed to feeling absolutely no remorse for what he had done.

The main reason for why Verzeni is of interest to students of the Ripper case lies in the descriptions of himself and his relatives that can be found in the book *Psychopathia Sexualis* (1886), written by the German psychiatrist Richard Krafft-Ebing:

> Cranium of more than average size, but asymmetrical. The right frontal bone narrower and lower than the left, the right frontal prominence being less developed, and the right ear smaller than the left (by 1 centimeter in length and 3 centimeters in breadth); both ears defective in

the interior half of the helix; the right temporal artery somewhat athe-
romatous. Bull-necked; enormous development of the cheek bone
and inferior jaw bone; penis greatly developed. Frenulum missing;
slight divergent alternating strabismus (insufficiency of the internal
rectus muscle, and myopia). Lombroso concluded from these signs
of degeneration, that there was a congenital arrest of development
of the right frontal bone. As seemed probable, Verzeni had a bad an-
cestry—two uncles were cretins; a third, microcephalic, fearless, one
testicle missing, the other anthropic. The father showed traces of pellagrous degeneration, and had an attack of pellagrous hypochondria.
A cousin suffered from cerebral hyperemia; another was a confirmed
thief.

Verzenis family was bigoted and low-minded. He himself had ordinary intelligence; knew how to defend himself well; sought to prove
an alibi and cast suspicion on others. There was nothing in his past
that pointed to mental disease, but his character was peculiar. He was
silent and inclined to be solitary. In prison he was cynical. He mastur-
bated, and made every effort to gain sight of women.

Here we can clearly see how the contemporary scientific world reasoned that
criminality often could be traced back to a genetic heritage that was lacking
in one way or another, and how a confirmation of a criminal disposition was
expected to be present in observable physical traits.

The «Lombroso» Krafft-Ebing speaks of in his text on Vincenz Verzeni is
Cesare Lombroso (1835–1909), an Italian physician and professor who is
traditionally regarded as the father of criminal anthropology. Criminal anthropology was the belief that criminality had its cause in biological properties within the criminals, and that these properties had been inherited on
either degenerative or atavistic grounds. Atavism in its turn speaks of how
properties that have been present within our ancestors, perhaps even in primitive stages of humanity, suddenly reemerge many generations later. Generally speaking, such properties could either be good or bad. But the Victorians
worked from the assumption that humanity will always move along a line
of constant positive evolution, meaning that bad properties will always give
way to good ones. Reemerging properties from long-lost times were therefore always likely to be bad ones in the Victorian mind. In other words, Vincenz Verzeni was an example of a degenerated person, revisiting the Victorian
world as the result of a whim of nature.

Cesare Lombroso and his theories about a link between physiognomy and

Cesare Lombroso, the father of criminal anthropology.

inner properties is a direct offshoot of the early nineteenth-century thought of the German physician Franz Joseph Gall, also known as the father of phrenology. The irony of this is that Lombroso was actually of Jewish descent. This means that he unwittingly contributed to legitimize the thoughts behind the Holocaust of World War II.

Today, Lombroso's theories are looked upon as unscientific nonsense, but during the closing decades of the nineteenth century he exerted a tremendous influence on Europe.

ENGLAND—AN EXCEPTION TO THE RULE?

It is oftentimes argued that England was an exception to the rule; here, phrenology and criminal anthropology were not given any leeway, according to many. England, it is said, was the one European country where physical deviations were not regarded as signs of the disposition of the soul.

But is this picture correct?

In 1869, the *British Journal of Mental Science* printed an article titled «The Hereditary Nature of Crime,» signed James Bruce Thompson. Thompson was a physician who, together with his colleagues David Nicolson and Henry Maudsley, worked from the idea that there was a «criminal type,» carrying a number of physiological as well as psychological deficiencies.

Thompson, Nicolson, and Maudsley preceded Cesare Lombroso, who did not formulate his theories until the mid-1870s.

At a later stage, the British physician and psychiatrist Havelock Ellis would in his book *The Criminal* (1890) lament that criminal anthropology had not got much of a hold in England. He thought that England had gotten left behind as Lombroso's research was acclaimed in the rest of Europe, and he thought that the pioneering work of Nicolson, Maudsley, and Thompson had not been awarded the recognition it deserved. Ellis went as far as to express a belief that England was lagging severely behind the civilized world.

A number of prison physicians and psychiatrists provided Ellis with their own findings from the world of criminal anthropology, but Ellis himself nevertheless expressed a disbelief about how many professionals he spoke to seemed to be totally unaware of the discipline.

The belief of Havelock Ellis that England was unaware of criminal anthropology at the beginning of the 1890s was not fully correct; instead, there was a situation where the British medical science and psychiatry thought that Lombroso's teachings frequently offered too blunt an instrument. There was a realization and acceptance that the practical experience offered by individual doctors and psychiatrists often were at odds with the generalized theoretical superstructure Lombroso offered. In many camps of the time, criminal anthropology was simply regarded as too simple or too incomplete an answer for what was a world of complex connections.

The built-in perils of the simplified perspective offered by criminal anthropology eventually caused a change of mind for Henry Maudsley. In 1889, he wrote that the time had come to abandon empty generalizations in favor of a method grounded on the many differences present in different cases involving criminals, and in the 1895 edition of his book *The Pathology of Mind* he wrote:

> It is easy to make too much of criminal instincts or dispositions and tempting to be content with them as a sufficient explanation of crime. But no criminal is really explicable except by an exact study of his circumstances as well as his nature; when there is a struggle in him between social habits and savage instincts it will depend much on the surroundings which shall gain and keep the upper hand.

Here, Maudsley very clearly distances himself from his earlier convictions. Back in 1874, he had written in his *Responsibility in Mental Disease:* «Multitudes of individuals come into this world weighed with a destiny against which they have neither the will, nor the power to contend; they are the stepchildren of nature and groan under the worst of all tyrannies—the tyranny of a bad organisation.»

It is important to note in this context how Maudsley in 1895 describes a struggle between hereditary and environmental factors. The underlining of the importance of these two opposed elements was to be implanted by many researchers of criminality in the following decades. The prison doctor James Devon wrote in his *The Criminal and the Community* in 1912 that it was impossible to measure to what degree different deeds are governed by heritage or environment, and that accordingly it was of the essence to analyze every case with great care. Devon also took the opportunity to taunt Lombroso by adding: «The criminal is a man or woman like the rest of us, and information about his head or heels, while it may have a special value in relation to his case should not be confounded with knowledge of himself. He is something more than a brain or a stomach.»

It is this development that has been brought up by those who mean that England was never under the influence of criminal anthropology. And yet, anybody who reads Devon must realize that he is arguing against criminal anthropology. And the reason why somebody argues against something is generally that there is somebody else arguing for the same matter.

We have already seen how Havelock Ellis rushed to the aid of criminal anthropology in 1890. His was in no way a solitary effort; anthropologist and psychiatrist Francis Galton gave Ellis's *The Criminal* a favorable review in *Nature* magazine, and went on to do work of his own, asserting that our behavior, including criminal facets of it, was conditioned by hereditary factors.

There was a battle of opinions in England. And among those who sided with criminal anthropology were a number of psychiatrists from mental institutions, such as Thomas Clouston of the Royal Edinburgh Sanatorium and Samuel Strahan at the Northampton County Asylum. Another proponent was the physician Alfred Tredgold, who in *Mental Deficiency* (1914) proved himself a criminal anthropologist by writing about morally perverse or habitually criminal types of people.

Interestingly, there are also examples of how criminal anthropology was lauded in the academic world. In the *British Medical Journal* of September 1889 there was an unsigned article that even discussed the Ripper murders from an angle of criminal anthropology:

> We are prepared to admit that habitual crime is a constitutional disease, which is often inherited and, like other diatheses, has its outward physiognomical expression. [… Lombroso's] may possibly be an accurate portrait of the wretch whose butcheries have for so long made a reign of terror in Whitechapel…

Cautiously, though, the article went on to admit that it would not be appropriate for any detective to arrest people solely on grounds of physical appearance.

Apparently, one year after the Ripper scare, this was accepted theorizing in the British academic world. Criminal anthropology's reasoning about a criminal heritage was found valid, as was the idea about typified criminal physiognomies, although it was pointed out that criminals would not always answer to more exact generalizations. As we move on, we will see how the road that is marked out here was to become a well-trodden one.

In 1892, the highly regarded medical journal *The Lancet* wrote that «there is surely a via media» between «the cautious attitude of the British law and the confident procedure of the Italian.» Similarly, the *British Medical Journal* wrote in July 1891 that criminal anthropology was rash in its way of deducing and immature in its classification of human beings—only to add in the next breath that it was «doubtless true that the degenerated classes have certain deficiencies of structure which show a hereditary weakness of constitution.» Three years on, the same magazine mocked those who looked for an «atypical confluence of the fissures of the brain,» only to then add «that there is a solid basis of truth in the teachings of Lombroso and his followers no physiologist would deny.»

This ambivalence, where criminal anthropology is first pointed out as being silly, only to be lauded as a kind of research representing a great value, was directly mirrored in the work of the Victorian police.

At the time of the Ripper murders, the police employed what was known as the «bertillonage»—a method using photo collections of criminals, taken in prison. The method was introduced by the French police officer and researcher Alphonse Bertillon and represented great progress for the identification process. The physiognomies of all kinds of criminals were photographed in great detail, and this made it possible to identify the ones who relapsed in crime after their respective jail terms.

The method was universally accepted as a scientifically reliable means of identifying multiple offenders, something that had previously not been possible. The problem was that many people involved in the judicial system believed that the bertillonage simultaneously provided a useful index of typified criminal physiognomies! And even if we in later days have seen a wish to clear Bertillon of any conviction linked to criminal anthropology, this seems not to have been a correct call. Already in 1882 Bertillon had, under the title «Les Races Sauvages,» presented research material where he generalized about cultural and moral failings within non-European people on anthropometric grounds. Anthropometry dealt with measuring different parts of the physiognomy in order to establish the underlying properties of different people. And in 1896, long after the bertillonage was presented, Bertillon put forward a thesis to the International Congress on Criminal Anthropology in Geneva. In it, he expressed a belief that when a sufficient number of criminals had been studied with his anthropometric method, it would become possible to establish the frequency of physical deviations and facial anomalies within different individuals, as well as the correlation between these anomalies and the criminal tendencies of the various individuals.

Once again, we note how genuinely progressive science linked arms with obscure, prejudiced typifications of criminals during the late Victorian era.

When we move forward to the mid-1890s, we can see how the academic world started to distance itself more clearly from criminal anthropology. In 1896, *The Lancet* wrote that criminals could not be reduced into distinct types by way of some sort of physiological identification, and the readers were warned not to stray from sense and experience.

Did this mean that criminal anthropology was now wholly dismissed by British science? Not at all. To clarify what was going on, we may take a look at the exchange between two of the aforementioned main figures in the debate, David Nicolson and Thomas Clouston. In 1895 the two were engaged in an exchange on the topic, after a speech Nicolson had made. In his speech, Nicolson had strongly attacked the teachings of Lombroso. By this point

C. Lombroso — *L'Homme criminel.* Pl. VII.

1. P. C., brigand de la Basilicate, détenu à Pesaro.

2. Voleur piémontais.

3. Incendiaire et cynède de Pesaro, surnommé *la femme.*

4. Misdea.

Examples of typified criminal physiognomies, three male thieves and a female pyromaniac, from Cesare Lombroso's «L'uomo delinquente» (1876).

Nicolson had joined sides with Henry Maudsley and abandoned criminal anthropology.

Thomas Clouston argued that it could well be that Continental colleagues of the medical profession were over-enthusiastic when interpreting Lombroso, but in the same breath he added that it would be totally at odds with the psychiatric findings of the preceding fifty years to deny that there was a link between criminality and heredity.

Nicolson's reply to the criticism is extremely elucidating. He said that Clouston had misunderstood what he had said in his speech, and that he had never suggested that criminal anthropology lacked a firm ground to stand on. «What I object to,» he went on, «is that a description—honest, true, verbose if you like—applicable to the few should be held up to the world as being applicable to the whole criminal class.» There were, Nicolson added, a number of people in jail who were «weak-minded,» and criminal anthropology could be applied to these, whereas it could not be applied to the rest of the criminal world.

What Nicolson claims here mirrors a line of thought that was accepted in the mid-1890s: there was hereditary criminality and there were physical traits coupled to this criminality, but these biological factors could only explain criminality within part of the criminal conglomerate. This part was described as «weak-minded» or «morally imbecile.»

In 1892, prison doctor John Baker, in his article «Some Points Connected with Criminals,» in the *Journal of Mental Science*, described a study of twenty-five male inmates, some of them «weak-minded» or «degenerate physically,» and it is easy enough to recognize these men as the exact category of criminals whom David Nicolson was to point to in his debate with Thomas Clouston three years later. Baker described how the majority of these twenty-five inmates had foreheads that were «generally low,» the frontal sinuses and zygoma «prominent,» the lower jaw generally «weak» (except in four cases of epileptic prisoners with «massive and square» jaws), and, most remarkable of all, he notes that the prisoners' palates were «frequently» abnormal. Only six of the twenty-five inmates cleared that particular hurdle.

For anyone looking for Jack the Ripper today, it is of the utmost importance to realize that those who took part in the same hunt back in 1888 quite probably believed that they were looking for a killer who carried a criminal inheritance that was in one way or the other visible on the outside. It was not until the mid-1890s that these prejudices slowly began to dissipate in England. The last to let go of them were seemingly those responsible for the country's mental institutions. Putting it differently, the prejudices lingered longest with the professionals who were responsible for the practical sector of the work with criminals, while those representing the higher academical spheres rid themselves of the burden of criminal anthropology somewhat earlier. The prejudices were phased out over a long period of time, but interestingly enough, they seem to have had their greatest support at the exact period of time when Jack the Ripper ravaged London. Had he emerged only ten years later, the inquiries would reasonably have been grounded on a much less murky thinking than the one prevalent during the scare. Accordingly, the chances of the killer having been apprehended would have been considerably larger.

Once we have reached this point, the time has come to introduce another scientist from the nineteenth century: Charles Darwin.

When Krafft-Ebing's *Psychopathia Sexualis* reached the bookstores, twenty-seven years had passed since the theory of evolution had wrenched the interpretation of what a human being really is out of the hands of religion. Back then, in 1859, Darwin's *On the Origin of Species* was published, and the concept of natural selection revolutionized our view of the world. The reasoning that man—and all other organisms—constantly develop and adapt to the surroundings, and that the individual that manages to adapt best is the likely survivor, formed the base of a new way of understanding the world.

Darwin's thought was extremely radical and modern and still forms the basis of how we look at evolution.

Factors that are rarely discussed in combination with Darwin's teachings are things such as justice and egoism. This makes sense, since evolution from Darwin's perspective is always about practical biology, not about morals and values. It is nevertheless interesting to take a look at how the new concept of evolution came to be regarded by the Victorians.

Darwin's basic idea is that if one individual adapts better than others, then this individual will be able to knock out the inferior competition in, for example, the hunt for food. Thus, he will eliminate less adapted individuals and groupings. Everybody's equal rights has to stand aside, biggest and best wins the day, and matters like moral and values do not enter the discussion.

In 1888, this message made for an alarming contrast to the prevailing conception of man being good by nature and prepared to share of his abundance to those in need, an idea much supported by religion. In the same way, the picture worked against the emerging demands for justice to the exploited laborers of the industrialized world. When the Victorians read about Scrooge, Bob Cratchit, and Tiny Tim in Dickens's *A Christmas Carol*, it was always obvious that Scrooge's greed and egoism could never be allowed to prevail over the Cratchit family's justified demand to take part in the assets of society.

It was—and remains—a beautiful thought, but it does not jibe with what Darwin claimed. Faced with the biological obduracy of evolution, Bob Cratchit and his family would soon succumb and Scrooge and his ilk would take over the world if Darwin was correct.

Since this truth must have been unpalatable to the Victorians, they instead opted to look at the theory of evolution as an entirety, comprising not only a biological applicability but also a moral one. This line of thinking is referred to as Social Darwinism: if mankind could develop biologically, then surely it could develop morally too?

According to these ideas, man would travel along a line of moral development that ultimately would wash away any bad properties in favor of the good ones. To the process of biological refinement, a moral refinement would be added, guaranteeing that every new generation would be morally sounder than the preceding one.

The logical extension of these thoughts would be that things like war and crime would dissolve over time and we would set course toward an upcoming ideal society. It is a refreshing perspective, but the period after the Victorian era has brought two world wars, innumerable genocides, and countless examples of human cruelty—together with a growing number of serial killers.

This is of course where the idea of atavisms enters the equation. If the expected positive development of the society did not arrive, and if people nevertheless chose to believe in a permanent bettering process of humankind from both a biological and a moral perspective, then a likely explanation to any shortcomings in that respect would be that properties that mankind should have lost a long time ago stubbornly persisted in returning to haunt society.

It is in the light of thoughts like these that one can understand how the western world of the late nineteenth century regarded criminals like Vincenz Verzeni. He was an evolutionary prank, a ghost from a primitive stage of mankind, when murder and moral deficiencies were the order of the day. And the actual proof for how Verzeni had been hurled from ancient times into the Victorian age was his physiognomy, with a skull deviating from what was normal, with a bull neck and marked cheekbones, with the protruding frontal skull, all reminiscent of the primates that, according to Darwin's teachings, we have developed from.

And this is where we come full circle. Here we have the last piece of the jig-

saw puzzle the Victorians tried to finish to find an explanation of the world
they lived in. The time has arrived to quote an article in the *Star* from September 8, 1888, written after Annie Chapman's demise and pointing the
police in which direction to look for the killer:

> A nameless reprobate—half beast, half man—is at large, who is daily
> gratifying his murderous instincts on the most miserable and defense-
> less classes of the community ... The ghoul-like creature who stalks
> through the streets of London, stalking down his victim like a Pawnee
> Indian, is simply drunk with blood, and he will have more.

The descriptions in the press of John Pizer, a Jew who was suspected of being
the character called «Leather Apron» and at one point regarded as possibly
being the killer, were no less colorful. This is how *The Atchison Daily Globe*
of Kansas, USA, described him on September 5, 1888: «He is a character
half way between Dickens' Quilp and Poe's baboon. He is short, stunted and
thick set. He has small, wicked black eyes and is half crazy.» Reading these
things today, we can see how they are outright ridiculous. To the Victorians,
however, they were schoolbook examples of descriptions that were grounded
in the latest findings and achievements of contemporary science.

If any reader should still be in doubt that there is an abyss of differences
telling today's world from the Victorian era, then let us put it all into a wider chronological perspective. The modern world is more than 130 years removed from the Ripper years. If we back down a further 130 years from 1888,
we find ourselves in the mid-1700s, where there were still ongoing witch trials in parts of Europe.

It is in the exact middle of the type of legal insights and human understanding that led to the burning alive of women as witches, and the high-tech
police work of our own time, coupled with today's knowledge about how
genetically close all representatives of humankind are to one another, that we
must fit in the hunt for Jack the Ripper. It is a staggering and sobering insight,
without which no real understanding can be had about the matter.

To make the picture complete when it comes to how it was reasoned what
type of person Jack the Ripper was, we also need to look at the thoughts expressed by Dr. Thomas Bond. Born in 1841, he was appointed surgeon to
the Metropolitan police's A division, covering Westminster, in 1867. He was
drawn into the Ripper investigation in late October 1888. He was also deeply
involved in the investigations into the Thames Torso murder series, together
with Dr. Charles Hebbert, who was a convinced criminal anthropologist.

It was the Assistant Commissioner of the Met, Robert Anderson, who requested Bond's participation in the Ripper investigation, and on November 10, 1888, the day after the murder of Mary Kelly, Bond performed the autopsy of Kelly together with George Bagster Phillips, police surgeon for the H division, covering Whitechapel.

In his report, Thomas Bond gave his view on what kind of man the Ripper was likely to be, something that has earned Bond an acknowledgement as being the first criminal profiler. When reading his thoughts on the perpetrator, we get a radically different picture from the one offered by criminal anthropology, and the general sense is that Bonds description is much more modern:

> The murderer must have been a man of physical strength and of great coolness and daring. There is no evidence that he had an accomplice. He must in my opinion be a man subject to periodical attacks of Homicidal and erotic mania. The character of the mutilations indicated that the man may be in a condition sexually, that may be called satyriasis. It is of course possible that the Homicidal impulse may have been developed from a revengeful or brooding condition of the mind, or that Religious Mania may have been the original disease, but I do not think either hypothesis is likely. The murderer in external appearance is quite likely to be a quiet inoffensive looking man probably middle-aged and neatly and respectably dressed. I think he must be in the habit of wearing a cloak or overcoat or he could hardly have escaped notice in the streets if the blood on his hands or clothes were visible.
>
> Assuming the murderer to be such a person as I have just described he would probably be solitary and eccentric in his habits, also he is most likely to be a man without regular occupation, but with some small income or pension. He is possibly living among respectable persons who have some knowledge of his character and habits and who may have grounds for suspicion that he is not quite right in his mind at times. Such persons would probably be unwilling to communicate suspicion to the Police for fear of trouble or notoriety, whereas if there were a prospect of reward it might overcome their scruples.

Here, Bond may insightfully seem to point to the exact type of serial killers we have in our own time—seemingly unobtrusive, discreet men with a talent for melting into the woodwork without anybody noticing them: Gary Ridgway, the Green River killer; Dennis Rader, the BTK killer; David Carpenter; Jeffrey Dahmer ...

However, it is just as likely that Bond had taken stock of the contemporary reports that spoke of how Vincenz Verzeni was a young man who didn't draw much attention.

Another character, also mentioned by Krafft-Ebing in *Psychopathia Sexualis*, was a native of Vittoria, Spain: the serial killer Gruyo. This man had a clean rap sheet and had been married to three different wives. This did not stop him from killing five women, tearing their kidneys and intestines out through their vaginas. After this series of murders, there was a ten-year hiatus before Gruyo killed again—and was arrested.

The reflection that can be made here is that Thomas Bond reasonably had access to the information that a sexually motivated serial killer can make a totally uncontroversial impression and melt perfectly into the society where he lives and works without anybody sensing what lurks under the seemingly harmless façade.

It is completely possible that these cases were what made Thomas Bond exert caution in his «profile» of the Whitechapel killer. Whether Bond expected that the killer, when caught, would exhibit physical traits akin to what had been found in Verzenis case is impossible to say.

Now that we have an understanding of the Victorian view of what a killer really was and looked like, we can see that a foreigner with a peculiar physiognomy, mental health issues, and a dislike for the authorities would make a very good contender for the Ripper's role. Conversely, an Englishman with no external hints at any sort of mischief, with a steady job and a family and with a propensity to help the police would be more or less in the clear.

The stage is set, the curtains are drawn, and the hunt is on. Let's now go back nearly a century and a half in time to the cobblestoned streets and alleys of the East End and have a look at the two series of murders that the Victorian police were at an understandable loss to understand—or solve.

THE MURDERS

THE RIPPER MURDERS

The so-called canonical Ripper murders were five. They encompassed Mary Ann «Polly» Nichols, killed on August 31, 1888; Annie Chapman, killed on September 8, 1888; Elizabeth Stride and Catherine Eddowes, both killed on September 30, 1888; and Mary Kelly, killed on November 9, 1888. In recent years, it has become common to add Martha Tabram to the tally. She preceded the other five and was killed on August 7, 1888.

These murders were knife murders, although it seems that there was strangulation or partial strangulation involved in a number of the cases. All five canonical victims had their throats cut. Four of them had their abdomens cut open from sternum to groin, with the exception of Elizabeth Stride. Three had organs taken out of their abdomens: Chapman, Eddowes, and Kelly.

Tabram was different from them all as regards the damage done to the body. She was stabbed thirty-eight times and only received a single cut wound. This wound did not open up the abdomen; it was on or close to her private parts, around three inches long and one inch deep.

The murders were all committed in a small area of the East End. The ones furthest apart had a distance between them that could be covered by a twenty-minute walk.

Although it has been recently challenged by historian Hallie Rubenhold in her book *The Five*, the broadly accepted view is that the victims were all prostitutes or part-time prostitutes. They were all poor and alcoholism was widespread among them. Therefore, it seems the victimology is more or less the same in all these cases.

All these six murders went down silently, at least silently enough not to spark much interest from those who were close to the murder spots. All the victims save one were killed in public spots: Tabram in the stairwell of a tenement building, Nichols out in the open street, Chapman in a backyard off a thoroughfare, Stride in a yard outside a working men's clubhouse, and Eddowes in a square. In all these cases, the murders seem to have taken place in very dark spots. Many would argue that Chapman was killed close to the sunrise, but I think that is a misconception.

The one victim who was not killed in a public spot was Mary Kelly, who was taken apart by the Ripper in her own lodgings—a dingy room in Millers Court, off Dorset Street.

It should also be noted that the two last victims, Eddowes and Kelly, both suffered facial mutilation. This was something the other four were not subjected to.

THE THAMES TORSO MURDERS

The canonical Ripper murders spanned a period of ten weeks only. The Thames Torso murders spanned at least a period of more than two years, from May 1887 to September 1889. Over the years, two murders from 1873 and 1874 have also come to be regarded as possible deeds of the Thames Torso killer as well an 1884 torso murder. My own view is that the 1873 deed was undoubtedly his work, that the 1884 murder was quite possibly so, and that the 1874 murder is so sparsely reported that it is impossible to say whether it had the same originator or not.

The bulk of the Thames Torso murders are the four murders committed in 1887–89. These were dismemberment murders, and the examining medico, Charles Hebbert, was quite certain that they all had the same originator. This was owing to how the cutting was performed: it was exceedingly skillfully done, and more or less the exact same cutting technique was employed in all these four murders. Just as in the Ripper murders, organs were missing from the victims. However, it is only in the one case where the victim was subsequently identified (as Elizabeth Jackson) that we can be certain that the organ removal was the killer's work. In Jackson's case, the uterus was taken out together with the fetus inside it; Jackson was pregnant at the time. Her heart and lungs were also removed from her body. In the other cases, there is the alternative possibility that the organs were lost in transport or during the time the body parts spent in water: the killer threw most of the body parts in the Thames, although some parts were also placed on dry land.

The 1873 victim was also dexterously and skillfully dismembered.

Almost all these victims were seemingly cut up close in time to their respective deaths. This was proven by muscle contraction at the cuts, something that can only take place when the cutting is done close to death. A general rule of thumb says that muscle contraction can only occur during the first thirty minutes after death.

It is impossible to say where the victims in this series met their killer, just as it is impossible to tell where they were actually killed. They were dismemberment murders, and all we know is where the dumped body parts were found. The bulk of them ended up in the Thames, and they floated ashore along the London banks of the river. Generally speaking, this meant that they were dumped somewhere to the west of the metropolis. In one case parts were dumped not in the Thames but instead in Regent's Canal, and a considerable amount of body parts were also dumped on dry land, in places spread all over London.

With the one exception of the 1884 deed, the heads from the victims in this series were never retrieved. It is possible that they were thrown into the Thames and sank to the bottom; heads will not float like other body parts. Of course, it may also be that they were significant to the killer, who may have kept them while throwing away the rest of the body. If so, the 1884 torso was either not connected to the series or an exception to the rule.

As for victimology, since only one of the Thames Torso killer's victims was identified, that victim is all we have to go by. Her name was Elizabeth Jackson. And just as the broadly accepted case was with the victims in the Ripper series, she was a woman of very small economical means and with a history of prostitution.

Let's look at the victims from both series individually now, and establish what kind of damage was done to them. I will present them in chronological order, meaning that Ripper victims and Torso victims will be mixed. For too long, they have been separated by students of the case. To get the full and correct picture, I believe the chronological aspect needs to be considered. Although there are dates for when the first body part in each respective torso case was found, I will give the corresponding month only in the headings, since it is more often than not difficult or impossible to establish the exact dates of death for these victims.

THE VICTIMS

SEPTEMBER 1873: THE FACELESS WOMAN (THAMES TORSO VICTIM)

On September 5, 1873, a part of the left side of a female torso was found floating in the Thames. It was fished out of the water by the crew of a police galley rowing in the vicinity of Battersea, and it marked the beginning of a series of finds of body parts that would ultimately prove to have come from the same body. The body had been taken apart in around a dozen pieces, and just about all the parts were retrieved from the Thames over a period of some two weeks.

What was never retrieved was the skull and some of the internal organs.

The discovery of a face and scalp floating in the Thames was a particularly horrifying detail of the 1873 torso murder.

It is not on record which exact organs had gone missing, but we know that part of the diaphragm was found in the body, as was part of the uterus and an ovary.

The victim was a «very stout» woman in her forties, as per Dr. William Henry Kempster, police surgeon to the V division of the Metropolitan Police. He identified a possible cause of death, due to a particularly gruesome find of one of the body parts. On September 7, a cut-away face and scalp had floated ashore at Duke's Shore, Limehouse. The killer had made two cuts, one vertical and one horizontal, at the back of the victim's head, and then he had meticulously pulled the skin forward over the skull, while using his knife to work the facial skin loose from it. The end result was a death mask, including eyelashes and ears, but with a few pieces of skin missing where the mask had not readily come off the bone as the killer cut. Part of the nose had also been cut away.

The haunting find was later put on a wooden block and displayed to the public. The police had high hopes of finding somebody who was able to identify the face, since they deemed it complete and recognizable. Nobody came forward to make a definitive identification, however.

The possible cause of death that Dr. Kempster identified was linked to how there was extensive bruising to the right temple of the cut-away face. It was obvious that the victim had received two very hard blows to the skull, likely fracturing it and quite feasibly being the cause of death.

One odd feature of the cutting work on the body was that it was quite dexterous. There were early reports in the daily newspapers that claimed that the cutting was sloppy, but this was refuted by an article in *The Lancet:*

> Contrary to the popular opinion, the body had not been hacked, but dexterously cut up; the joints have been opened, and the bones neatly disarticulated, even the complicated joints at the ankle and the elbow, and it is only at the articulations of the hip-joint and shoulder that the bones have been sawn through.

The dismemberment had been performed using a sharp knife and a fine-toothed saw, implements that would later resurface in the reports covering the 1887–89 torso murders.

The horrific inclusion of the death mask was in some way rivaled in gruesomeness by the doctor's information that it could not be excluded that the cutting had commenced while the victim was still alive. Muscle contraction proved that the victim must at the very least still have been quite warm as she was cut up.

However, another peculiarity tells us that the victim actually would have been dead as she was dismembered. It was discovered that there was not a drop of blood left in the body. This in its turn must have come about as the result of the body being positioned in a way so as to allow for a complete exsanguination. *The Lancet* was satisfied that the blood had left the body as the head was severed, opening up all the vessels in the neck. But if the severing of the head had taken place as the victim lay on the ground, not all blood would have left the vessels. The blood closest to the ground would have stayed in the body, meaning that we can conclude that the victim must have been strung up, presumably by the feet, in order to completely drain the body of its blood.

The police speculated that the body parts had been dumped in the river at about the place where the Wandle joins the Thames, at the westernmost part of London. None of the parts were wrapped in anything; all parts were found naked.

MAY 1887: THE RAINHAM VICTIM
(THAMES TORSO VICTIM)

The Rainham murder of 1887 is the first murder in a series of four where we have a renowned doctor, Charles Hebbert, who gave his professional view that there could be little doubt that the same man was responsible for all four cases. Hebbert based his belief on how the four cases were «in almost every respect,» as he put it, «similar to each other.» These cases were the Rainham case of 1887, the Whitehall Mystery of 1888, followed by two cases in 1889, the Elizabeth Jackson murder, also referred to as the Horsleydown murder, and the Pinchin Street case.

The first part of the Rainham victim was found in the village to the east of London that has given the case its name. On May 11, 1887, lighterman Edward Hughes saw a bundle floating in the Thames. Fishing it out of the river and unwrapping the sacking cloth that had been wrapped around it, he found part of a female torso, severed from the pelvic part at the third lumbar vertebra and from the shoulder part at the fifth dorsal ditto.

The absolute bulk of the body parts of this case were retrieved along the shores of the Thames. The last find, however, was made in Regent's Canal, where a sack with two lower legs was found floating. Apparently, the killer had made a conscious choice not to dump all the parts in the Thames. Moreover, the condition of the various parts found made it clear that not all the parts had been thrown into the water at the same time. Interestingly, the police also concluded that not all the parts found in the Thames had been dumped at the same spot.

The post-mortem carried out on the remains was conducted by Dr. Edward Galloway. Giving evidence at an inquest into the case on May 14, he said that he believed the victim had been dead for around two weeks, taking the estimated time of death to somewhere around the beginning of May. He gave the probable age of the victim as somewhere between the late twenties up to the mid-thirties.

What is most remarkable about Galloway's observations is that he was initially convinced from the skill of the cutting to the body that the killer had «a thorough knowledge of surgery,» thereby implicating someone in the very same medical profession to which he himself belonged. The disarticulations of the limbs had been clinical and clean, and the cutting angles were absolutely straight, leaving no traces of jaggedness. The implements used were a very sharp knife and a fine-toothed saw.

At the time of the inquest, not all parts had been found. New finds were continuously being made, eventually leading up to a second inquest. On June

5, another sacking-cloth-wrapped parcel was found, this time in the vicinity of Temple Pier. Having examined the cutting work on the thigh found inside the parcel, Dr. Galloway stated, «These body parts have been removed with skill, not simply torn off to hide a murder.»

The press understandably latched on to the notion of a possible surgeon killer, and the excitement was great. This was somewhat dampened when on August 13, at the second inquest, Edward Galloway expressed the view that «the body had been divided by someone who knew the structure of the human frame, but not necessarily a skilled anatomist.»

It is both possible and probable that Galloway had been subjected to pressure from his fellow physicians, and therefore decided to take his foot off the gas pedal when it came to pointing out a medico as the killer.

At the second inquest, Dr. Thomas Bond, who was to become involved with the Ripper murders the following year, stated that the removal of the head had been made «not for the study of anatomy, but was done for the purpose of covering up a murder.» Here he sided with the contemporary general conception of what dismemberment murders were really about: hiding a murder or the identity of the victim. As was the norm in this series of murders, the head was never retrieved.

Dr. Bond and Dr. Charles Hebbert were both officially called in to examine the body parts of the Rainham victim before the second inquest. Charles Hebbert was the expert who set out to dissolve the picture of a murderous surgeon, by actually claiming that no surgeon would be as skilled as the killer of the Rainham victim was. Hebbert instead claimed that the cutting was more probably the work of somebody who had much more cutting experience than the average surgeon, like a butcher or a hunter.

Regardless of which occupation the killer had, he had cut his victim open from sternum to groin. From the thorax, the heart and lungs had gone missing. These organs were described as being «absent» from the thoracic cavity, meaning that it was not determined whether they had been lost as a result of being thrown into the Thames or on account of the killer having cut them out. The organs in the abdominal cavity were still in place but for the small intestine from the duodenum and part of the colon.

AUGUST 7, 1888: MARTHA TABRAM
(RIPPER VICTIM)

Martha Tabram was found dead in George Yard Buildings, off Old Montague Street. Her dead body was discovered by a working man living there, John Saunders Reeves, on his way to work. Tabram was lying on a staircase landing just outside a toilet compartment. She had been stabbed thirty-seven times with an implement that the examining medico, Dr. Timothy Killeen, believed to be a smallish knife, like a penknife. She had also received a relatively shallow cut, three inches long and one inch deep, to the lower part of her abdomen, possibly to her genitals. Finally, she had been stabbed through the sternum and heart by a weapon that Killeen said would have been a long, strong one, suggesting a dagger or a bayonet. Killeen was adamant that the thirty-seven smaller stabs were not dealt with the same weapon that pierced the heart.

Dr. Killeen was also the medico who executed the post-mortem, and although not all thirty-nine wounds were specified at the inquest, some of them were. The left lung had been hit five times, the right lung had received two stabs, the liver was pierced five times, the spleen twice, and the stomach was stabbed six times. And then there was the stab to the heart. This accounts for twenty-one wounds. We are to a degree guided by Killeen as to where the other stabs were found by his claim that the main focus of the attack were the breasts, the belly, and the groin. It may well be that the wounds unaccounted for simply did not harm any of the inner organs, traveling through muscle tissue and sinews only.

Martha Tabram was a plump woman of some thirty-nine years of age. She stood five feet three inches tall and had dark hair and a darkish complexion. Dr. Killeen estimated that she would have died around 2:30–2:45 A.M., which was roughly three hours before when Timothy Killeen first examined the body.

Martha Tabram has always divided those who study the case into a group where she is reasoned to be a Ripper victim and another group where she is considered the prey of another unnamed killer.

There are various elements that speak for an inclusion. First and foremost, she shares the timing, the geography, and the victimology with the Ripper victims. But there is more.

When found, Tabram was on her back in a provocative position with her clothes thrown up and her legs spread. This is consistent with how the majority of the Ripper victims were found.

Her fingers were tightly clenched, possibly suggesting that the killer had deprived Tabram of breathing air. Signs of strangulation or suffocation were also present in the Ripper murder series.

There was also evidence that Tabram had received a blow to her head, either by the killer or by falling head first to the floor. As has been pointed out, the 1873 torso victim had received two blows to her temple, and when Polly

John Saunders Reeves finding the body of Martha Tabram in George Yard buildings on the morning of the 7th of August 1888.

Nichols died, the examining medico, Dr Llewellyn, pointed out that there was bruising to her jaw that was consistent with a blow from a fist. This may have been part of incapacitating the victims.

Last but not least, the dwellers of the house where Tabram was found dead had not heard any signs of a struggle, although some of them lived only feet away from where she was found. Combining silence with extreme brutality was a trademark inclusion in the Ripper murders; it was one of the details that had the Londoners speculating about dealing with a superhuman phantom of death.

AUGUST 31, 1888: MARY ANN «POLLY» NICHOLS
(RIPPER VICTIM)

Polly Nichols was discovered in Buck's Row in the early morning hours of August 31, 1888. The traditional way of presenting the case is that the carman Charles Lechmere found her on his way to work. However, as will be discussed later, there is no initial corroboration for Lechmere's claim. What we actually know is that another carman by the name of Robert Paul found Charles Lechmere standing out in Buck's Row, some little way from Polly Nichols's body. We also have on record the information that PC John Neil on his beat had at around 3:15 A.M. passed over the spot where Nichols was subsequently found. At that stage, the spot was empty.

The information about the wounds to Polly Nichols's body is sparse. There was a large gash running from sternum to groin in her abdomen, and there were a number of smaller cuts running alongside it. The throat had been cut twice, the injuries reaching all the way down to the spine and severing all major vessels in the neck. The tongue was slightly lacerated and there was a bruise to the right side of the jaw, possibly from a blow of some sort delivered by the killer. There was also some bruising on the left side of the face. Two small stabs to the private parts were reported by the responsible medico, Dr. Rees Ralph Llewellyn. The doctor's estimation about the knife that had caused the damage was that it would have been long-bladed and moderately sharp.

Dr. Llewellyn likely arrived at the murder site somewhere around 4:05–4:10. His estimation was that the woman had not been dead for more than half an hour at most, putting the time of death at around 3:35 at the very earliest. It should be remembered that estimating the time of death by means of feeling for warmth and other parameters was not a fully reliable art, and so we may need to be careful about taking Llewellyn's estimation as gospel. What can be said is that Lechmere's proven presence at the murder scene falls within the estimate Llewellyn made.

The doctor also offered the view that the killer would have had at least some rough anatomical insights, since he seemed, as Llewellyn put it according to the *Daily News* of August 3, to «have attacked all the vital parts» of the body.

In contrast to the Tabram case, there was nothing provocative about how the body of Polly Nichols was found. She was on her back with her legs stretched out, and her clothes covered the wounds in her abdomen, although they left her thighs exposed. It was reported that neither Lechmere nor Robert Paul was able to see any blood in spite of the fact that Nichols had been the victim of a horrific knife attack.

Polly Nichols had turned forty-three five days before she was killed. She stood five feet two inches tall and had dark complexion and brown hair that was in the process of turning gray. She was a smallish woman with delicate features.

Just as in the Tabram murder, there were people close by the murder scene, some of them sleeping with open windows. No witness, however, had heard any struggle or scream.

SEPTEMBER 8, 1888: ANNIE CHAPMAN
(RIPPER VICTIM)

Annie Chapman was born in September of 1841. She stood five feet tall and was a stout woman with wavy brown hair. She was found dead in the back-yard of 29 Hanbury Street by the carman John Davis, who resided in the house on the premises. She was lying in a narrow recess between some stone steps leading up to the door opening on to the backyard and a wooden fence, separating the premises from the neighboring lot. Chapman was found around 6:00 A.M., and the examining medico, Dr. George Bagster Phillips, police surgeon of the H division, arrived at 6:30.

With Annie Chapman, the Ripper series returns to the victim being found in a provocative position. Her clothes were flung up over the body, and Phillips described how «the legs were drawn up, the feet resting on the ground, and the knees turned outwards.»

The Nichols murder is the only canonical Ripper murder where the true finder (Charles Lechmere) was not depicted in the papers. Instead PC Neil was represented as the finder.

Chapman had suffered a very extensive mutilation. Her abdomen had been cut open from pubes to ribs, and the killer had taken out her uterus from it along with the upper part of the vagina and two-thirds of the bladder. These parts were not in place at the site; evidently, the killer had taken them with himself as he left. The intestines of the body had been severed from their mesenteric attachments. After that, they had been lifted out of the abdominal cavity and placed over the right shoulder of Chapman, arguably to allow for easier access to the abdominal organs. The killer had also cut away Chapman's abdominal wall in four flaps. Three of these flaps were placed on her shoulders, but the fourth had been removed from the site. This fourth flap was arguably attached to the part of the reproductive organs that was taken away by the killer. Dr. Phillips was impressed by how skillfully this particular operation had been done, stating that it «indicated a certain amount of anatomical knowledge.» He added that his own impression was that the killer's anatomical knowledge «was only less displayed or indicated in consequence of haste.» The publication that is most explicit when quoting Dr. Phillips is *The Lancet*, where Phillips words on the skill of the killer were recorded like this:

> Mr. Phillips … stated that the mutilation of the body was of such a character as could only have been effected by a practiced hand. It was appears that the abdomen had been entirely laid open; that the intestines, severed from their mesenteric attachments, had been lifted out of the body, and placed on the shoulder of the corpse; whilst from the pelvis the uterus and its appendages, with the upper portion of the vagina and the posterior two-thirds of the bladder, had been entirely removed. No trace of these parts could be found, and the incisions were cleanly cut, avoiding the rectum, and dividing the vagina low enough to avoid injury to the cervix uteri. Obviously the work was that of an expert—of one, at least, who had such knowledge of anatomical or pathological examinations as to be enabled to secure the pelvic organs with one sweep of a knife, which must therefore, as Mr. Phillips pointed out, have been at least five inches long.

Here we can see how Dr. Galloway's words about surgical insights in regard to the killer of the Rainham victim in the Thames Torso series were echoed. The impression that a murderous expert anatomist or surgeon was on the loose caused a sensation with the papers and the public.

Annie Chapman's face was swollen and her tongue, likewise much swol-

*Annie Chapman was found dead in the backyard of 29 Hanbury
Street by the carman John Davis.*

len, protruded between the front teeth. This was in line with suffocation of
some kind. The neck had been cut twice, severing it down to the bone. Two
parallel cuts, divided by half an inch, were found in the left side of the spinal
vertebrae. The damage done to the muscular structures at these cuts led Phillips to speculate that an attempt had been made to decapitate Chapman.

When Phillips examined the body, he found it cold apart from a «certain
remaining heat, under the intestines, in the body.» There was also a stiff-
ness of the limbs that was «not marked, but commencing.» The doctor also
described the blood as being «well clotted.» Weighing these factors together, he stated that Chapman had been dead for at least two hours, but probably more so when the initial 6:30 examination was made. This estimate has
been the subject of much discussion among the students of the case, since
three witnesses subsequently appeared who all seemed to make the doctor's estimate impossible. The subject will be discussed at length later in the
book.

There was some bruising to the upper part and head of Chapman's body,
some of which had come about as the result of an earlier fight with another
woman, Eliza Cooper, in the Britannia Public House. The row was about a
man and resulted in Chapman receiving a black eye and a bruised chest.

Dr. Phillips was also able to tell that the two cheap brass rings that Chapman were in the habit of wearing had been wrenched from her finger and
taken away.

SEPTEMBER 1888: THE WHITEHALL CASE
(THAMES TORSO VICTIM)

The first part of the so-called Whitehall victim that was found was a right arm. It was separated from the body at the shoulder. It was retrieved from the muddy banks of the Thames at low tide by a laborer named Frederick Moore, close to where today's Chelsea Bridge spans the Thames, on September 11, 1888. Back then, there was another bridge in the same spot, namely Victoria Bridge. Oddly enough, the arm had a string tied tightly around it as a ligature, not far from where the shoulder would have been.

The arm was originally examined by a Dr. Nevill, who noted that it had been removed with a great amount of skill. Five days later, on the 16th, a re-examination was made by Thomas Bond and Charles Hebbert, who were also able to note that the arm had been amputated in a very clean fashion, using seven separate cuts. Hebbert added that the veins of the arm were «full of black fluid blood» which had «been kept in by the ligature.»

Some two weeks after Bond and Hebbert's examination, on October 2, the headless torso from which the arm had been removed was found. It consisted of the full thorax, both arms missing, down to the fourth lumbar vertebra, where the lower abdomen and pelvis had been separated from it. This time, the find was made not in the Thames or along its banks. Instead, the torso was discovered in the cellar vaults of the New Scotland Yard building, which was at the time still under construction. Deep down in its foundations, and in a vault where a number of construction workers kept their tools so as not to have them stolen, was where the torso had been placed. It was wrapped in paper that had been carefully tied around the flesh with some lengths of string of various origin. The spot where the ghoulish parcel had been placed was so dark that the man who found it could not make out what it was. He settled for thinking it was an old coat, as he was groping around for his working tools. It was only after a couple of days that the parcel was fetched out of the vaults and examined.

The torso was badly maggot-infested, and the wall against which it had leant in the vault had turned black. This made Thomas Bond suspect that the torso had been in place in the vault for several days. The presence of the maggots furthermore made it clear that the decomposition of the torso had taken place in air.

At the inquest, opening on October 8, Bond and Hebbert suggested that death had taken place as far back as early August. Part of the paper wrapping from the torso was from a newspaper, the *Echo*, of August 24. Typically for the Thames Torso victims, the incisions on the body were clean with well-defined edges. In Hebbert's «An Exercise in Forensic Medicine,» a dissertation

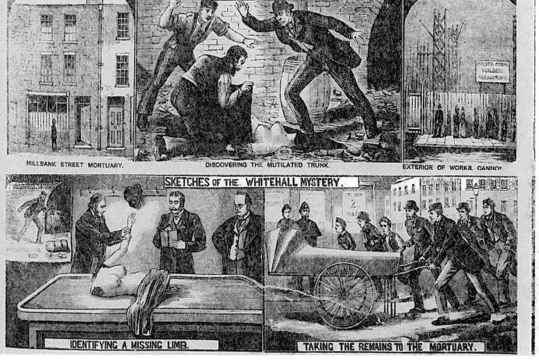

The Whitehall torso was discovered in the cellar vaults
of the New Scotland Yard building.

in two parts from 1888 and 1889 detailing the four Thames Torso cases from 1887–89, he remarked upon how similar the cutting was to that performed on the Rainham victim from the year before:

> As will be gathered from the description, the arm in the second case (the Whitehall case) had been cut from the trunk in a precisely similar manner to that in the first case (the Rainham case), in fact, as soon as I saw the arm I was struck by the close resemblance of the modes of separation, and the mutilation of the trunk was in every respect identical.

The skin of the neck had been divided opposite the cricoid cartilage by two lateral cuts, and a fine-toothed saw had been employed to take the spine off through the sixth cervical vertebra.

On October 17, a London journalist by the name of Jasper Waring managed to persuade the police to allow him to search the premises where the torso had been found. Waring had a dog, a Russian terrier, that quickly set about digging in the soil. A left lower leg and foot was unearthed as a result of the dog's efforts. The leg had been amputated at the knee joint and the patella was absent. Once again, the amputation had been made in a very clean and exact manner.

The leg had lain in the ground and was partly covered with mold. The leg, the arm, and the torso were in different stages of rotting, owing to how they had decomposed in soil, water, and air, respectively.

The organs of the thorax were all in place inside the torso, but since the pelvic area had been removed the organs of the lower abdomen could not be accounted for.

SEPTEMBER 30, 1888: ELIZABETH STRIDE
(RIPPER VICTIM)

Elizabeth Stride was one of two women who were killed on September 30, something that has given rise to the term «The Night of the Double Event.» The general conception at the time—and since—is that the killer was interrupted after having cut Stride's throat. This, it was reasoned, prevented him from being able to move on to the abdominal mutilations that have always been regarded as a significant trait of the murder series.

Elizabeth Stride was born on November 27, 1843, on a farm called Stora Tumlehed, outside Gothenburg, Sweden. She emigrated to Britain in 1866 and married John Stride three years later, thereby gaining her British name. Standing five feet five inches tall earned her the nickname «Long Liz.» Her complexion was pale and she had gray eyes and brown hair.

The spot in which Stride was found dead was called Dutfields Yard, and lay off Berner Street. One of the houses of the yard was a three-story building housing the International Working Men's Educational Club, attended by social democrats and anarchists. The club hosted lectures on politics and economics as well as concerts and dances. The steward of the club, Louis Diemschitz, was the person who found Stride at around 1:00 A.M., when he arrived with his pony and cart at the entrance of Dutfields Yard. As he tried to enter the yard, the horse shied to the left and Diemschitz realized that there was a dark bundle lying on the ground up close by the clubhouse wall to his right. Half a minute and a lit match later, Diemschitz alerted the people inside the clubhouse to the fact that there was a woman lying in her own blood outside their yard door.

Stride was found lying on her left side in Dutfields Yard, with the body resting on her left arm. Her right hand was on her belly and smeared with blood. She had had her throat cut, but not to the dramatic extent that had been the case with Nichols and Chapman. The post-mortem was performed by the aforementioned Dr. Phillips with the assistance of the medico who

Louis Diemschitz, steward of the working men's club on the premises, found Elizabeth Stride dead in Dutfield's Yard.

had first been called to Dutfields Yard on the murder night, Dr. Frederick William Blackwell. Phillips described the cut to the neck in detail:

> There was a clear-cut incision on the neck. It was six inches in length and commenced two and a half inches in a straight line below the angle of the jaw, one half inch in over an undivided muscle, and then becoming deeper, dividing the sheath. The cut was very clean and deviated a little downwards. The arteries and other vessels contained in the sheath were all cut through.
>
> The cut through the tissues on the right side was more superficial, and tailed off to about two inches below the right angle of the jaw. The deep vessels on that side were uninjured. From this is was evident that the hemorrhage was caused through the partial severance of the left carotid artery.

Around her neck, Elizabeth Stride had tied a scarf, and that scarf had been cut together with her throat. The fraying of the scarf indicated that the knife used had been a sharp one.

Over the shoulders and in front of the chest there was a bluish discoloration that probably emanated from how Stride had been thrown to the ground by a man seen in her company at around 12:45, a quarter of an hour before she was found dead. While this man may have been the killer, there can be no certainty that this was so. There was ample time, a full fifteen minutes, for an alternative killer to have arrived at the spot. Regardless of who the killer was, nobody inside the clubhouse seems to have heard the murder.

SEPTEMBER 30, 1888: CATHERINE EDDOWES (RIPPER VICTIM)

Catherine Eddowes was found dead and mutilated in Mitre Square, roughly a fifteen-minute walk from Dutfields Yard, at around 1:45 A.M. on the same night as Elizabeth Stride was killed. It was assumed that she was killed to quench the thirst for blood and evisceration that the killer had not been able to satisfy when killing Stride.

Catherine Eddowes was found in the darkest corner of the square by PC Edward Watkins on his beat. Once again, the body was left in a provocative manner, on its back with the lower abdomen exposed and one leg, the right one, drawn up and bent at the knee. Her arms were alongside the body with the palms of her hands turned upwards and her fingers slightly bent.

Catherine Eddowes was a small and thin woman of forty-six years of age, with hazel eyes and dark auburn hair. She stood five feet tall. She was examined in situ at around 2:20 A.M. by Dr. Frederick Gordon Brown, a police surgeon who subsequently also did the post-mortem. The damage done to her body was terrifying. In his post-mortem report, Brown described the cutting of the throat like this:

> The throat was cut across to the extent of about six or seven inches. A superficial cut commenced about an inch and a half below the lobe below, and about two and a half inches behind the left ear, and extended across the throat to about three inches below the lobe of the right ear.
>
> The big muscle across the throat was divided through on the left side. The large vessels on the left side of the neck were severed. The larynx was severed below the vocal chord. All the deep structures were severed to the bone, the knife marking intervertebral cartilages. The sheath of the vessels on the right side was just opened.
>
> The carotid artery had a fine hole opening, the internal jugular vein was opened about an inch and a half—not divided. The blood vessels contained clot. All these injuries were performed by a sharp instrument like a knife, and pointed.

The mention of how the intervertebral cartilages of the neck had been marked by the knife lends itself to speculation whether the killer had attemp-

PC Edward Watkins found the body of Catherine Eddowes in Mitre Square on his beat.

ted to decapitate Eddowes, just as Phillips had suggested in the Chapman case.

Catherine's abdomen had been ripped open all the way down from the sternum to the groin, and through the opening the killer had drawn out her intestines and draped them over her right shoulder. The liver was slit and stabbed and the pancreas was also cut. The left kidney had been carefully taken out from the front and removed, cutting through the renal artery to allow for it. Dr. Brown suggested that the killer must have had some anatomical knowledge to locate the kidney behind the peritoneal lining behind which it is hidden.

The lining membrane over the uterus was also cut through, and the uterus had been sliced through horizontally, leaving a portion of three-quarters of an inch in the body, while the rest of it was taken away by the killer.

This time, the killer had also attacked the face of his victim. Brown detailed the damage in his post-mortem report:

> The face was very much mutilated. There was a cut about a quarter of an inch through the lower left eyelid, dividing the structures completely through. The upper eyelid on that side, there was a scratch through the skin on the left upper eyelid, near to the angle of the nose. The right eyelid was cut through to about half an inch.
>
> There was a deep cut over the bridge of the nose, extending from the left border of the nasal bone down near the angle of the jaw on the right side of the cheek. This cut went into the bone and divided all the structures of the cheek except the mucous membrane of the mouth.
>
> The tip of the nose was quite detached by an oblique cut from the bottom of the nasal bone to where the wings of the nose join on to the face. A cut from this divided the upper lip and extended through the substance of the gum over the right upper lateral incisor tooth.
>
> About half an inch from the top of the nose was another oblique cut. There was a cut on the right angle of the mouth as if the cut of a point of a knife. The cut extended an inch and a half, parallel with the lower lip.
>
> There was on each side of cheek a cut which peeled up the skin, forming a triangular flap about an inch and a half. On the left cheek there were two abrasions of the epithelium under the left ear.

Dr. Brown suggested that the knife used was one with a sharp blade of at least six inches.

One gruesome and mystifying detail of this murder was specifically commented on by Dr. Brown. It concerned the colon: «A piece of about two feet was quite detached from the body and placed between the body and the left arm, apparently by design.» Why the killer would have taken out this part of the large intestine and stretched it out alongside the body of his victim remained a mystery.

Once again, the murder was perpetrated without anyone hearing a sound, although there was a night watchman working in a tea warehouse in the small square, with his door slightly ajar.

NOVEMBER 9, 1888: MARY JANE KELLY
(RIPPER VICTIM)

Mary Kelly has traditionally been regarded as the last of the Ripper victims. One of the reasons for this is that she was always seen as the end point for an escalation on behalf of the killer in terms of the damage done to his victims. Kelly was by far the victim who suffered the worst and most far-reaching damage.

Nobody has ever been able to track down Mary Kelly in the records, possibly because the name she used was not her real one. We know that she was supposedly around twenty-five years of age, that she stood five feet seven inches tall, and that she was said to be «possessed of considerable personal attractions.»

Mary Kelly was found dead in her room in Millers Court, off Dorset Street, at around 10:45 A.M. by Thomas Bowyer on November 9, 1888. Bowyer was working for John McCarthy, who owned the building where Kelly rented a room. The reason for Bowyer's searching out Kelly was to collect the rent from her. Looking through the window, he saw Kelly lying dead and horribly mutilated on her bed. The door of the room was locked, and it was not until 1:30 P.M. that it was broken open by John McCarthy, Mary Kelly's landlord, on the request of the police.

Dr. Thomas Bond was called in to assess the Kelly murder, although the medico who made the first examination was George Bagster Phillips. Bond wrote an extensive post-mortem report on the damage which is as sober as it is nightmarish:

> The body was lying naked in the middle of the bed, the shoulders flat but the axis of the body inclined to the left side of the bed. The head was turned on the left cheek. The left arm was close to the body with the forearm flexed at a right angle and lying across the abdomen.

The right arm was slightly abducted from the body and rested on the mattress. The elbow was bent, the forearm supine with the fingers clenched. The legs were wide apart, the left thigh at right angles to the trunk and the right forming an obtuse angle with the pubes.

The whole of the surface of the abdomen and thighs was removed and the abdominal cavity emptied of its viscera. The breasts were cut off, the arms mutilated by several jagged wounds and the face hacked beyond recognition of the features. The tissues of the neck were severed all round down to the bone.

The viscera were found in various parts viz: the uterus and kidneys with one breast under the head, the other breast by the right foot, the liver between the feet, the intestines by the right side and the spleen by the left side of the body. The flaps removed from the abdomen and thighs were on a table.

The bed clothing at the right corner was saturated with blood, and on the floor beneath was a pool of blood covering about two feet square. The wall by the right side of the bed and in a line with the neck was marked by blood which had struck it in a number of separate splashes.

The face was gashed in all directions, the nose, cheeks, eyebrows, and ears being partly removed. The lips were blanched and cut by several incisions running obliquely down to the chin. There were also numerous cuts extending irregularly across all the features.

The neck was cut through the skin and other tissues right down to the vertebrae, the fifth and sixth being deeply notched. The skin cuts in the front of the neck showed distinct ecchymosis. The air passage was cut at the lower part of the larynx through the cricoid cartilage.

Both breasts were more or less removed by circular incisions, the muscle down to the ribs being attached to the breasts. The intercostals between the fourth, fifth, and sixth ribs were cut through and the contents of the thorax visible through the openings.

The skin and tissues of the abdomen from the costal arch to the pubes were removed in three large flaps. The right thigh was denuded in front to the bone, the flap of skin, including the external organs of generation, and part of the right buttock. The left thigh was stripped of skin fascia, and muscles as far as the knee.

The left calf showed a long gash through skin and tissues to the deep muscles and reaching from the knee to five inches above the ankle. Both arms and forearms had extensive jagged wounds.

Thomas Bowyer, sent to collect the rent from Mary Kelly, discovered her through the broken window lying dead and mutilated in her own bed.

The right thumb showed a small superficial incision about one inch long, with extravasation of blood in the skin, and there were several abrasions on the back of the hand moreover showing the same condition.

On opening the thorax it was found that the right lung was minimally adherent by old firm adhesions. The lower part of the lung was broken and torn away. The left lung was intact. It was adherent at the apex and there were a few adhesions over the side. In the substances of the lung there were several nodules of consolidation.

The pericardium was open below and the heart absent. In the abdominal cavity there was some partly digested food of fish and potatoes, and similar food was found in the remains of the stomach attached to the intestines.

Bond's words about how the vertebrae of the neck were deeply notched have often been regarded as pointing to a parallel to what happened to Annie Chapman. Consequently, it has been argued that the killer tried—and failed—to decapitate Mary Kelly. As has been pointed out, the markings of the knife to Catherine Eddowes's intervertebral cartilages of the neck may well bear witness to the exact same thing. If so, we have three possible cases of attempted decapitation in the canonical Ripper series.

The two medicos, Bond and Phillips, estimated the time of death differently. Whereas Bond settled for somewhere around 1:00 to 2:00 A.M., Phillips put the time as late as 5:15 to 6:15 A.M. Two witnesses spoke of a cry of «Murder!» that could have come from Kelly's room, and they put the time of the outcry at around 3:30 to 4:00 A.M.

JUNE 1889: ELIZABETH JACKSON
(THAMES TORSO VICTIM)

June 4, 1889, was a warm day. On it, a young woodcutter by the name of Isaac Brett along with two friends decided to take a bath in the Thames as they were walking through Battersea. Cooling themselves down in the river, they noticed a parcel wrapped in white cloth floating therein. Fishing it out of the water and unwrapping it, they found a human thigh inside, and immediately set off for the nearest police station. There, it was noticed that the ladies' underclothing in which the thigh was found bore a marking. It carried the name L. E. Fisher in black ink. There was also part of a tweed ulster found with the parcel.

On the same day, but some five miles away from the spot where Brett and his friends had found the thigh, a riverside laborer named John Regan noticed how a band of boys were throwing stones into the Thames, trying to hit a parcel floating in it. Regan got hold of the parcel and opened it, finding human remains inside it. The contents were two large flaps of skin from the abdominal wall, wrapped around the uterus, placenta, and cord of a woman.

The very same doctor, Felix Kempster, who had worked on the Rainham case two years before was called in together with Thomas Bond to look at the case as various parts of the body were found and turned over to the police. Kempster's examination of the thigh led him to determine that the murder

*In the Elizabeth Jackson case, body parts were found
both on land and floating in the Thames.*

was not far removed in time: he initially believed it had been committed the day before the find, on June 3, but it was later thought that the murder was committed one or two days earlier.

Most of the parts were retrieved from the Thames, but there were two exceptions to that rule. On June 6, a gardener named Joseph Davis while at work in Battersea Park noticed a parcel lying on the ground. The area, some 200 yards from the Thames, was closed to the public and not many people would frequent it. The parcel contained the upper part of a woman's trunk. From it, the heart and lungs had been removed, while the spleen, both kidneys, and portions of the intestines and stomach were in place. The abdomen had been cut open from sternum to groin, and the sternum itself had also been sliced open.

The other parcel found on land was to cause much controversy owing to where it was found. On June 8, a journalist by the name of Claude Mellor noticed a parcel lying in a private garden on Chelsea Embankment underneath some bushes. Broken bush tops disclosed that the parcel would have been thrown over the railings surrounding the estate, which—remarkably—belonged to Sir Percy Shelley, whose mother was Mary Wollstonecraft Shelley. Mary Shelley was of course the author of *Frankenstein; or, The Modern Prometheus*, a horror novel about a scientist creating a man out of dead body parts and giving life to the abomination.

At the time of the Elizabeth Jackson murder, Percy Shelley was not living in the house. He had rented it to Arthur Charles, who had been appointed a judge to the Queen's bench in 1887. Charles, in his turn, was on vacation on the Isle of Wight in June 1889, which was when the parcel (containing one of Elizabeth Jackson's thighs) was deposited in the garden.

Whether or not it was all a coincidence that the thigh was found in the garden of a man related to the author of *Frankenstein* remains open to discussion. At any rate, the fact that the same killer had previously dumped body parts from the Whitehall torso in the cellar vaults of the New Scotland Yard building makes it a tantalizing possibility that he was mocking society. And there can be little doubt that it was the same killer: Charles Hebbert was, as has been pointed out before, adamant about this in his *An Exercise in Forensic Medicine:* «The mode of dismemberment and mutilation was in all similar, and showed very considerable skill in execution, and it is a fair presumption from the facts, that the same man committed all the four murders.»

Hebbert's assertions were to a large degree strengthened by a detail present in both the Elizabeth Jackson case and the Whitehall case: body parts had in both cases been found that were tied up in parcels using Venetian blind cord.

Elizabeth Jackson was the only victim in the Thames Torso series who was ever identified. The *Times* of June 26, 1889, reveals how this was achieved:

> After more than a fortnight of patient and unremitting investigation the metropolitan police have at length been able to place practically beyond doubt the identity of the woman, portions of whose mutilated remains have been found in the Thames from time to time since the 4th inst. By means of certain scars, and the clothing incautiously or recklessly left by the murderer, a number of persons have been able to declare in the most positive manner that she was Elizabeth Jackson, well known in some of the common lodging-houses in the Chelsea district. She was last seen alive on the 31st of May.

Elizabeth Jackson was a young woman of twenty-four years of age, who was pregnant at the time of her death. One of the things that had been discovered at the post-mortem was that there was a mark on a finger of the victim, indicating that the killer seemingly had removed a ring from it. Once Elizabeth Jackson was identified, it was confirmed that she had worn a ring on the finger in question.

SEPTEMBER 1889: THE PINCHIN STREET TORSO (THAMES TORSO VICTIM)

The torso found dumped in a railway arch in Pinchin Street on the morning of September 10, 1889, represents the final victim involved in the case made in this book against Charles Lechmere. This time, the damage done was different and less severe: no organs were cut out and the body was dumped in the East End. But we have Charles Hebbert to tell us that this victim nevertheless fell prey to the exact same man as the other three 1887–89 victims. It was the same «very considerable skill» once again, and there was even evidence that the killer had evolved when he killed the Pinchin Street victim:

> In the first two cases the vertebrae had been sawn through, in the third the sixth cervical vertebra was sawn through, but the dorsal and lumbar vertebrae were separated by cutting through the intervertebral substance, and in the fourth the intervertebral substance in the neck was cut, showing that the man was aware of the projecting anterior lip on the under surface of the vertebra, and suggesting he was becoming more expert in his work...

The sequence is a very clear one. It shows how the killer always wants to decapitate by way of knife and almost gets around to it in the Jackson case, but only solves the problem in Pinchin Street.

There were other matters that seemingly distinguished the Pinchin Street victim from the other torso victims. It is the only case where only one part was found, and it is the only case in the 1887–89 tally where limbs were left attached to the torso. Both arms were in place, whereas both legs had been taken off, along with the head. And while the others had all had their abdomens opened up—in the Rainham and Jackson cases by way of cutting from sternum to groin and in the Whitehall case by severing the body across the abdomen at the fourth lumbar vertebra—the Pinchin Street victim had only a shallow cut to her abdomen. It was fifteen inches long and ran from two inches below the ensiform cartilage down to the genitals, just opening the vagina. The abdominal cavity, however, was left unopened by the cut.

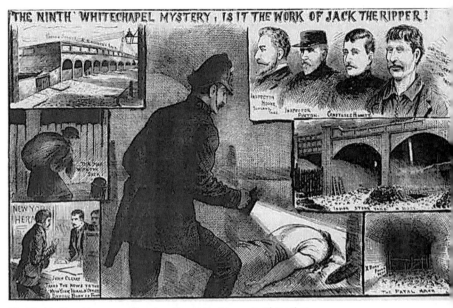

The Pinchin Street torso was found on Ripper territory, something that told this victim apart from the other Thames Torso victims.

The final matter that separates this victim from the other torso victims is, as Hebbert wrote, that there was no contraction of the muscles, meaning that for once it seems the killer did not set about cutting up the body immediately after having killed his prey. This, however, did not mean in any way that Hebbert thought the Pinchin Street victim didn't belong to the series. On the contrary, he was adamant that it did.

THE ONES LEFT BEHIND

In this book, I have chosen to exclude a number of possible victims from my presentation. As I have pointed out, I do so because these victims do not materially change anything when it comes to Charles Lechmere's viability as the combined Ripper and Thames Torso killer. I also feel there is a risk that they would detract from the clarity of the overall picture I am presenting.

It should be pointed out that these victims do not in any way present any obstacle for Lechmere being the killer; if anything, some of them actually strengthen that suggestion. Let's take a very quick look at them before we move on.

The 1874 Torso victim (suggested Thames Torso victim): This victim is very sparsely commented on in the sources. A headless body of a woman with no arms but one leg remaining was found at the Putney Riverbank in June 1874. This victim tends to be looked upon as a parallel case to that of 1873.

The Tottenham Court Road torso (suggested Thames Torso victim): This victim was found in October 1884, and may very well have been part of the Thames Torso series. She was skillfully cut up, and the head was found together with other body parts. On the head, there were wounds that were reminiscent of the ones in Ripper victim Catherine Eddowes's face.

Emma Smith (suggested Ripper victim): Prostitute Emma Smith was attacked in early April 1888. She was beaten up and raped and had a blunt object shoved into her vagina with such force that her perineum was ruptured, eventually killing her some days after the attack. Before succumbing to her injuries, she was able to state that she had been attacked by three or four young men. It has been suggested that this could have been the Ripper's work and that Smith, unwilling to admit that she was a prostitute, disguised the affair as a gang robbery.

Rose Mylett (suggested Ripper victim): Mylett was found dead in December 1888, and there was a clash of opinions about whether she had been strangled by a killer or had fallen down and choked to death on her own collar. There was no other physical damage done to the body. It can be pointed out that Mylett died in the vicinity of two Pickfords depots.

Alice MacKenzie (suggested Ripper victim): «Clay Pipe» Alice MacKenzie was found dead in Castle Alley in July 1889, in the midst of the murder spots lining Charles Lechmere's logical routes to work. She had had her left carotid artery severed and there were two stabs in her neck. A seven-inch-long cut ran between the bottom of her left breast down to her navel, and there was a small cut across the mons veneris.

Frances Coles (suggested Ripper victim): In February 1891, Frances Coles was attacked in Swallow Gardens and had her throat cut. She was found very shortly afterwards by PC Ernest Thompson. He noted that Coles opened and shut an eye as he looked at her, meaning that the deed was extremely fresh. Generally, a sailor named Thomas Sadler is regarded the main suspect for the Coles murder. He stood trial but was acquitted.

And there we are: We have singled out eleven dead women who have traditionally been perceived as coming from two sets of murders. One of the series was always believed to have been committed by a disorganized opportunist who shoved his deeds in the face of society, whereas the other was thought to have been perpetrated by a cool and calculating dismemberer with an intention to hide what he was up to.

The evidence as such has always been there to prove that these notions are misconceptions, to a massive degree led on by a lacking insight about the criminal mind on behalf of the Victorians. This factor should, however, not have been allowed to obscure the likely truth for such a long time. We have experienced more than a hundred years of gaining new insights about what sexual serial killers are about, and we are very far removed from the Victorian views on these matters. Nevertheless, what was framed as truths and hung on the walls back then has remained hanging and gathering dust ever since.

The time has come to clear that dust away and replace stale old misconceptions with an investigation that relies on modern-day investigative tools. In short, the time has come to introduce the East End carman Charles Allen Lechmere.

MEET
CHARLES LECHMERE

Anybody examining the case of Jack the Ripper is quite likely to start out by meeting Charles Lechmere. Since the Ripper series has traditionally been regarded as involving five cases only, and since the same tradition has dubbed the murder of Polly Nichols on August 31, 1888, the first murder in the series, this is logical on account of how Lechmere is on record as the person who found Nichols's body. Consequently, when the story of Jack the Ripper is told, we are normally invited to join Charles Lechmere on his work trek through Buck's Row in Whitechapel in the early morning hours of that ominous August day.

Charles Allen Lechmere was born on October 5, 1849, at 28 Church Street in the parish of St. Anns, Soho, London. He was the son and second child of John Allen Lechmere, a bootmaker, and Maria Louisa (Roulson) Lechmere. His parents married in 1846 in Hereford, and they had their first child, a daughter named Emily, the same year.

Charles was two generations removed from wealth and influence; his grandfather Charles Fox Lechmere (1782–1834), who squandered the family money he had received from birth, was in turn the third son of John Scudamore Lechmere (1746–1801), who was the master of Fownhope, the Lechmere estate in Herefordshire, where the family was very prominent. Historically, the Lechmeres have provided Britain with several important and distinguished characters. One such example is Vice-Admiral William Lechmere (1752–1815), who served under Horatio Nelson.

In the 1851 census listings, John Allen Lechmere is no longer present when his family is reported as staying in Blue School Lane of Hereford. He had abandoned the family at this stage and taken up a new life. Maria Louisa Lechmere, the mother of Charles, is listed as a twenty-five-year-old straw bonnet maker.

Seven years later, in 1858, we find the family in Whitechapel. Maria Louisa remarried the same year, to a police constable named Thomas Cross. Thomas was Maria Louisa's junior by nine years. The marriage was bigamous, since John Allen Lechmere was still very much alive and Maria Louisa's marriage to him had not been dissolved.

The next time the family crops up in the census listings is in 1861. At this stage, the four members of the family are all given as being named Cross. Charles Lechmere was now eleven years old, and this is the only proven existing public record where he carries the name Cross. Two years earlier, in 1859, he and his sister had both been baptized Lechmere. This took place a year after Charles and Emily's mother married Thomas Cross. It is not known who supplied the information to the census taker, but the likelihood is that it was Thomas Cross who did so.

Charles Lechmere's life is defined by documents with his name on them, from an early age and up until his death. There are more than a hundred documents with Charles's name on them, and with this one exception of the 1861 census listing, they all give his name as Lechmere. There is, however, a further possible link to the name Cross built into a case of violent death as early as 1876. We will return to that link later on, when we discuss the name issue as a possible pointer to guilt on the carman's behalf.

One interesting fact is that the family at the time of the 1861 census was living in Thomas Street, later renamed Pinchin Street. It is a street that will emerge frequently in the Lechmere family history, but also in connection with the murderous activities going on in the East End in the late 1880s.

In the next census, that of 1871, we find that Charles has left home and is now staying in Mary Ann Street. This street also surfaces on a number of occasions when the Lechmere family is researched. That is to be expected; the typical Eastender of the late Victorian London was a person who moved frequently, but rarely long distances. Many families were listed as living on dozens of different addresses over periods of only a few years, and many times those addresses only involved one or two streets.

In Mary Ann Street, Charles was kept company by his wife Elizabeth Lechmere. Both were twenty-one years old at the time, and they had married the year before, 1870, in Christchurch, Spitalfields. Elizabeth was born Bostock on May 20, 1849. Her father was Thomas Bay Bostock, a lighterman, and her mother was Susannah Ann Bostock, née Bland. Elizabeth, as well as both her parents, were illiterate. There were thirteen children in the Bostock family.

The year before Charles Lechmere married, 1869, his sister Emily passed away from phthisis exhaustion in the middle of the summer. She was only twenty-two years at the time.

As we move on to the 1881 census, we get a new address for Charles and his family. Now the family is staying in James Street, and four children have been added, ranging between one and seven years of age. Ten years later, the

*The armorial bearings of the Lechmere family of Fown-
hope with vulning pelicans. Drawing blood from
their own chests, they signify a will to
sacrifice themselves.*

number of children has doubled (the couple eventually had eleven children) and new lodgings have been taken up in 22 Doveton Street. This address is where Charles Lechmere lived when the Ripper murders were committed. He had moved there with his family in June 1888.

At this remove in time his mother had long since remarried, and once again the marriage was bigamous. John Allen Lechmere, Charles's father, died in 1879, seven years after Maria Louisa wed the shoemaker Joseph Forsdike, ten years her senior. Maria Louisa herself gave her occupation as a dressmaker in the 1881 census.

Living with the couple, who resided in the aforementioned Pinchin Stre-et, formerly Thomas Street, was a young girl of six years by the name of Mary Jane Lechmere. She was one of Charles Lechmere's children. Why she did not live with her father and mother is unknown, but we can see from the 1891 census listings that she stayed on with her grandmother. Maria Louisa had by now moved to George Street in St. George and taken up a new occu-pation, that of a horseflesh dealer. Joseph, her husband, had died in late 1889 after a long-term hospital admission.

In 1899 and at the age of twenty-six, Mary Jane Lechmere married Harry

Alfred Goodson, a printer's compositor. The couple did not take up lodgings of their own. Instead, Harry and Mary Jane stayed together with Maria Louisa in Old Gravel Lane. Charles Lechmere's mother had now reached the ripe age of seventy-four, but she had nevertheless once more managed to change occupations and was now a corn chandler. She lived on to see a new century arriving and died in late 1901 in St. George in the East.

Charles Lechmere himself was fifty-two when his mother passed away, and still living in Doveton Street, although not in number 22. By 1894, he had moved to Sceptre Street in Mile End, and from there he returned to Doveton Street and took up lodgings in the house next to his old one, number 24, around the turn of the century. He then moved in to 24 Carlton Road around 1902.

During his last few years, Lechmere lived in Rounton Road. He had opened up a general store and sweetstuff shop in the early years of the new century: he was listed as a grocer in 24 Carlton Road in 1902, and left a tidy sum of 262 pounds to his wife when he died on December 23, 1920, from a brain hemorrhage. Elizabeth survived him by two full decades and only passed away in 1940. The couple were buried in Tower Hamlets Cemetery in Bow, although not in the same lot. Charles was buried in a common grave when he died, whereas Elizabeth was laid to rest in a marked grave of her own in the opposite end of the cemetery. Her gravestone is long since gone, while her husband never had one in the first place.

These are the basics of what we know about Charles Lechmere's private life. Now let's turn to why I believe he was a serial killer and single out one of the eleven murders described above and look at it in minute detail. The murder is that of Mary Ann Nichols on August 31, 1888, and the reason for scrutinizing it so closely is that I think it holds—and always held—the key to the identity of Jack the Ripper.

BUILDING A RIPPER CASE AGAINST CHARLES LECHMERE

Anomalies, Inconsistencies, and Disagreements

The earliest details on record when it comes to how Mary Ann «Polly» Nichols was found dead in Buck's Row have all been handed down to us as a result of how Charles Lechmere told his story at the second day of the inquest proceedings. Three days had then passed since the Friday morning when Nichols was discovered, and it was Monday, September 3. The fact that it is Charles Lechmere who shaped this part of the story is logical: he was initially the only person in the presence of the body. However, this book will tell the story from Robert Paul's perspective, although he was only the second person to reach the murder scene.

The reason for this is not that I believe that Paul was a very good witness. As we shall find out, we can easily see that his narrative has serious flaws in it. Whether this was Paul's own fault or not is an open question.

The reason that I have chosen to tell the story from Robert Paul's perspective is of course that I believe that Charles Lechmere was the killer. I think that he killed Polly Nichols and lied his way out of it, and so I am not as willing to allow him to shape history as generations of Ripperologists have been. The main problem about accepting what Lechmere said as the truth is that until Robert Paul arrives at the murder scene, everything we are told about the proceedings is uncorroborated and coming from the same source: Charles Lechmere himself.

Let's therefore turn the tables and deprive Charles Lechmere of the advantage he has been handed for so many years. Let's instead tell the story about the murder of Polly Nichols as it should always have been told. Here is the corroborated version of what has traditionally been regarded as the first murder of Jack the Ripper.

In the early morning hours of August 31, 1888, Robert Paul stepped out of his dwellings in 30 Foster Street, setting out for his walk to work. Paul was a carman employed in Corbett's Court off Hanbury Street, and on this particular morning he was late. To make up for the lost time, he hurried along the dark streets. His walk took him down Foster Street for some forty yards, after which he arrived in Bath Street, where he made a right turn. He passed outside a well-lit brewery in Bath Street and then he traversed Brady Street and proceeded into Buck's Row. When he had walked about a hundred yards down Buck's Row, making his trek on its northern pavement, he noticed a man standing out in the street. This man was Charles Lechmere, a fellow carman. Neither man recognized the other. They were strangers to each other.

Knowing that the neighborhood was a rough one, Paul was unsettled by Lechmere's presence in the street. He reasoned that he could be a robber, not least since Lechmere stepped closer to himself as the gap between the two men was gradually closed. Since Robert Paul wished to avoid Lechmere, he stepped out into the street to round him, but to no avail: Charles Lechmere proceeded to close the distance to Paul and put his hand on Paul's shoulder, saying «Come and look at this woman.»

Robert Paul now noticed that there was someone lying on the southern pavement, right outside the gates of Brown's Stable Yard. The two men jointly walked over to her. There, they knelt by the body and Paul felt it for warmth, noticing that the hands and face were cold. He did, however, believe that he felt the body stir as he put his hand on the woman's chest. Accordingly, he told Charles Lechmere that he thought that the woman could be alive, but only just. In order to try and resuscitate her, Robert Paul now suggested that they should prop the woman up. However, Charles Lechmere said that he did not wish to do so and the measure was therefore never taken.

Once the cursory examination was over, Robert Paul informed Lechmere that he was late for work, and suggested that he should walk on and try to find a policeman to send to Buck's Row. At this stage, Lechmere said he was late himself, and the two therefore made off together in a westerly direction. Before they did, Robert Paul made an effort to pull the woman's dress down over her legs. When Paul first saw her, the clothing was up over her thighs and Paul did not want her to be indecently exposed. The dress would only come down to the knees, so that was how she was left lying as the carmen abandoned the scene.

A few minutes after Charles Lechmere and Robert Paul had left the site outside Brown's Stable Yard and reached Baker's Row at the far western end of Buck's Row, turning into its northerly stretch, they bumped into PC Jonas Mizen some way further up the street. Mizen was at this stage positioned at the junction of Baker's Row and Hanbury Street. The constable was in the process of knocking people up. The knocking up business was something the PC's were required to do; they knocked on doors and windows to wake people up who were due at their workplaces soon after.

PC Mizen was now informed about how there was a woman lying on her back in Buck's Row. This is actually all we can be certain about when it comes to the amount and character of the information passed on. There were three people involved in the process, and they all gave different versions of what occurred in Baker's Row. In order to get a clear picture of the matter, let's divide the three up and see what they said.

Robert Paul differs from the two others because there are two sources for how he described the event. All three witnesses gave evidence at the inquest, Mizen and Lechmere on September 3 and Paul on the 17th. Robert Paul was also interviewed by a paper, *Lloyd's Weekly Newspaper*, at some stage before the inquest proceedings. The interview took place on the afternoon of the murder day, and was published on September 2, since *Lloyd's Weekly* was a Sunday newspaper. Here it is in its entirety:

> On Friday night Mr. Robert Paul, a carman, on his return from work, made the following statement to our representative. He said:—It was exactly a quarter to four when I passed up Buck's-row to my work as a carman for Covent-garden market. It was dark, and I was hurrying along, when I saw a man standing where the woman was. He came a little towards me, but as I knew the dangerous character of the locality I tried to give him a wide berth. Few people like to come up and down here without being on their guard, for there are such terrible gangs about. There have been many knocked down and robbed at that spot. The man, however, came towards me and said, «Come and look at this woman.» I went and found the woman lying on her back. I laid hold of her wrist and found that she was dead and the hands cold. It was too dark to see the blood about her. I thought that she had been outraged, and had died in the struggle. I was obliged to be punctual at my work, so I went on and told the other man I would send the first policeman I saw. I saw one in Church-row, just at the top of Buck's-row, who was going round calling people up, and I told him what I had seen, and I asked him to come, but he did not say whether he should come or not. He continued calling the people up, which I thought was a great shame, after I had told him the woman was dead. The woman was so cold that she must have been dead some time, and either she had been

lying there, left to die, or she must have been murdered somewhere else and carried there. If she had been lying there long enough to get so cold as she was when I saw her, it shows that no policeman on the beat had been down there for a long time. If a policeman had been there he must have seen her, for she was plain enough to see. Her bonnet was lying about two feet from her head.

So here we have Robert Paul being quoted as having said that «I told him what I had seen» about the encounter with Jonas Mizen. However, we can clearly see that Robert Paul tells a story in which he does not mention that Charles Lechmere was also present in Baker's Row. He claims to have told Lechmere that he himself would go looking for a PC, and then he says «I went on» instead of «we went on,» effectively taking Lechmere out of the story.

From the inquest, we know for certain that the two carmen walked together and found Mizen together, so when it comes to the *Lloyd's Weekly Newspaper* interview, we must conclude that either Paul exaggerated his own role or the reporter did it for him. This is further emphasized by noting that Paul claims that the woman was so cold that she must have been long dead, although we know from the inquest reports that he actually thought Nichols was probably still alive, as he felt her chest and noticed a stirring movement inside it. Whether this inconsistency is the work of an inventive reporter or whether Paul actually gave two differing accounts of the matter is impossible to say. It may, however, be that Robert Paul was a person who did not like the police, and so he took a chance to accuse them of slack work when speaking to the paper, whereas he was more truthful when testifying at the inquest, for fear of being exposed as a liar. The papers had reported from the inquest that Charles Lechmere had mentioned Paul's detecting movement when feeling the chest of Nichols. A further indication of how Paul may have been hostile to the police lies in how we know that he did not willingly come forward to the inquest, but had to be sought out and fetched from the East End streets. It seems clear that the *Lloyd's* article contains material that needs to be treated with caution.

When we turn to the inquest proceedings, we get a different picture of the carmen's interaction with PC Mizen. Robert Paul gave his testimony on September 17, two weeks after Lechmere and Mizen had contributed their views on the matter. We do not have the original inquest reports, so we must rely on the various newspapers. These do not always give the exact same version of what was said, meaning that we have to try and make as good sense as possible of the respective articles after having weighed them together. Generally speaking, we may conclude that Paul now gave a different version from the one in his paper interview. The essence of what he said is well captured in the *Times:* «Witness (Robert Paul) and the other man (Charles Lechmere) walked on together until they met a policeman at the corner of Old Montagu-street, and told him what they had seen.» This version is roughly representative of what the newspapers reported, but there is actually one paper that seemingly tells a different story. It is the *Morning Advertiser*, where Paul is quoted as saying:

> I am a carman, and on the morning of the murder I left home just before a quarter to four. As I was passing up Buck's-row I saw a man standing in the roadway. When I got close up to him, he said, «Come and look at this woman;» and together we went across the road. There was a woman lying across the gateway, with her clothes disarranged. I felt her hands and face; they were cold. I sent the other man for a policeman.

We now have all three possibilities covered by various statements ascribed to Robert Paul. The *Lloyd's Weekly Newspaper* interview only speaks of Paul walking to Baker's Row and meeting Mizen, the bulk of the inquest articles have the two walking in tandem to Baker's Row, and the *Morning Advertiser* has Paul sending Lechmere to find a PC. How shall we understand these differences?

As has been pointed out, we can see that the *Lloyd's Weekly Newspaper* is incorrect. We know that the carmen walked to Baker's Row together. Does that mean that we must also rule out what we may refer to as the *Morning Advertiser* conundrum? Not necessarily, no. And the reason for this lies in how the papers many times condensed what was said to a significant degree. Once we know that, a possible solution to the *Morning Advertiser* conundrum can be gleaned. We will return to the solution of that riddle in due course, but first we need to look at what PC Mizen said about the developments on that fateful morning. Let's pick two different papers and see where we end up.

«Police-constable Mizen said that at a quarter to four o'clock on Friday morning he was at the crossing, Hanbury-street, Baker's-row, when a carman who passed in company with another man informed him that he was wanted by a policeman in Buck's-row, where a woman was lying.» (*Daily Telegraph*)

The information here is consistent with what most papers said. However, as we move on to the next paper, the *Morning Advertiser*, we will find out that the information in the *Daily Telegraph* was condensed, as earlier suggested:

> Police constable George Maizen [*sic*], 55 H, said—On Friday morning last, at 20 minutes past four, I was at the end of Hanbury street, Baker's row, when someone who was passing said, «You're wanted down there» (pointing to Buck's row). The man appeared to be a carman. (The man, whose name is George Cross, was brought in and witness identified him as the man who spoke to him on the morning in question). I went up Buck's row and saw a policeman shining his light on the pavement. He said, «Go for an ambulance,» and I at once went to the station and returned with it. I assisted to remove the body. The blood appeared fresh, and was still running from the neck of the woman.
>
> The Coroner—There was another man in company with Cross?
> The Witness—Yes. I think he was also a carman.

Here we can see that PC Mizen originally only spoke of one of the carmen. One man only had spoken to him, it would seem, and that man was not Robert Paul but instead Charles Lechmere (who is called Cross in the article, as he used that name at the inquest). The coroner actually had to remind the PC about Robert Paul's presence. It was not until he did so that Jonas Mizen acknowledged that Paul had also been on the scene.

No other paper clarifies how the coroner asked this question, although this detail is of course absolutely vital to understand how things went down.

Let's now turn to the third part in the drama, Charles Lechmere, and see how he depicts the matter. Did he say that Paul was the one contacting Mizen, does he claim that he did so himself, or does he describe it as a joint venture? Let's begin with the *Daily Telegraph*. The report therein is roughly consistent with how the other papers had it:

> He [Lechmere] and the other man [Paul] left the deceased, and in Baker's-row they met the last witness [Mizen], whom they informed that they had seen a woman lying in Buck's-row. Witness said, «She looks to me to be either dead or drunk; but for my part I think she is dead.»

There we have it. Lechmere claims that it was a joint effort, that both he and Paul walked to Baker's Row together and informed Mizen about the woman.

Another version with the same basic information can be found in the *Morning Advertiser:* «We left together, and went up Baker's row, where we met a constable. I said to him, ‹There is a woman in Buck's row on the broad of her back. She is dead, or else drunk.›»

Another element is added in the description in the *Echo:*

I said to a constable—the last witness—«There's a woman lying in Buck's-row. She looks to me as though she was dead, or drunk.» The other man then said, «I believe she is dead.» I don't know who this man was; he was a stranger, but appeared to me to be a carman.

So here we have vital information left out by the other two papers. Lechmere says that Paul also informed Mizen verbally about the find the two carmen had made and actually quotes his fellow carman.

We can immediately see that what Lechmere claims is not in line with what PC Mizen said. Generally, all the papers present Mizen as having said that «a» man who looked like a carman had come up to him and spoken. No paper has Mizen saying that two men jointly informed him about the woman. And we know from the *Morning Advertiser* that the coroner even had to remind Mizen about Paul's presence. The question that this offers up is evident: If both men actually did speak to Mizen, then why did he not say so at the inquest?

This apparent anomaly was one of the first things to catch my eye when looking at the role of Charles Lechmere in the murder of Polly Nichols. It would be followed by numerous others, each of them adding more and more to the feeling that something was not quite as it should be. Let's move on now to these anomalies and take a look at how they fit into the story.

THE DISAGREEMENT BETWEEN
LECHMERE AND PC MIZEN

There was a number of PC's involved in the early stages of the Polly Nichols murder. They can all be accounted for except for one—a phantom PC whose existence came to light at the inquest but who could never be verified to have existed. Let's return to the above quote from the *Daily Telegraph*, and listen to how PC Mizen spoke of this mysterious PC: «Police-constable Mizen said that at a quarter to four o'clock on Friday morning he was at the crossing, Hanbury-street, Baker's-row, when a carman who passed in company with another man informed him that he was wanted by a policeman in Buck's-row, where a woman was lying.»

We clearly have Mizen saying that Charles Lechmere told him that he was wanted by a policeman in Buck's Row. But we know from the statements made by Lechmere and Paul that there was no policeman in Buck's Row. So why does this other PC suddenly crop up in the *Daily Telegraph*'s inquest article?

Charles Lechmere informing PC Mizen about Polly Nichols. Interestingly, in the drawing, made some years after the Ripper deeds, the artist has left Robert Paul out of the scene..

Well, the PC does actually not only crop up there. He is present in the bulk of the articles, although not in all of them. The fact that Mizen did speak of Lechmere having alleged that there was a PC present in Buck's Row who had requested his colleague's presence there is firmly established. In some of the papers, like the *Daily News*, we learn that the matter was picked up on by a juryman:

> A juryman—Did you tell Constable Mizen that another policeman wanted him in Buck's row?
>
> The Witness (Lechmere)—No; because I did not see a policeman in Buck's row.

When it comes to Robert Paul, we get no further information about this matter. Although he could have been asked about it as he made his appearance at the inquest a fortnight after the two other participants in the drama, this never happened. And Paul offered no information about the issue on his own account.

A further anomaly lies in how Lechmere and Mizen made differing claims about how the status of the woman in Buck's Row was reported. Charles Lechmere claimed that Mizen was told that she was either drunk or dead. This is consistent throughout the various papers. Equally consistent is how Jonas Mizen says that he was merely told that there was a woman lying on her back in Buck's Row. There is even a passage in the *Star* of September 3 where we can see how Mizen explicitly declared that he had not been informed about how the woman was possibly dead: «Cross told him a policeman wanted him. He did not say anything about murder or suicide.»

What does all this add up to? That depends on who we listen to. If we listen to Lechmere, we get a picture of a law-abiding citizen who gave the correct information and did his best to help Polly Nichols. But if we listen to PC Mizen, we can begin to outline a scenario where Charles Lechmere coolly and cleverly lied his way out of having killed Polly Nichols himself.

If we accept that Charles Lechmere killed Polly Nichols, we can understand how he would have been well served by implying to Mizen that the woman in Buck's Row was not in grave danger. If, as Mizen tells us, Lechmere only spoke of a woman on her back, it would have looked like a tedious errand about a woman who had had too much to drink. If he furthermore told Mizen that another PC was present in Buck's Row, then Mizen could rely on this other PC to attend to the matter at hand.

Obviously, if this other PC had found Lechmere and Paul with the body, he would not have sent them on their way. Therefore, Mizen would feel certain that the carmen had arrived as mere spectators in Buck's Row after the other PC found the woman, and that they had been sent as messenger boys to himself by that other PC.

It would have been an ingenious method to allow for Lechmere to circumnavigate PC Mizen, and indeed, this was exactly what happened. Jonas Mizen accepted what he had been told, and sent the carmen on their way as he himself set out toward Buck's Row to find the woman and the fellow PC. He did not even take the carmen's names—why would he, if he had a colleague in charge in Buck's Row who had assessed them already?

Of course, if Charles Lechmere lied to PC Mizen, it would require that Mizen was never informed that Lechmere himself was the finder of the body. It goes without saying that if this vital information had been given to Mizen, the PC would not have let the men go, least of all without taking down their names.

Here we have the makings of a perfect crime, cleverly thought out and executed. This is where the inquest should have picked up on the potential explosiveness of what was said, but it never did. If the juryman who asked whether Lechmere had really told Mizen of another PC had pressed the point further, we would perhaps have had an entirely different outcome. But the moment—and opportunity—passed.

The main reason for how a seemingly apparent lie was allowed to pass on the murder morning lies in a truly amazing addition to the story: when Jonas Mizen arrived to the murder site in Buck's Row, there was actually a second PC in place! This was PC John Neil, who walked a half-hour-long beat that included Buck's Row. He had turned into the street on his round, and had found Nichols lying on the ground. He then shone his lantern on the woman and saw that there was a pool of blood forming under her cut throat.

As Mizen arrived to the murder spot, alerted to it by Charles Lechmere, Neil's presence there will of course have served for Mizen as confirmation of what he had been told by the carman. In fact, neither of the two PC's involved would have found any reason to believe that something was wrong, and this all boiled down to sheer luck on Lechmere's behalf. John Neil told the inquest that he had signaled the two PC's at either end of Buck's Row by means of flashing his bull's-eye lantern. He acknowledged that they had both duly arrived shortly afterwards. However, if a thorough check had been made, it would have been discovered that from the murder site it was impossible to see all the way up to where Buck's Row reached Baker's Row. For Neil to have been able to see the junction, he would have had to walk over to the northern side of Buck's Row. And even if he did, he would see only a few yards of the junction. Moreover, for Neil to be able to signal to Mizen, the latter would have to be passing those few yards at the exact time when Neil was looking west along Buck's Row.

The reasonable implication is that Neil only could see Jonas Mizen because he was already some way down Buck's Row and en route to the murder scene, summoned to go there by Charles Lechmere. John Neil nevertheless came away with the logical conviction that he had signaled Mizen down by way of his lantern. Mizen, on the other hand, was under the impression that Neil had called upon him by way of sending Charles Lechmere in his direction.

Neither belief was true.

But both beliefs served the purpose of getting Charles Lechmere out of harm's way.

When Mizen arrived at the murder scene, neither he nor PC Neil had any reason to check the validity of their respective beliefs. Mizen did not ask if Neil had sent for him, since he already believed that this was so—the carman's story had panned out. And Neil did not have to ask Mizen if he had arrived because Neil had signaled to him with his lantern—this was very obviously so, as far as John Neil was concerned.

And so, all the pieces fell in place, and although there were some confusing contradictions involved, the inquest satisfied itself that there was no foul play involved.

We can actually—to a degree—check in retrospect whether Mizen was really told about the phantom PC. If Charles Lechmere had been truthful and told Jonas Mizen that he himself was the finder of Polly Nichols, then when John Neil testified on the first inquest day on September 1 and claimed that he was the finder of the body, Jonas Mizen should have informed his colleagues that this was not so. If Mizen had done this, Neil would further not have claimed at a press conference held by the police on the 2nd that there were never any two men who were the real finders.

But Jonas Mizen never protested against John Neil's claim to be the original finder, and why would he? He was of course under the impression that Neil's claim was absolutely true.

One can only imagine Mizen's surprise when he subsequently found out that it was the other way around, that the carman who had spoken to him was the true finder.

Did Jonas Mizen at this stage think that he must have misunderstood Lechmere? Probably. At any rate, he seems not to have made it clear to his colleagues that there was a tangled web of misunderstandings, misinformation, and misleading involved in the matter.

In many ways, this is understandable: it was not until a few years ago that this potential key to unlocking the Ripper riddle was found. Not only the inquest, but also the contemporary police and press as well as generation after generation of researchers and Ripperologists have all missed out on the explosive potential of this detail.

The story about the phantom PC and the disagreement between Lechmere and Mizen is an extremely important red flag. Anomalies like these matters are what the police must always search for in the witness statements when looking for the perpetrator of a crime.

Are there any more such anomalies and inconsistencies to strengthen the case against the East End carman? Indeed there are—lots of them. Moreover, we have the distinct advantage of having the complete picture of the many murders committed back in the East End of late Victorian London. This means that we can piece things together with full hindsight. This was not an option open to the inquest in September 1888. They had the one case only (although Annie Chapman was added before the inquest was brought to its end) and could not outline the kind of pattern that offers itself up when we look at the full material.

So let's stay firmly on the track of the killer, more than a century after his murders, and let's do it the way a police force would have done today. We have our suspect, Charles Allen Lechmere, and we have begun to see how his path through the murder night is lined with anomalies and inconsistencies. What more can we pick up on?

THE PULLING DOWN OF THE CLOTHES

As has been pointed out, a prudent Robert Paul pulled down the clothes of Polly Nichols to her knees so as not to have her thighs indecently exposed. This element would not have meant anything at all to the inquest, for the simple reason that Polly Nichols was the first victim in the series. There were no further cases where there was the certainty of the same killer, and no comparisons could thus be made. When Annie Chapman was added on September 8, she was seemingly posed in a degrading manner, but no clear line had yet formed in this respect.

To those studying the murders today, however, we can see that there is very good reason to believe that the ensuing Ripper victims were left displayed post-mortem by the killer. It seems he took pride in what he did, and wanted to present his deeds explicitly to the world. This is a quite common feature in many sexually driven murders. However, in the Nichols case the many horrific wounds were not on display. Polly Nichols had had her neck ferociously cut down to the bone, severing all the major vessels inside it. Her abdomen had been cut open between sternum and groin, together with a number of lesser cuts alongside the larger one. But when Robert Paul arrived on the scene, he could see no wounds, because the clothes were pulled down over them all. And instead of having her legs obscenely spread like the bulk of the Ripper victims, they were only slightly apart as she lay on her back. She must have presented an almost peaceful image in comparison to what was to come, looking as if she had fallen asleep in the open street.

What this tells us, of course, is that the wounds were covered up before Robert Paul arrived, and the logical guess is that the killer did it himself. The question that follows is why a killer who seemingly took pride and pleasure in displaying his deeds would instead cover up the wounds in this particular case? If he had fled the scene, it would have taken him some time to do it—time that could have proven very dear when trying to escape. And why would he not be proud of what he did to Nichols, when it seems he was very proud of what he did in the latter cases?

The solution to that question is obvious: It is only if you are still present at the scene when the body is found that covering up the body can be an advantage, namely if you do not want any oncoming member of the public to find out what you have done.

The suggestion becomes one of Charles Lechmere choosing to stay put at the scene as Robert Paul approached, banking on how he would be able to fool him. Lechmere would then have used the minute it took Robert Paul to walk down Buck's Row to cover up the wounds, stash the murder weapon, and step out into the street, away from the body. It seems to point Lechmere out as an extremely cool character, and one who was able to think on his feet. It outlines a type of personality that is actually very common among serial killers, that of a psychopath. We will turn to that topic later, but first let's return to the listing of points of circumstantial evidence against the carman.

THE REFUSAL TO PROP NICHOLS UP

The next inclusion in the accusation act is how Charles Lechmere refused to help Robert Paul prop Polly Nichols up. This is in evidence from the many paper reports. Robert Paul thought he felt a slight stirring movement inside Polly Nichols as he touched her chest, and he therefore suggested that he and Lechmere should prop Nichols up, to try and see if she would come around. We can see what happened next in the *Times*, for example: «The other man (Paul), having put his hand over her heart, said ‹I think she is breathing.› He wanted witness (Lechmere) to assist in shifting her, but he would not do so.»

It was Charles Lechmere who called on Paul for assistance with Nichols. Together with Paul, he examined the woman. But then, when asked to help prop her up, he refused to do so. That is decidedly odd for somebody who has himself initiated a rescue effort.

But of course, once we reason that Lechmere was the killer, we can see that propping Nichols up would have given away what had happened to her, since her head only hung on to her body by the spine.

LECHMERE'S CLAIM ON PAUL'S BEHALF

In the material we have looked at, we have seen that Charles Lechmere claimed that Robert Paul told PC Mizen that he believed that the woman in Buck's Row was dead. But we have also seen that Robert Paul actually believed that she could be breathing—he thought she stirred as he touched her chest. So why would Paul tell PC Mizen that he thought she was dead if in fact he believed that she could well be alive?

One reason for Lechmere to make this claim could be that he wanted to

Eastenders of Victorian London, separated from Buckingham Palace by a few miles only, but living in an entirely different world.

present a picture where Mizen was fully informed about how the carmen thought that the woman was either drunk or dead. Also, of course, if Lechmere lied to Mizen without Paul being close enough to be able to hear it, he would not want that element to be known. He would have preferred to give the picture that Paul had been present, since that would guarantee that Lechmere was not lying about it.

This is where we return to the so-called *Morning Advertiser* conundrum, referred to some pages back. Let's recap what was said in the paper, Robert Paul speaking:

> I am a carman, and on the morning of the murder I left home just before a quarter to four. As I was passing up Buck's-row I saw a man standing in the roadway. When I got close up to him, he said, «Come and look at this woman;» and together we went across the road. There was a woman lying across the gateway, with her clothes disarranged. I felt her hands and face; they were cold. I sent the other man for a policeman.

This quotation has always been looked upon with great skepticism, since it sounds as if Paul sent Lechmere from Buck's Row to Mizen, while we know full well that this was not the case. We also know that Paul never made such a claim at the inquest. However, if what we have here is another example of a condensed report, it may be that what Paul said was that the two walked together to Baker's Row where they saw a PC, and that Paul at that stage sent Lechmere to talk to him. It should be noted that Paul is not quoted as having said that he sent Lechmere to look for a policeman, only that he sent him for a policeman.

Suddenly, the wording makes a whole lot of sense. And in addition, there is another quotation, this time from the *Echo*, where Paul is described like this: «There was another man in company of Cross when the latter spoke to witness. The other man, who went down Hanbury-street, appeared to be working with Cross.»

Here, it seems that Paul actually proceeded to walk down Hanbury Street as Lechmere did the talking to Mizen. Once we look at things this way, it clearly points a further finger of accusation at Charles Lechmere. It looks as if he saw to it that Paul would not be able to reveal what Lechmere actually told PC Mizen.

THE BLOOD EVIDENCE

One topic that has been hotly debated in recent years is the blood evidence. This, as in so many other issues, is a result of the many different reports in the newspapers. However, we can easily see that there is an overall consistent and logic picture when we take a look at the timeline. And it is in perfect line with Charles Lechmere being the killer of Polly Nichols.

The logical outcome of a blood flow is easy enough to establish. When a wound is opened up, blood will pass through it and end up on the outside of the body. A comparison would be to make a hole in a plastic bag filled with water and hang it from a tree branch: the water will of course pass out through the hole and end up outside the bag. However, what governs how much water will pass through the hole is where the hole is made. If we make it in the bottom of the bag, it will lose more or less all its water. But if we make it high up, all the water that is positioned below the hole will remain in the bag. If the hole we make in the bag is big, the water will pass through it very quickly. If we make a tiny hole with a needle, it will take a lot more time.

Basically, the same rules apply to a human body when blood vessels are cut open. The more and the larger vessels that are cut, the quicker the blood will leave the body. If many enough large vessels are cut open, there will be an exsanguination that involves all the blood that is positioned over the position of the cut, whereas the blood positioned under it will remain in the body. Theoretically, if we hang a human body by the neck from a tree branch and cut open one or more of the large vessels in the neck, the blood that will flow out is the blood over the cut, whereas the blood under the neck will remain in the body. If we instead cut off the feet, then all the blood will flow out, leaving the body drained.

There are, however, a few things that distinguish us from water-filled bags, and these things will have an impact. For instance, we have hearts that pump the blood through our bodies. This means that a body hung from a tree branch with one or more large vessels in the neck cut open will actually empty blood from below the cut too. This is because of how the heart pumps the blood out of the body under pressure. And the heart would keep pumping for some time even after the neck vessels were cut open. Eventually, the blood loss would cause the heart to stop pumping and whatever blood that remained in the body would be trapped inside it. Similarly, the beating of the heart would speed up the draining process in the example with the cut-away feet, but in that case, once the heart stopped beating the blood would still drain out more or less completely, only at a decreased speed. It would not require any pressure to drain the body out; it would be a simple matter of gravity.

There are other factors that may have an impact. Vessels can actually contract and close themselves when cut. It is a defense reaction our bodies are capable of—to a degree. The body is also able to mend itself when it comes to cut vessels on many occasions, depending on the severity of the damage done. Generally speaking, arteries are under higher pressure and therefore more dangerous to cut than veins, where the low pressure makes for a better chance for the vessel to seal.

When looking at the Polly Nichols case, it is vital to add the information that nobody who has all the major vessels in the neck severed—and this was the case in Buck's Row—can have a vessel contraction stopping the blood flow. It is impossible, as per the medical expertise. No contraction can occur if all the large vessels in the neck are cut open.

Having taken stock of this information, it is easy to see why the observations of the blood flow in the Nichols murder form a logical sequence. Charles Lechmere and Robert Paul said at the inquest that the darkness prohibited them from seeing any blood, but in all likelihood there was not much blood to see as the carmen examined the body.

The blood pool that formed under the neck was never a large one. Dr.

Llewellyn, who examined the body in situ at around 4:05–4:10, said that the amount of blood in the pool under Polly Nichols's neck would be «about enough to fill two large wine glasses, or half a pint at the outside.» And let's keep in mind that the doctors' observation was made after the blood had stopped running, whereas it is obvious that it was still running from the neck, not only as the carmen were in place but also several minutes afterwards. Basically, what Llewellyn saw was the total amount of blood that had run into the pool, while the other observers saw the pool in different stages of growth.

Keeping in mind that the carmen could see Polly Nichols's hat on the ground, some two feet away from the body, that Lechmere said that he saw a shape lying outside Brown's Stable Yard from the opposite pavement, and that Paul saw that the clothes were pulled up over the thighs and was able to grab onto them and pull them down to the knees, we understand that it was not pitch dark. Therefore, if there had been any dark blood visible, the carmen would arguably have been able to see that too. What light there was would have been reflected in the surface of the blood. The suggestion must be that there was probably at this stage only a small pool of blood and that this pool was more or less hidden under the neck in a manner that prevented the carmen from noticing any of it.

The next person to comment on the blood was PC Neil. He improved the lighting conditions by shining his bull's-eye lamp on Polly Nichols, and stated afterwards that the first thing he noticed was the pool of blood under the neck. He also noted that there was a gaping cut in the throat, an inch or two wide. Neil described the blood as «oozing» from the wound, but also as «running» from it. Regardless of what we make of those terms, we can note that the blood flow was still ongoing as Neil saw Nichols. The PC was in place a few minutes only after the carmen, but we should nevertheless accept that the pool of blood would have grown at that stage, now making it easier to notice.

Once Neil was made aware of what had happened, he heard his colleague PC Thain passing at the junction of Brady Street and Buck's Row, around one hundred and thirty yards away to the east, and signaled him down. PC Thain, however, does not mention having taken a look at the blood flow as he arrived at the spot. He is the only policeman of the three PC's initially involved who offers no information on this point. He was informed about the cut throat and sent off to fetch Dr. Llewellyn, who had his practice at 152 Whitechapel Road, a quick two- or three-minute walk from the murder spot.

Next up to pass comment on the blood was PC Mizen. After he was informed about the woman in Buck's Row, he made his way there. He arrived at the site when PC Neil was present by the side of Polly Nichols, but after PC Thain had already been sent for Dr. Llewellyn.

Mizen commented on the blood at the inquest. He said it was «still running» and «appeared fresh» and that is was in the process of coagulating in the pool.

Here we must return to the paper reports from the inquest and their various wordings. A handful of reports described Mizen's part in the errand, such as the *Morning Advertiser:*

> On Friday morning last, at 20 minutes past four, I was at the end of Hanbury street, Baker's row, when someone who was passing said, «You're wanted down there» (pointing to Buck's row). The man appeared to be a carman. (The man, whose name is George Cross, was brought in and witness identified him as the man who spoke to him on the morning in question). I went up Buck's row and saw a policeman shining his light on the pavement. He said, «Go for an ambulance,» and I at once went to the station and returned with it. I assisted to remove the body. The blood appeared fresh, and was still running from the neck of the woman.

We may note here that Mizen seems to place his observation of the blood flow at the time when he assisted in removing the body. However, such an assumption poses some serious problems. Mizen was sent by Neil to fetch an ambulance (which was basically a stretcher on wheels), and he did so up at Bethnal Green police station. The trip back and forth would have taken him around twenty or even thirty minutes, and to this we must add that Nichols was cut a number of minutes before Mizen spoke to Neil. And as Mizen arrived back with the ambulance and Nichols was put on the ambulance, the blood from under her neck had stopped flowing, as would be expected. PC Thain, who helped to lift the body onto the stretcher, said that there was at this approximate remove in time «a large quantity of congealed blood» under the neck.

Why then would PC Mizen say that the blood was «still running» and that it «looked fresh» if around half an hour had passed since Nichols would have been cut and if the blood under her neck was already congealed? Jonas Mizen would of course be fully aware that it had stopped bleeding, and he would know that the wounds in the neck were not fresh at all. A clear indication of how Mizen was aware of the congealing properties of blood can be found in the *Star* of September 3: «He noticed blood running from the throat to the gutter. There was only one pool; it was somewhat congealed.» Ergo, Mizen knew that the blood had started congealing as he first saw it. And since blood will start congealing roughly around four minutes after it exits the body, we have exactly what we should expect, since Mizen must have arrived more than four minutes after Nichols was cut. The blood that had originally left the wound would be in the process of congealing, whereas the blood that had only recently exited the wound and was «still running,» as per Mizen, would be perfectly uncongealed and looking fresh.

Once again, we seem to be looking at a condensation of the material on behalf of the papers. The solution to the conundrum of what Mizen claimed is presented by one paper only, the *Echo*, where the conversation from the inquest is recorded in a fuller manner, albeit with faulty time given (the *Echo* says that PC Mizen encountered Lechmere at twenty minutes past four, whereas all other sources say 3:45 A.M.):

> Police-constable George Myzen, 55 H, said that on Friday morning, at twenty minutes past four, he was at the corner of Hanbury-street, Baker's-row, when a man, who looked like a carman, said, «You are wanted in Buck's-row.» Witness now knew the man to be named Cross, and he was a carman. Witness asked him what was the matter, and Cross replied, «A policeman wants you; there is a woman lying there.» Witness went there, and saw Constable Neil, who sent him to the station for the ambulance.
>
> The Coroner—Was there anyone else there then?
>
> —No one at all, Sir. There was blood running from the throat towards the gutter.

We suddenly realize what happened. When Mizen went through his account and ended up at the sequence where he was sent for the ambulance, the coroner actually stopped him and asked him whether there was anybody but Neil present at the site as Mizen arrived there. It is only then that Mizen says that there was nobody else in place at that particular stage, and adds that the blood was running from the throat to the gutter.

So there we have it: the other papers missed out on reporting how Mizen was directed back in time by the coroner. His observations were linked to when he first arrived at the scene, and when the blood flow and coagulation mentioned by the PC are perfectly logical inclusions.

Last, but not least, we can see how Mizen adds a very interesting detail to the issue: At the stage when he arrived outside Brown's Stable Yard, the pool of blood under the neck had started to flow into the gutter. This is perfectly in line with the rest of the information: The carmen could not notice any blood because the pool was still small and obscured by the neck, whereas PC Neil immediately noticed the pool that had grown at that stage. When Mizen arrived it had run over the brim and started to pour into the gutter.

What does all this mean? It means that when Paul and Lechmere examined Polly Nichols, the wounds to the neck were very fresh. My belief is that they had been inflicted a minute or so only before Paul came upon Lechmere, and that the latter was the one who inflicted them. Recalling that neither carman said that he saw any wound or blood, it of course seems odd that the gaping wound to the throat was not observed by them. A possible reason for this could be that Lechmere used the pulled-up clothing to cover the throat cut alongside the abdominal cuts. The reason that Neil observed the cut immediately as he shone his lantern on Nichols could be that the wound became visible as Paul pulled down Nichols's clothes to her knees. This was done after the examination, and the wound may beforehand have gone unnoticed.

In a conversation with Professor Jason Payne-James, a specialist in forensic and legal medicine and consultant forensic physician and the forensic expert taking part in the documentary *The Missing Evidence—Jack the Ripper*, I inquired about how long time a woman with the damage that Nichols had would bleed from the neck before the blood had been emptied out and stopped running. I asked whether it could be a matter of perhaps three, five, or seven minutes. Professor Payne-James's response was that all three suggestions could per se be correct, but he personally favored three or five minutes as the likelier answer. It should be noted that Professor Payne-James was well acquainted with the total damage done to the body of Polly Nichols.

My own estimation of the timing is that many minutes would have passed after Nichols was cut and before Mizen could possibly have reached the murder spot. Coupling that with Payne-James's view, the outcome of the equation is obvious; it was in all probability Lechmere who cut the throat of Nichols. If it was somebody who preceded Lechmere, it would push the time into a less credible stretch.

A further factor of great interest here is how Robert Paul actually thought he felt a stirring movement as he touched Polly Nichols's chest in Buck's Row. It could well be the last movement there was within the body, testifying to how very close in time she had been killed when Paul put his hand

Whitechapel High Street in 1890, a teeming artery of the East End.

against her. If Lechmere cut her throat at around 3:45, then it would be perfectly logical for the body to still be able to stir a minute or two afterwards. It could even be a faint heartbeat Paul had felt.

The vital information linked to the observations of the blood flow means that a timeline can be formed. Along this timeline, the three observations made by the carmen and the PC's can be placed as waypoints, and Lechmere's potential as the culprit can then be tested against each of them.

The first waypoint is when Lechmere and Paul examined the body of Polly Nichols. At this stage, although the carmen did not notice it, the blood was already flowing from the wound to the neck, and the cut must have been made at least a minute earlier (if Lechmere was the culprit) or more than so (if there was another killer).

The second waypoint is when PC Neil arrived and noticed the blood flow, around five minutes later. At this stage, the blood would have been running for a minimum of six minutes.

The third waypoint is when PC Mizen joined his colleague outside Brown's Stable Yard, arguably around another three minutes later. At this stage, the blood was still running from the neck wound, and the blood in the pool under the neck was partly coagulated and running into the gutter.

The blood flow would have been ongoing for many a minute at this remove in time.

These estimations of the timing will have to take a number of factors into account. Let's outline in greater detail the kind of time perspective we are looking at.

We will work from Robert Paul's estimate that he arrived in Bucks Row at 3:45, and make the assumption that hearing Paul was what made Charles Lechmere switch from cutting into Polly Nichols's abdomen to cutting her throat in order to make sure that she was dead and unable to speak or in any way point a finger at him.

Accepting this course of action on Lechmere's behalf, we have put the cutting of the throat at as late a stage as possible. There is every possibility that the throat was cut before Paul stepped into Buck's Row, in which case the accusation against Lechmere is further strengthened. But let's work from the assumption that the throat was cut at 3:45.

We then have Robert Paul proceeding down Buck's Row from Brady Street, a stretch of some 130 yards, meaning that he could not have arrived at the body before 3:46.

After that, Charles Lechmere halts Robert Paul in the street and directs him to the body on the pavement, and an examination is made where the carmen feel the body for warmth, discuss the matter, and pull the clothing down over Nichols's thighs. That will have taken a minute or two. To understand the approximate time span involved, we can look at what Robert Paul said at the inquest as per the *Daily Telegraph:* «The man walked with him to Montague-street, and there they saw a policeman. Not more than four minutes had elapsed from the time he first saw the woman.»

If this is true, then we have a combined time of four minutes to add to 3:46 before Robert Paul and Charles Lechmere reached PC Mizen up at Baker's Row/Hanbury Street. This takes us to 3:50, if we want to land on the four-minute estimate that Robert Paul made.

We then have an exchange of information between Charles Lechmere and PC Mizen that we have no time measurement for, and we also have PC Mizen finishing his knocking up business before he set out for Buck's Row. If those two factors took a minute and a half, we are now at 3:51:30.

PC Mizen then had a stretch of roughly 300 yards to cover before he was at the murder site. If we have him walking at a brisk speed of two yards per second, it would take him two and a half minutes to cover that stretch, and he would arrive at the body of Polly Nichols at 3:54:00.

There are other factors to check the process by. PC John Neil, who was the first policeman on the site, arrived in Buck's Row from Thomas Street. The stretch to the murder site from Thomas Street was around 145 yards. The regulation day speed of a PC walking his beat was two and a half miles per hour, but it has been suggested that nighttime patrolling was speedier, reaching a speed of three miles per hour. Three miles per hour translates into 88 yards per minute, and so covering 145 yards would take PC Neil around a minute and 35 seconds.

Before we can find a starting time for Neil at the junction of Thomas Street and Buck's Row, we must get the two carmen out of Buck's Row and around the corner into Baker's Row. PC Neil did not see or hear them, and so realistically the carmen must have turned the corner and walked some little way from it before Neil arrived in Buck's Row. If we have Lechmere and Paul reaching Mizen at 3:50 as suggested, they would first have had around 80 yards to walk from the corner of Buck's Row/Baker's Row before they arrived at the junction Baker's Row/Hanbury Street, where Mizen was positioned. That means that at a walking speed of two yards per second, it would take the carmen forty seconds to walk from the corner of Buck's Row/Baker's Row up to Mizen. Once again working from the assumption that they arrived at 3:50, they would then have turned the corner at 3:49:20. If we give them a further ten seconds to disappear out of earshot from PC Neil, that means that Neil arrived into Buck's Row from Thomas Street at 3:49:30 at the very earliest, after which he had a walk of a minute and a half down to the murder site. He would therefore have arrived there at 3:51.

On his arrival at the murder site, PC Neil noticed the body of Nichols on the southern side of Buck's Row and walked over the street. He flashed his bull's-eye lamp and saw that the woman had had her throat cut, whereupon he examined the body. He felt her arm and found it quite warm from the joints upwards. Let's assume that the whole of this combined process took a minute only. We then arrive at 3:52. PC Neil then notices the sound of a fellow officer, PC John Thain, patrolling up at Brady Street, and signals him by way of his lamp. Thain duly arrives at the site after having walked the 130 yards from Brady Street. Another minute has now passed and we are at 3:53. Neil informs Thain about what has happened and sends him for Dr. Llewellyn.

PC Neil then turns to the other end of Buck's Row and notices another PC. It is PC Mizen, who has been sent to the site by Charles Lechmere. Neil now signals Mizen down with his lamp and the latter arrives at the murder site. If we accept that the information given to Thain and the signaling down of Mizen and his trek to the murder spot took only a minute, we get a time of

3:54 for PC Mizen's arrival at the body of Polly Nichols. It was at this stage he looked at the blood flow from the neck.

These timings allow us to see that there would have been a time span of around some nine minutes between when Nichols had her neck cut and when PC Mizen observed that the blood was still running from her neck as he arrived. If, that is, she was cut a mere minute before Paul arrived by Lechmere's side in Buck's Row. If not, then we need to add even more time.

These timings and observations of running blood play a pivotal role when making a case against the carman. If there had been no blood running as the carmen met at the body of Nichols, then Charles Lechmere would not make a very good suspect. He would in all probability have been nothing more than the finder of the body, some significant time after the real killer had left. But the blood was flowing as the carmen examined the body, and so Lechmere enters a stage of possible culpability.

If the blood had stopped flowing when PC Neil saw the body, then Lechmere would still not be in the clear. A body may well bleed out in a minute or two only, if the damage done to the body is large enough.

The space for another killer would nevertheless have been more pronounced if the body had stopped bleeding before PC Neil arrived at the murder site. This was not so, the blood was still running—and Lechmere becomes an even better suspect for the murder.

Finally, if there had at least been no blood flow when PC Mizen arrived, it would have somewhat improved the case for Lechmere's innocence, although it would not in any way exonerate him. We would already have had a case of around a six-minute blood flow, and that is more than ample time for the body to have bled out completely. In actual fact and as has been pointed out, Professor Payne-James suggested that three or five minutes were likelier suggestions than seven minutes when asked about the timing. But the blood had not ceased flowing even at the late stage when Mizen arrived at the murder site, and we now have a bleeding time of around nine minutes. In accordance with that, Lechmere of course becomes an even likelier suspect.

We can see that every one of the waypoints could have improved the case for innocence on Lechmere's behalf if only the blood had stopped running at any of these three stages. It is of course only the first waypoint that could have provided a really good reason for that innocence.

What we can also see is that out of the various possible outcomes of this test, Lechmere is handed the worst possible one. Each and every waypoint is completely in line with his guilt.

The alternative solution to Lechmere's guilt is to accept that another person cut the throat of Polly Nichols at least a minute or two before Lech-mere arrived at the murder site. The blood would then have been running for around ten or eleven minutes or even longer from the neck of Polly Nichols as Jonas Mizen saw her. This alternative killer would furthermore not have been seen or heard by anybody in the vicinity, and he would also for some unfathomable reason have pulled the clothes of Polly Nichols down over her wounds before he left the stage.

It is perhaps possible, perhaps not. It all depends on how long Polly Nich-ols bled. The one thing we can say with certainty is that an alternative killer is decidedly unlikely already from the outset as per Jason Payne-James's es-timate—and that such a person becomes even less likely with every passing second.

There is, however, nothing at all that takes Lechmere out of the frame. He is firmly caught in the eye of the storm.

There is one further element that needs to be added to the discussion of the blood evidence in the Polly Nichols case. From the above, we can see that although the amount of blood in the pool under Nichols's neck grew over time, there was never any great amount of blood in it. We know from PC Neil that the cut to the neck left a wound that was wide open, and we know that Polly Nichols was lying on her back, meaning that gravity would not stop much of the blood from leaving the body. We also know that the vessels could not have contracted so as to diminish or stop the blood flow. So why was there not a large pool of blood, one of liters of blood, under the neck?

The answer to the question is easy: because Nichols had also suffered very much damage to her abdomen. It was cut open in a large gash extending from sternum to groin and there were other cuts alongside the large one. Dr. Llewellyn was of the opinion that the wounds to the abdomen came first, and he said that they in themselves would have sufficed to kill Nichols. After having carefully examined the body, he indicated that much of the blood had collected in the abdominal cavity.

This is the logical reason for the small amount of blood from the neck. It was also said that much of the blood from the neck had soaked into the clothing of the victim, and that would further have reduced the blood on the ground.

At this stage, it is time to listen to a colleague of Jason Payne-James, namely Professor Ingemar Thiblin. He is a professor of forensic medicine at the Uni-versity of Uppsala, Sweden. He is also a senior doctor at the Unit of Forensic Medicine of Rättsmedicinalverket, the expert medical forensics authority serving the Swedish judicial system. For fifteen years, he was the chairman of the Association of Swedish Forensic Medicine.

Having looked at all the details of the Nichols murder, he concluded that Dr. Llewellyn would in all likelihood have been correct in his assessment about the abdominal wounds coming first.

Ingemar Thiblin laid down the basics of a case like that of Polly Nichols. Around twenty per cent of the blood pumped from the heart goes to the head. A grown woman has a blood volume of around five liters. The volume of blood pumped out by the heart in a resting body is around five liters per minute, and under a lot of exertion that figure raises to around 30 liters per minute. Reasonably, Thiblin says, in a case like this the body will go into a stage of stress, meaning that perhaps around 20 liters of blood are pumped out per minute. Therefore, there can be little doubt that a large amount of blood would have been visible around the neck a minute or two after the deed if the neck wounds came first.

However, Professor Thiblin thought it more probable that the cutting of the throat had occurred when Nichols was already dead or almost dead, reasoning that the blood that was observed running from the neck was passively emptying out from the head of Polly Nichols. The main reason behind the bleeding would likely be gravity.

Ingemar Thiblin also stated that there may have been some little heart activity involved in the bleeding, and added that even if this was not so, there could be a fair amount of blood seeping out from damaged vessels and inner organs. To establish just how long such a seeping bleeding could go on is hard to do, he noted, not least since there is for obvious reasons not much empirical data to go on. Ingemar Thiblin's own feeling was that it could possibly be a process of up to, at the very longest, ten to fifteen minutes. However, he very much agreed with Professor Payne-James about how three or five minutes of bleeding were more likely suggestions than seven minutes and added that although we may have to allow for longer than that, the likelihood is that this kind of bleeding must decrease with every passing minute.

And there we have it. Two professors in forensic medicine, renowned specialists in the field, agree that as we arrive at the seven-minute mark of continued bleeding, we have entered a time span where they are both are inclined to think it likely that the bleeding should have stopped. What we have on record is instead seemingly a nine-minute bleeding time if Lechmere was the killer. Worse still, if we want to find another killer, we need to add a further minute or two, at the very least, ending up at a time span that is even further removed from what should be realistically expected.

Since there are no cases to compare from and since every case is unique, neither professor excludes the possibility that Nichols could have bled for a period of time that could perhaps have allowed for another killer. The message from these specialists is nevertheless loud and clear: Charles Lechmere is very much likelier to have been the cutter than another killer preceding him in Buck's Row.

In short: The bleeding times involved in the Polly Nichols case leave us with only one truly reasonable candidate for the killer's role.

THE TIMING ASPECT

There are two aspects of timing that are crucial to the question about Lechmere's guilt. The first one has already been covered, pointing to how the passing minutes at the crime site in combination with the blood evidence speaks loudly for Lechmere being the probable culprit. The second aspect has to do with when in time Lechmere was found standing in close vicinity to the victim in Buck's Row by Robert Paul.

There is contradictory information regarding the matter, as so often in the Ripper case. We have Robert Paul's *Lloyd's Weekly Newspaper* interview to begin with. In it, he states that it was «exactly» 3:45 as he passed down Buck's Row, heading for his job. At the inquest, he gave information that is in total agreement with this very precise timing, since he said that «on the morning of the murder I left home just before a quarter to four.» The stretch he had to cover to arrive in Buck's Row from his Foster Street home would not take more than a minute or two to cover, so everything pans out. He left home at 3:43–3:44 and was therefore walking up Buck's Row at exactly 3:45. Presumably, his wording tells us that he kept close track of the time, using a clock.

The problem with Robert Paul's timing is that the three policemen who were involved in the initial stages of the case, PC's Neil, Thain, and Mizen, all said that they got engaged in the case at 3:45. Whether they came to this conclusion on their own, man by man, or whether they discussed it beforehand and settled together for 3:45, is unknown. But if Paul walked down Buck's Row at 3:45, he would have arrived at the murder site at 3:46 (the stretch was more than a hundred yards from Brady Street), where he examined the body of Polly Nichols together with Charles Lechmere. As shown in the previous chapter, the carmen will not have turned the corner up at Baker's Row any earlier than around 3:49:20. After this, as has been pointed out, we should add another minute and a half at normal patrolling pace for Neil to walk down to the murder site from where he turned into Buck's Row, seemingly at the junction with Thomas Street. We are now at around

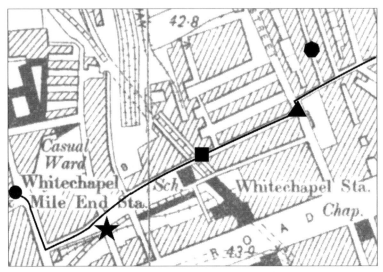

Some important positions from the Nichols murder night, with the line representing Charles Lechmere's path. Heptagon: 30 Foster street, where Robert Paul lived. Triangle: The junction of Bucks Row and Brady Street. Cube: The murder spot. Star: The junction up at Thomas Street where PC Neil entered Buck's Row. Circle: Where Lechmere spoke to PC Mizen.

3:51 as PC Neil arrives at the body of Polly Nichols, a full six minutes after 3:45.

It is quite possible that all three PC's were actually engaged at roughly the same time. Neil may have flagged down Thain close in time to his finding the body, and Mizen may more or less simultaneously have been contacted by Lechmere up at Baker's Row.

Two police reports signed by Donald Swanson, the man who was made responsible for collecting and sorting all information pertaining to the Ripper case by Robert Anderson, concern themselves to a significant degree with the Nichols case. In the first, dated September 19, the time given for when Lechmere and Paul met at the murder site is 3:40. In the second report, from October 19, the timing is amended to 3:45, so it would seem that the police ultimately settled for Paul's timing being correct. Very clearly, and although the suggestion that the carmen met at the murder spot at around 3:40 is better in line with the PC's all claiming to have been called into action at 3:45, the earlier timing was ultimately rejected in favor of the 3:45 timing. And there are important factors pointing to this being absolutely correct.

One such factor has to do with when Dr. Llewellyn was woken up, got dressed, and found his way to the murder spot, escorted by PC Thain. Llewellyn had his practice at 152 Whitechapel Road, and he stated at the inquest that he was called up by a policeman (who would be PC Thain) at «around four o'clock» in the morning. As discussed in the previous chapter, if Paul's 3:45 timing was correct, then PC Thain would have arrived at the murder spot at around 3:53. He was then informed by PC Neil about the woman and sent to fetch Dr. Llewellyn. From the murder spot, he would have had a two- or three-minute walk to 152 Whitechapel Road. If he took off from Buck's Row at 3:53, he should have reached Llewellyn's practice at 3:55–3:56. And although Llewellyn at the inquest said that he was called up at around four o'clock, the doctor actually made an earlier statement that was recorded in the *Daily News* and the *Evening News*. In these papers, he was quoted as having said that he was awakened by Thain's arrival at «about five minutes to four.» If this was correct, we can see how it dovetails perfectly with Thain having left at Neil's request at 3:53. It also fits quite well with how Llewellyn would have arrived at the murder scene at around 4:05–4:10.

The exact time of arrival for Llewellyn is somewhat unclear, for a couple of reasons. In the *Daily Telegraph*'s report from the inquest, it says about PC Thain: «About ten minutes after he had fetched the surgeon he saw two workmen standing with Neale.» The *Times* makes it clear that this was the exact moment when PC Thain arrived back: «On his return with the doctor, Neil and two workmen were standing by the body.»

Since it would have taken Llewellyn a few minutes to get dressed and get his bag, we can work from the suggestion that he would have left his practice at the earliest around around 4:00 if he was woken up by Thain at 3:55. And it is not until Llewellyn leaves his practice that it can be said that PC Thain «had fetched» the doctor.

If the ten-minute estimation is correct, we should then have PC Thain and the doctor arriving at the scene at about 4:10. Walking back together with the doctor, carrying his bag, PC Thain would likely have traveled significantly slower than he had done in the opposite direction.

However, even if Thain and Llewellyn walked at a relatively slow speed, it would reasonably not have taken as much as ten minutes to reach the murder scene from Llewellyn's practice. Therefore, it seems that when Thain speaks of having fetched the doctor, he may be referring to the whole process taking ten minutes: five minutes for waking Llewellyn up, waiting for him to get dressed and get his bag, and another five minutes to walk to Buck's Row.

So if the two left in tandem at 4:00, it seems reasonable to suggest that they arrived at the murder site at around 4:05.

If, on the other hand, the information Llewellyn gave at the inquest was correct, stating that PC Thain only arrived at his practice at four o'clock, then it could well be that Llewellyn and the PC arrived at the murder scene at around 4:10.

The exact point of time at which Llewellyn arrived at the murder spot is not instrumental in how we must look at matters. Regardless of whether it was 4:05 or 4:10, Lechmere's presence at the murder spot is nevertheless in perfect line with being the killer. The time span after Polly Nichols's death that Llewellyn opted for was at most thirty minutes, so we should expect the murder to have taken place somewhere after 3:35—if we accept Llewellyn's suggested time window as gospel.

And of course, the earlier Llewellyn arrived at the murder spot, the wider the window of time for an alternative killer becomes. But the blood evidence has already shown us that this window would have been very narrow indeed—if it ever even existed.

There is another factor that fixes the time when the body of Polly Nichols was found to 3:45. When the coroner summed up the inquest on September 22, 1888, he gave his view on the timing issue like this, as per the *Daily Telegraph* of September 24: «The time at which the body was found cannot have been far from 3.45 A.M., as it is fixed by so many independent data.» Coroner Baxter did not present the data he was referring to, but it must be accepted that there was such data available. Of course, we can see how Baxter's stance is subsequently echoed in Swanson's earlier mentioned report from October 19.

If we work from the 3:45 timing, we can also take a look at how this dovetails with what Charles Lechmere said about his own departure time on the murder morning. Here too we have varying information. Most papers speak of Lechmere saying that he left home at 3:30, but the time 3:20 is also mentioned in one paper. It seems possible that he told the inquest that he normally left home at 3:20, but that he left at 3:30 on the murder morning. It would make sense if this was so, since we know that Lechmere told Paul that he too was late for work.

I have walked and timed the distance from Lechmere's home at 22 Doveton Street down to the murder site. The walk there, in normal walking tempo, took me seven minutes and seven seconds. However, the walk between the two addresses is not the same today as it would have been back in 1888, because of later changes in the infrastructure and layout of the area. Author

Michael Connor suggests that the trek would only have taken around six minutes back in 1888. But working from my seven-minute estimate we can see that if Lechmere left Doveton Street at 3:30, he should have been at the murder site at 3:37. If he left at 3:20, he should have been in place at 3:27.

So what was he doing in Buck's Row at 3.45? Why would a seven-minute walk take a quarter of an hour, more than the double amount of time—on a day when Lechmere was late for work and presumably in a hurry?

Why was he in Buck's Row when he should have been halfway down Hanbury Street?

Of course, timings are by and large not all that safe in late Victorian London. But since Lechmere was aware that he was running late, he must have checked the time. The inference is obvious. Charles Lechmere was seemingly in place in Buck's Row long before Robert Paul arrived. Long enough to have butchered Polly Nichols.

THE CONVENIENT ARRIVAL OF ROBERT PAUL

Let's now take a closer look at the stage when Robert Paul arrived at the crime site. How was that event described by himself and Charles Lechmere at the inquest? A representation that covers Pauls version of the events nicely could be found in the *Times:*

> Robert Baul [Paul], a carman, of 30, Foster-street, Whitechapel, stated he went to work at Cobbett's-court, Spitalfields. He left home about a quarter to 4 on the Friday morning and as he was passing up Buck's-row he saw a man standing in the middle of the road.

This version does not differ materially from what Paul had stated in the *Lloyd's Weekly Newspaper* interview: «It was dark, and I was hurrying along, when I saw a man standing where the woman was.»

Paul stating in the interview that Lechmere was standing «where the woman was» does not make it incompatible with the suggestion that Lechmere stood «in the middle of the road.» To begin with, Buck's Row was narrow, a mere 25 feet wide from wall to wall. And the expression «in the middle of the road» should not necessarily be understood as meaning the exact middle of it. Anybody standing somewhere out in as narrow a road as Buck's Row could well be described as standing «in the middle of the road.»

The one thing that matters is that Lechmere was in close proximity to the body. He may well have been able to back away from it very quickly in a few steps as he heard Paul turning into Buck's Row.

Over to Charles Lechmere now: what does he say about the encounter? We turn to the *Daily News* to find a fair representation of it:

> Charles A. Cross, carman, said he had been in the employment of Messrs. Pickford and Co. for some years. On Friday morning he left home about half past three to go to work, and passing through Buck's row he saw on the opposite side something lying against a gateway. In the dark he could not tell at first what it was. It looked like a tarpaulin sheet, but walking to the middle of the road he saw it was the figure of a woman. At the same time he heard a man about forty yards away coming up Buck's row in the direction witness had himself come.

There are papers that speak of thirty yards too, and the reasonable thing to do would be to think that Lechmere may have mentioned both estimates, along the line that he heard Paul coming as he was thirty or forty yards away.

A significant problem with Lechmere's claim about when Robert Paul arrived is that the street was silent at night. There are numerous testimonies speaking about how the streets in the area were even more quiet than usual, such as in the *Evening Standard* of September 1: «Mrs. Green, Mr. and Mrs. Perkins, and the watchmen in two neighbouring factories agree that the night was unusually quiet.» PC Neil himself gave a similar description of the night in the *Daily News* of the 3rd: «He had not heard any noise that night. On the contrary, the place was unusually quiet…»

At the time, the typical footgear of a working man would be hobnail boots. Every step taken in them would sound like hammer blows against the cobblestones underneath, but nowhere does either man, Lechmere or Paul, say that they were aware of the other man walking close by. If Paul was a mere thirty or forty yards behind Lechmere, the two should reasonably have heard each other and be aware of each other's presence. Paul would effectively have followed Lechmere for a minute or two, in between rows of houses that lined the narrow streets, making them act like acoustic tunnels, more or less. And as he stepped out of his lodgings in Foster Street, Paul would have been around forty yards from the bright lights shining outside the brewery in Bath Street, situated where Foster Street spilled out into Bath Street. If Lechmere was a mere thirty or forty yards in front of Paul, then why did not Paul see him passing outside the brewery?

In this context, we should keep in mind that PC Neil was able to hear his colleague John Thain's footsteps as the latter passed up at Brady Street when Neil himself was over a hundred yards away, tending to Nichols out-

side Brown's Stable Yard. But Robert Paul seemingly never noticed Lechmere before he came upon him standing still at the murder site.

There is another fact that makes it even more confusing that Paul did not
notice Lechmere. Buck's Row was very poorly lit, and what few lamps there
were seem to have been malfunctioning or broken with a few exceptions. In
his testimony at the inquest, PC Neil said that there was a lamp burning at
the end of the row, but he does not specify which end he was speaking about.
The one lamp that supposedly did burn regardless of this was a lamp outside
Schneider's Cap Factory. Making caps was a typical Whitechapel branch of
business, and the factory in Buck's Row would become one of the largest cap
manufacturing businesses in London, remaining in the same street into the
1960s. On the night in question, however, it was still a minor factory. But
outside it, there was a lamp shining.

The factory was situated around a hundred yards up Buck's Row after
having turned into the street from Brady Street, and on the northern side
of the street. This was the opposite side of where Polly Nichols's body was
later found some twenty-five yards further into Buck's Row. Both Charles
Lechmere and Robert Paul walked down Buck's Row on the northern side,
the side on which the Cap Factory was situated. This means that Robert
Paul would have had a light burning behind Charles Lechmere as the latter walked forty yards in front of himself. Accordingly, he should have seen
Lechmere in silhouette. Strangely, he never said he did. He only noticed
Lechmere as he arrived outside Brown's Stable Yard.

One logical solution to this enigma is of course that Lechmere was in
place in Buck's Row many minutes before Paul arrived, that he killed and cut
Nichols at this stage, and that he only aborted what he did when he heard
Robert Paul turning into the street up at the Brady Street junction.

If Lechmere noticed Paul as he turned into Buck's Row, he would have
had around a minute to cover up the wounds, stash his knife in his pocket,
and get up and silently back out into the street before Paul arrived. And if he
did, it explains why Robert Paul never heard or saw Lechmere until he came
upon him.

One thing the alleged distance to Paul of 30–40 yards conveniently does
is to provide Lechmere with a makeshift alibi. If Robert Paul had been closer
as Lechmere allegedly made his way out into the middle of Buck's Row, Paul
would have seen him do so. But he never did: he clearly points out in his own
testimony that Lechmere was already standing in place in the middle of the
road as he saw him.

What if we turn things around and take a look at what happens if Paul had instead been a few minutes behind Lechmere? Well, in such a case Paul would not help out with an alibi, because Lechmere would have had time alone with Polly Nichols, time he could have used to kill and mutilate her.

Isn't it very practical, then, that Robert Paul arrived in that exact minuscule window of time that disallowed him to see Lechmere stepping out in the street but allowed him to provide an alibi on Lechmere's account?

A summing up of the timings gives food for thought: If Lechmere left home at 3:30—as he himself claimed he did—he could have been in place at the murder scene for nine minutes when Robert Paul arrived there. If he left earlier, he could of course have been there any amount of time. But the blood timings suggest that Nichols was only very freshly cut at the time of Paul's arrival, putting a likely time of the cutting of the neck not too far from 3:45, weighing in the varying pieces of information we have.

THE NAME

A much discussed element of the case against Charles Lechmere is the name issue. It was only at some point in the first years of this century that it was actually found out that the carman's name was Lechmere. Until this was revealed, research efforts into him were always destined to fail, and much of the material that points a finger at him was out of reach.

Using an alias was no uncommon thing in the Victorian East End. There are numerous police reports that call people by two different names and make it clear that although you may be recorded by a specific surname in the registers, you could choose to use another name colloquially. In Charles Lechmere's case, he had a connection to the name Cross. He had a stepfather called Thomas Cross from 1858 to 1869, when Thomas Cross died: therefore, it is perhaps not unreasonable to think that Charles may have taken on that name, although he was always registered by the name Lechmere. However, around a hundred documents have been found with the carman giving his name to different authorities, either by having his name signed for him or by signing it himself. And on each and every one of these documents, he signs himself Lechmere, year in and year out. There are documents from 1888 with that name on them. There is one document only with the name Cross, and that is the census listing from 1861, when Charles was eleven years old. It may well be that his stepfather signed that document for him. And it should be noted that Charles and his sister Emily were actually baptized in 1859, the year after Thomas Cross had married their mother—and they were baptized Lechmere, not Cross.

It is also a fact that when Charles Lechmere's relatives of today were spoken to, none of them recognized that the name Cross had ever been used by any of the Lechmeres they know of.

Since the police reports involving his name do not tell us that Cross was an alias, the only conclusion must be that the police were not aware of his real name. Therefore, he must have chosen not to give that name to the police. He withheld it, for whatever reason.

Obviously, one such reason could have been a wish to stay unidentifiable to people in general. This suggestion does not work on all levels, though. We know from the reports that Charles Lechmere volunteered his home address of 22 Doveton Street and his working place at Pickford's of Broad Street to the police. He did so in addition to giving them the name Charles Cross. The information is included in Donald Swanson's aforementioned report from September 19. The one thing that he seems to have kept from the police is his real name of Lechmere.

The inference becomes that he was acutely aware that if he was investigated by the police, any lie that he produced could then be revealed and very troublesome for him. He could not say that he worked elsewhere than at the Pickford's Broad Street station, he could not claim that he lived anywhere else than at 22 Doveton Street—but he could give the name Cross, because when asked about it, he could always claim that he honored his former police stepfather by using that name. There was never any law against using aliases.

However, much as he gave this information to the police, he seems not to have given the same information at the inquest, in front of the reporters who would market the story in their papers. And this is odd to a degree, since the witnesses would always have been asked to give their names, addresses, and occupations. Accordingly, we can note how the amateur witnesses (excluding the police and medicos, for example) normally always give this information in the inquests of the time. The Nichols inquest was no exception; the reporters gave the addresses in their articles, although they did not always get the information correct. Robert Paul was in some papers called Robert Baul, and his address was variously given as 30 Foster Street or 30 Forster Street. The reporters relied on their hearing and it was easy to get the information wrong. Edward Walker, the father of Polly Nichols, was described as living in 15, Maidwell-street, Albany-road, Camberwell by the *Daily Telegraph*, in 16 Maidswood-road, Camberwell by the *Times*, and in 16 Maidwood street, Albany road, Camberwell by the *Daily News*.

Although these mistakes were quite common, they tell us one important thing: the papers would always try to write the address, although the reporters were not always certain of what they heard. And this is where we arrive at another anomaly in Lechmere's case. One paper and one paper only, the *Star*, had any information about the carman's address. And they gave it as «22 Doveton Street, Cambridge-road»—which is exactly how it should be spelled. It would seem at a glance that the *Star* reporter had no problem picking up on the information, and the inference would accordingly be that Lechmere spoke very clearly as he gave it.

But if this was so, then why did the other papers not have the address? We know that they gave it a shot regardless of whether they could hear it well or not, but in Lechmere's case—nothing.

An explanation to this enigma could be that Lechmere never stated his address at the inquest, and that an ambitious *Star* reporter simply asked the address from a clerk afterwards, to enable him to give the full information in his article. And this is where we suddenly need to make a leap back in time to December 29, 1876, when the *Islington Gazette* reported a lethal accident out on the London streets:

> An inquiry was held on Wednesday, at the Coroner's Court, touching the death of Walter Williams, aged four years, who was run over by a Pickford's van.
>
> Walter Williams, of 36, Cloudesley-road, a jeweler, and father of the deceased, said on Thursday last he was told that his boy was run over and killed. He made inquiries, and he had reason to blame the driver, believing he had not exercised proper care.
>
> George Porter, a traveler, said on Thursday, at about four o'clock in the afternoon, he was outside his brother's shop, 3, Elizabeth-terrace, when he witnessed the accident. He saw a Pickford's van going towards Liverpool-road, and he saw deceased and another child about to cross the road. The driver called out, and the witness then saw deceased reel against the near side shaft of the van about two feet from the pavement. The driver tried to pull up but the wheels went over deceased.
>
> Henrietta Owen, of 100, Aldenham-street said she was in Elizabeth-terrace on the day in question, and saw the child run over. The van was going slowly. One child drew back, but deceased was caught by the wheel.
>
> Dr. Hindhaugh, of Barnsbury-road, deposed that deceased was bro-

ught to his surgery in a dying state. The cause of death was internal injuries and fracture of an arm.

William Warner, of 25, Henry-street, deposed to seeing the accident, and said he heard the driver shout, but the horse was then on the child.

Charles Cross, carman to Pickford and Co., said he was crossing with his van from Copenhagen-street to Elizabeth-street, when two children seemed to come from behind a trap that was standing on the off-side, all in an instant, running against his horses. He tried to pull up, but found it was impossible.

The jury expressed the opinion that the driver was not to blame, and they returned a verdict of «Accidental death.»

Here we once again have the name Charles Cross figuring. And this Charles Cross was «a carman to Pickford & Co.» It would be odd in the extreme if there were two carmen with that same name working for Pickford's, and so the likelihood that this man is identical with «our» Charles Cross is very high. The Polly Nichols witness stated that he had been working for Pickford's for twenty years, meaning that he seems to have been hired by the company back in 1868—which was when the Broad Street station originally opened up for business.

An interesting matter is how the father of the boy who was run over and killed entertained suspicion about the carman not exercising proper care after having made inquiries. He initially blamed the driver, but in the end the verdict was one of accidental death.

How is all this helpful to us? Well, not least because we can see that four of the six witnesses who are quoted in the article apparently stated their addresses at the inquiry. One of them, George Porter, is stated to be «a traveler,» and it may be that he did not have a fixed address. He nevertheless mentions his brother's address as 3 Elizabeth-Terrace, and thereby he makes himself identifiable to the readers.

But the man who ran over the four-year-old boy, the carman Charles Cross, seems to have withheld his address.

This means that if we are dealing with the same man—and everything points in that direction—we are dealing with a man who twice seems to have declined to give up his address in connection with inquests that both concerned themselves with violent deaths.

The question that follows is an obvious one: What would Lechmere stand to gain from such a thing? Well, have a look at how the papers were able to present him: a carman named Charles Cross, working at Pickford's of Broad Street—where hundreds of carmen plied their trade.

Would even his wife—who was in fact illiterate and unable to read—be able to recognize her husband from such a description, if he never called himself Cross otherwise? Or would she think the description was that of a colleague of his?

This is where we may see the outlines of a deception: although the police would know that it was him, even his own family and friends would likely not do so if the name Cross was otherwise not used by him. And going by the more than one hundred signatures we have, he always called himself Lechmere. His children went by that name, his wife did, his post would reasonably have had that name on it, and so on.

It seems he did not want those who knew him to find out about his involvement in the Nichols murder—or the death of young Walter Williams. Of course, if he was the killer, it makes a good deal of sense that he wanted to keep that knowledge from those who could follow his movements on a daily basis.

THE WORKING CLOTHES

One further straw in the wind points in the exact same direction as the name issue. And once again, we owe our knowledge about it to a single newspaper that reported something the other ones left out. This time we are dealing with *The East London Observer* where it was written: «Charles A. Cross, a carman, who appeared in court with a rough sack apron on, said he had been in the employment of Messrs. Pickford & Co. for some years.»

Here we are informed that the carman did not arrive to the inquest in his best clothes, something that otherwise seems to have been the rule for the amateur witnesses. This is why the reporter remarked upon how the carman turned up in his working clothes, even brandishing his sack apron—it was unusual and unexpected. But what possible significance does it have? If we couple it with the way the carman seems to have hidden this home address from the inquest on two occasions of violent deaths, it may well point to how he never told his family he was going to attend the inquest.

Dressing up nicely would have given away that something was very much out of the ordinary.

Setting off in the morning in his usual work attire would make it seem likely to his wife and children that the head of the family was simply heading off to another ordinary working day.

As always, the devil is in the details.

GEOGRAPHY—THE LITMUS TEST

What distinguishes Charles Lechmere from more or less all the other Ripper suspects is that his presence at one of the murder sites in the Ripper series is firmly established. Luckily, we also have on record his own claims about why he was there and what he was doing at the spot. This means that we can approach the case in the way a modern police investigation would. It is long overdue; back in 1888, no such investigation into Charles Lechmere seems to have taken place. If it had, we would have had the carman's true name recorded by the police.

Alas, the Victorian police failed to pick up on the obvious red flags connected to Charles Lechmere. This would have been a result of two factors: how Lechmere did not fit the contemporary perception of a criminal and how he, seemingly out of a desire to help, contacted the police himself on two different occasions.

What we have done in this book is what the police failed to do back in 1888. We have identified multiple anomalies and oddities in the records. That is always the initial task of a police force looking to identify their prime suspect. We have also noted how the physical evidence of the case is in line with the carman's guilt.

Once a person of this character has been found, all efforts must be focused on mapping the life of the suspect. In the Nichols case, the geography and timings would not be something the police needed to go looking for, since they already knew that Lechmere had been in place at a time that seemingly corresponded well with when Nichols died. In a modern investigation, other parameters would, however, have been looked for: did he have a police record, did he have a history of violence, did he have access to a weapon that matched the damage done to the body, was there any blood on his clothing that could perhaps be linked to the case, had he spoken to somebody after the deed in a manner that implicated guilt, and so on. These are matters where we cannot go into in much detail today, whereas the sources would have been there to a much greater degree in 1888—but they were left untapped.

However, we have the advantage of being able to look at all the murders of the period, likely Ripper murders as well as only possible ones, and apply what we know about the carman's geography and timings on them. And this is the precise thing that the police look for when they are researching a string of murders that they believe—or actually know—are connected. The geography factor is the litmus test, as it were, of an investigation into a case of serial murder.

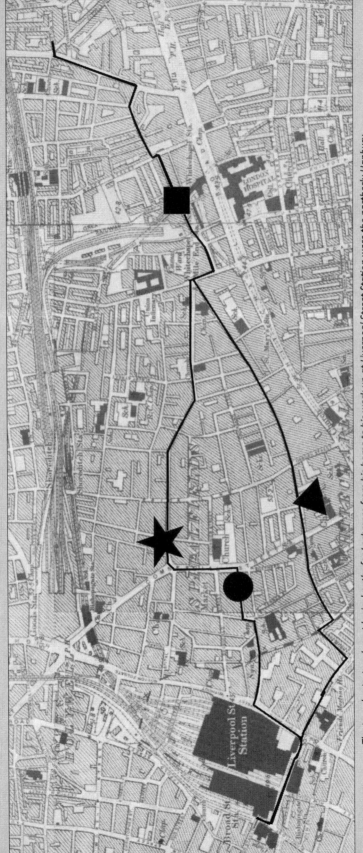

The two shortest and most logical paths for Lechmere from his home to his work up at Liverpool Street Station were the northerly Hanbury Street route, veering off to the north. The murder spots are marked. Triangle: Martha Tabram. Cube: Polly Nichols. Star: Annie Chapman. Circle: Mary Kelly.

Serial killer and pedophile Robert Black, who was arrested in 1990, is a typical example of how and why this kind of police work is conducted. Black was caught after having been observed abducting a six-year-old girl in the village of Stow in Scotland and driving away with her in his van. The observer of the deed took down the license number of the van and alerted the police. The van was located and stopped, and a relieved father could step into it and find his bound and gagged daughter inside a sleeping bag in the luggage compartment of the van.

Black was arrested, and criminal profiler Paul Britton was asked to look at the abduction case. He immediately noticed far-reaching similarities with at least three other cases where young girls had been abducted and subsequently found molested, murdered, and dumped. The three cases Britton referred to were those of eleven-year-old Susan Maxwell, who disappeared on her walk home to Cornhill-on-Tweed after having played tennis in Coldstream on July 30, 1982; five-year-old Caroline Hogg, who disappeared from outside of her home in the Portobello suburb of Edinburgh on July 8, 1983; and Sarah Harper, who went missing on March 16, 1986, after having left her home in Morley outside Leeds to buy a loaf of bread in a shop 100 yards away.

The girls were found dead far from their respective homes: Maxwell beside the A518 road near Uttoxeter, 425 kilometers from where she had been abducted, Hogg in a ditch along the M1, close to Twyford, 500 kilometers removed from Portobello, and Harper floating in the Trent river, off Nottingham, 113 kilometers from home.

It was clear that whoever the killer was, he traversed Britain in all directions, and he probably did so on account of his work. And Robert Black had worked since 1976 for a Hoxton firm that delivered posters and billboards all over Britain and Ireland, and indeed also as far away as continental Europe.

A search of Black's van produced «assorted ropes, sticking plaster, and hoods, a Polaroid camera, numerous articles of girls' clothing, a mattress and a selection of sexual aids,» pointing to Black being a very good candidate for the killer's role. Black then claimed to be in the habit of dressing up like a little girl and masturbating, and said that the items found in his van were on occasion used as implements to that end. His home was full of child pornography, but that of course did not prove him to be the abductor and killer of the girls.

What the police needed to do, therefore, was to put Robert Black at the locales where the girls had disappeared. And they needed to put Black at these locales at the relevant times. This was also exactly what they achieved, mainly by means of petrol receipts. It turned out, when the police researched the cases named by Paul Britton, that Robert Black had been near all three locales whence these girls had disappeared. He had always filled up on petrol close in time to the deeds and saved the petrol receipts afterwards, making the police believe that the receipts were actually kept as trophies.

This circumstantial evidence was ultimately what helped to send Black down, in spite of his pleading innocent at the second trial against him, in 1994. The first trial had covered the abduction of the girl from Stow, and in that trial Black could not possibly plead innocent since he had been caught red-handed. Accordingly, Black was found guilty and a horrified judge concluded that the red rush of blood that Black had claimed as leading up to the abduction was in fact a barefaced lie; all the elements involved pointed to a very deliberate and planned act. Black was consequently handed down a sentence of life imprisonment.

At the second trial, the defense claimed that Black was no murderer, that he never had any intention of killing anybody, although he was a professed pedophile. He had always intended to let the Stow girl go, it was said, and it was alleged that Robert Black had become a convenient scapegoat for a police force that had failed to solve the murders of Susan Maxwell, Caroline Hogg, and Sarah Harper. It was also pointed out that there was not a single piece of physical evidence linking Black to the three abductions and murders. The fact that Black could be put close to each spot from where the girls had disappeared was suggested to be merely coincidental.

In his closing arguments, prosecutor John Milford pounced on this suggested coincidence and said that if the defense was correct in their assessment, then it would be «the coincidence to end all coincidences.» Milford did not buy the reasoning for a second. Neither did the judge and jury; Robert Black was given a guilty verdict in each of the three cases, and sentenced to serve a minimum of thirty-five years for each murder. He only managed to serve out twenty-two years, dying in prison in 2016.

What we can learn from Black's case is that there is a limit for how far a string of coincidences can be stretched before it breaks. In the case of Charles Lechmere, there are no petrol receipts and the Pickford's records from the time are no longer in existence. But what we can do is to take a long, hard look at how his logical routes to work correspond with the Ripper murder locations and the timing of the deeds. What we will find when doing so is that Lechmere would reasonably always pass through Buck's Row to reach his work in Broad Street. It was the only logical passageway taking him past the railway that cut through the area. To avoid Buck's Row would mean a substantial addition of time to his morning trek.

Of course, we also know that he did use this exact passage on the morning of the Nichols murder.

Looking at the other murders in the series—and I am adding the Martha Tabram murder of the 6th of August into the mix—we can see that after Buck's Row, Lechmere had two choices of roads if he wanted to use the quickest way to work. From Buck's Row, he would turn right into Baker's Row and he would then arrive at a junction where he could either turn into a southerly route along Old Montague Street, or he could use a northerly route by way of Hanbury Street. The two stretches are very close to each other in terms of the time it would take to walk them, although the Old Montague Street route is a fraction quicker. A third option would be to turn left after Buck's Row and go down to Whitechapel Road to proceed westwards on it, but that route would be considerably longer and more time-consuming than the other two, making it an unlikely choice.

We of course know that Lechmere made use of the Hanbury Street route on the Nichols murder morning. As a carman, he would have been very well acquainted with the different options. If we accept that the two quickest routes were the ones he chose from, we are faced with some pretty astonishing information.

Martha Tabram was found dead the fewest of yards from Old Montague Street on the morning of August 7. The examining medico said that she would have died around three hours before he examined her, putting the time at 2:30–2:45. If he was slightly off, we would end up at the approximate time when Lechmere would have passed en route to work if he chose the Old Montague Street route that day.

Annie Chapman was discovered dead in the backyard of 29 Hanbury Street on September 8, perhaps five or ten yards from where Lechmere would have passed on his route to work if he used the Hanbury Street option, as we know he did on the Nichols murder morning. Witnesses indicated that Chapman died at around 5:30, but the examining medico laid down that she had been dead for at least two hours as he first examined her, and probably longer than that. That examination took place at about 6:30, so the suggestion was that she died at the very latest at a time leading up to 4:30—but in all probability considerably earlier than that.

Mary Kelly was found butchered to pieces in Miller's Court, off Dorset Street, on November 9. Dorset Street represents a shortcut from the Hanbury Street route toward Broad Street. The medicos could not agree on the time of death in the Kelly case. Dr. Bond suggested a time between 1:00 and 2:00 A.M., whereas Dr. Phillips opted for the space between 5:15 and

6.15 A.M. Two witnesses claimed to have heard an outcry of «Murder!» somewhere around 3:30 and 4:00 A.M., representing not only a middle point between the doctors' estimates, but also a timing that is entirely consistent with when Lechmere would have passed.

Charles Lechmere could have worked anywhere in London, north, south, west or east of 22 Doveton Street. Instead, his working place was positioned in the only minuscule area that is geographically in perfect line with him having been the killer of the four Whitechapel victims, right between where the Old Montague Street and the Hanbury Street trails ended up.

It would be remarkable if these four murders all occurred out of sheer coincidence on streets where Lechmere had reason to pass—unless the carman was the killer. To find out just how remarkable, we need to turn to the census listings, where inhabited streets were listed. The listing closest to 1888 is the 1891 census listing. In Whitechapel alone, 1012 inhabited streets are listed here. This enables us to make a rough calculation.

We can see that if Charles Lechmere used the two shortest routes to work suggested here, he would have walked on roughly twenty Whitechapel streets on his way to work. This means that he would have walked on around two per cent of the Whitechapel streets. And astonishingly, the four murders committed in Whitechapel were all perpetrated along these exact logical routes of his. All of them.

Let's now turn to the field of mathematics, and try to take a look at what the material suggests. We must start by pointing out that there are unknown factors involved. Much as we know that Charles Lechmere passed through Buck's Row and along the Hanbury Street route on the morning Polly Nichols was killed, we of course do not have any evidence that he did his early morning trek on the days when Martha Tabram, Annie Chapman, and Mary Kelly lost their lives. All we can do is to accept that he very likely did and to calculate from that assumption.

It may also be that Lechmere used more than twenty streets when traversing Spitalfields. When calculating likelihoods relating to material like this, we must accept that many factors we do not weigh in could have had a massive importance, either strengthening or weakening a case.

What can be said without any doubt is that out of all the hours of the clock, the four Whitechapel murders all went down in the early morning hours. If we were to add that information, the case against the carman would be very much strengthened. For simplicity's sake, we will leave the chronological factor untouched, together with all other possible factors. We will only put the twenty streets I am assuming Lechmere would have walked against the one thousand inhabited streets of Whitechapel and see what happens.

I was kindly helped by Rolf Larsson, professor in Applied Mathematics and Statistics at Uppsala University, when doing the calculations. He was able to tell me that we need to use a binomial distribution when calculating the likelihoods. This is how it is done:

We begin by naming the different murders A, B, C, and D. The likelihood that murder A was committed on one of Lechmere's twenty streets is 0.02, two percent (or 20 out of a thousand). The likelihood that murder B was committed on another street than Lechmere's twenty streets is 1 − 0.02 = 0.98, or 98 per cent. The same is true for murders C and D. The outcome of this information is that the likelihood that murder A was committed along one of Lechmere's streets and that the other three crimes were all committed on other Whitechapel streets is 0.02 x 0.98 x 0.98 x 0.98.

Once we have reached this far in our calculations, we must allow for the possibility that it was murder B, not murder A, that was committed along Lechmere's streets, while all the other three murders were committed on the rest of the Whitechapel streets. Or that it was murder C or D that took place along Lechmere's streets, with the other murders going down on the remainder of the Whitechapel streets. This means that we actually have four (excluding) murders with the same likelihood as mentioned above, 0.02 x 0.98 x 0,98 x 0.98.

Therefore, the likelihood that one of the murders went down along any of the twenty Lechmere streets is 4 x 0.02 x 0.98 x 0.98 x 0.98 = 0.075. Putting it differently, it was a 75 in 1000 likelihood that this should happen. Less, that is, than a one in ten chance.

Once we have this formula, we can calculate the chances of two of the murders taking place along the Lechmere streets. Since we now have six possible pairs of murders, A/B, A/C, A/D, B/C, B/D and C/D, we get 6 x 0.02 x 0.02 x 0.98 x 0.98 = 0.0023. In other words, we have roughly a 1 in 500 chance of this happening.

Moving on to the suggestion of three of the murders happening along the Lechmere streets, we get 4 x 0.02 x 0.02 x 0.02 x 0.98 = 0.000031. We have now moved on to roughly a 1 in 30,000 chance of getting the outcome sought for.

The final mathematical exercise we need to undertake is the one with all four murders happening along Lechmere's streets. We have now ended up with the formula 0.02 x 0.02 x 0.02 x 0.02 = 0.00000016. Making this figure more understandable, we are now talking about a 16 in 100,000,000, or roughly reshaping the figures, a one in five million chance.

As has been pointed out, many factors could have had a smaller or larger influence of these numbers. Overall, though, the kind of numbers we get when doing these exercises says a lot about what we are up against if we want to claim that the correlation between Lechmere's logical work treks and the four Whitechapel murders would have been merely coincidental.

We are at this stage either looking at a very likely confirmation of guilt, bordering on certainty, or a truly remarkable coincidence. Putting it in the words prosecutor John Milford used in the Robert Black case, it would certainly be «the coincidence to end all coincidences.»

We could go further. If we extend our playing field to the East End in general, we get many more thousands of streets to throw into the calculations. And substantially more than ninety-nine per cent of these streets could not be linked in any way to Lechmere's work trek.

This rises a vital question: Why did not a single one of these four murders take place in any of those streets? It would go a long way to exonerating Lechmere. Instead, all the murders take place within the fewest of yards from where it can be logically reasoned that he would have passed—and, roughly speaking, seemingly at the approximate time he would have passed them.

Before we take our leave of Professor Larsson, it must be pointed out that what he calculated was not the likelihood that Charles Lechmere was the killer. Instead, he calculated how likely it was that an alternative, unknown killer would by pure chance have happened to commit the four Whitechapel murders along the routes that have been suggested as the logical morning routes Charles Lechmere used on his way to work. The conclusion Rolf Larsson reached is accordingly not that it is a five in a million chance that Charles Lechmere was not the killer, but instead that it is a five in a million chance that somebody else just happened to commit all his or their four murders along the twenty streets Lechmere logically would have walked to work on.

Of course, once we identify Charles Lechmere as a suspect, Professor Larsson's calculations have a massive bearing on the case. To understand how that works, we will once more turn to the Robert Black case.

Over the years, the geographical implications of Charles Lechmere's morning trek to work have been discussed on the Internet boards covering the case. The defense for Lechmere has been much the same as it was for Robert Black. It is asserted that what looks very much like a perfect congruence is probably only coincidental and—not least—it is said that there were thousands of people who used the same set of streets that Lechmere used for his morning work trek.

Indeed, there were many people who had one reason or another to make use of these specific Whitechapel streets. But to begin with, the streets were more or less empty at the time Lechmere and Paul traversed them, as witnessed about by numerous people; it is clear from the evidence that it was a strangely quiet and desolate night, more so than normal. Moreover, passing the streets at noon would not make you a suspect; it was only those who were close to the body as it was still bleeding that would fill the requirements for such a status.

Once we look at how the geographical matters were dealt with in the Robert Black trial, we can see how the carman gets into all sorts of trouble. Susan Maxwell was abducted from between two villages inhabited by a total sum of around 2000 dwellers. But Caroline Hogg was abducted from an Edinburgh suburb, and Edinburgh houses around 480,000 people. And Sarah Harper lived in a suburb of Leeds, and there are some 715,000 people living in the area of the City of Leeds. Regardless of this, the jury singled out one man out of this bulk of more than a million people, and for what reason? Because he was a suspect who was checked by way of the litmus test of all serial murder investigations—the geography.

The case for Lechmere being the Ripper is to a decisive degree built on the exact same ground—a correlation between his logical morning trek paths combined with a chronological conformity. And the outcome of the test singles out Charles Lechmere in much the same way as Robert Black was singled out a century later.

There are two further murders involved in the series that very clearly did not take place in streets Lechmere would have had a reason to pass on his road to work. Can these murders be linked in any way to the carman?

The answer is yes, they can.

These two murders involved Elizabeth Stride, who was found dead on September 30 in Berner Street, at around 1:00 A.M., and Catherine Eddowes, who perished in the minutes leading up to 1:45 in Mitre Square on the same date. The two slayings are referred to as the Double Event, since the killer supposedly claimed two victims on the same night. Elizabeth Stride had her throat cut but was not mutilated, and it is reasoned that the killer was disturbed and fled toward Aldgate, where he found, killed, and mutilated Eddowes. She payed dearly for the dammed-up urges from the Stride scene; her murder was the most gruesome one thus far, involving ripping the abdomen open, retrieving inner organs, and adding severe mutilations of the face.

So we have two cases where Lechmere did not kill en route to work. But the fact of the matter is that he reasonably did not work at all on the night of

the Double Event; it was a Saturday night, a night off for just about everybody involved in the working class.

But how do we link Lechmere to the murder spots? To answer that, we
must begin with Berner Street and the Stride murder.

Lechmere's place of residence was 22 Doveton Street during the Ripper
scare. He had moved there in June 1888. Before moving to Doveton Street,
he had been living many years in James Street down in St. George in the
East—only a short distance away from Berner Street. In fact, the many addresses where Lechmere grew up as a boy and where he became a young man
all neatly surrounded the Berner Street murder site.

Not only that, a stone's throw away from the murder site, Charles Lechmere's mother was living in 1 Mary Ann Street at the time of the Double
Event, together with one of his daughters. Lechmere had eleven children,
and for some reason one of them spent her life living together with Maria
Louisa, Lechmere's mother.

What does a working man do on his day off? Perhaps he goes to visit his
mother and daughter in St. George in the East. Perhaps he goes for a pub
round with his old friends and neighbors. Either way, we can see that Lechmere had very good reason to visit the grounds where Elizabeth Stride met
her fate. And we can see how the early timing suddenly makes sense. Was
she killed by Lechmere as he was making his way back to Doveton Street?

How about Mitre Square, then? How is Lechmere linked to that site? The
answer lies in the fact that he lived for many years in James Street before his
move to Doveton Street in June 1888. If we draw a direct line from James
Street (today's Burslem Street) to the Broad Street station, we find that it will
pass right by Maryann Street, where Lechmere's mother lived at the time
of the Stride murder. It also goes right by Berner Street (today's Henriques
Street), where Stride was killed. And it passes close by Mitre Square. In short,
the road the killer took from Berner Street to Mitre Square would have been
the very same road that Lechmere used to get to the Broad Street station for
numerous years when living in James Street.

Charles Lechmere would also have been very much acquainted with how
St. Botolph's church was the last point of call on his trek before reaching Mitre Square. And St. Botolph's church was known as «the prostitutes' church»
back in 1888. Here, the so-called unfortunates walked in circles around the
church, waiting for business. It was forbidden to stand still. If you did, you
were regarded as a prostitute, but as long as you walked you would not be
subjected to any interest of the police.

In the Mitre Square case, one intriguing element is added. That element

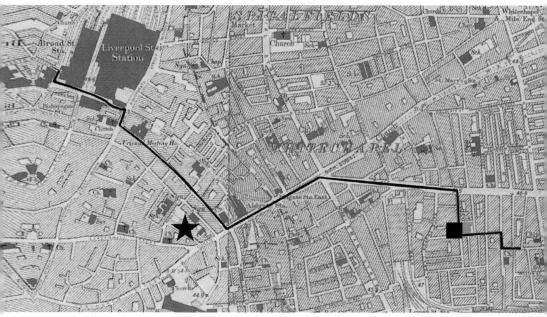

The murders of the so called Night of the Double Event on the 30th of September 1888. The first victim was Elizabeth Stride, marked by the cube. The second victim was Catherine Eddowes in Mitre Square, marked by the star. The path from Berner Street to Mitre Square would have been part of Lechmere's old working trek from James Street to Broad Street.

is the only known physical clue ever to have been left behind by the Ripper, a portion of Catherine Eddowes's apron. It was cut away at the murder site by the killer, and subsequently dumped in the doorway of 108–119 Wentworth Model Buildings in Goulston Street. And if we draw a straight line on a map from Mitre Square to 22 Doveton Street, we find that this line cuts right through Goulston Street, not far from where the apron was discarded. In other words, if Charles Lechmere killed Catherine Eddowes and cut the apron piece away in Mitre Square, and from there set off toward his home in Doveton Street, the dumping of the rag in Goulston Street would fit the picture perfectly.

An important matter to note is how the murders are not interchangeable between the Tabram-Nichols-Chapman-Kelly group of Whitechapel murders and the Stride-Eddowes group of St. George-in-the-East/Aldgate murders. If any of the former murders had been committed on a Saturday night, the logical link to the carman's morning work trek would vanish, and we would find ourselves wondering what he was doing on his work trek at that remove in time. Similarly, if any of the victims in the latter group had died at around 3.30 A.M. on a working day, we would have to ask ourselves what Lechmere was doing in St. George-in-the-East or Aldgate at a time when he should have been en route to work along Hanbury Street or Old Montague Street.

When we realize the intricacy of these matters, we can see that every little detail fits like a glove. And the forefinger of that glove points very clearly and steadily toward Charles Lechmere.

So there we have it: All six murders can be logically linked to Lechmere's routes and timings. And that really means the game is up. If a suspect can be linked to the murder sites involved in an investigation into a case of serial murder in a credible manner, the suspicions entertained have been confirmed and the police will have their culprit. In this case, the culprit's name is now clearly established: Charles Allen Lechmere.

We have our Ripper, at long last. What remains to do is to link him to the Thames Torso murders. The time has arrived to bridge that gap, and we will do so by building three bridges. Once we have walked over these bridges, there will be no returning to the idea that Jack the Ripper could not possibly have been the same man as the Thames Torso killer.

BRIDGING THE GAP

Getting it Wrong 1: Sir Melville MacNaghten—
*«Now the Whitechapel murderer had 5 victims
& five victims only ...»*

The man behind the suggestion that there were five Ripper victims was Sir Melville MacNaghten, promoted to assistant commissioner of the Met in 1903. In his famous memorandum of 1894, he made the claim that «Now the Whitechapel murderer had 5 victims & five victims only,» thereafter listing Polly Nichols, Annie Chapman, Elizabeth Stride, Catherine Eddowes, and Mary Kelly. Although it is impossible to know on what exact grounds MacNaghten built his conviction, it is reasonable to assume that similarities between the murders would have been instrumental in the process. It is a sound approach, and one that is universally employed by the police whenever a number of murder cases surface in a defined geographical area.

One of the more common questions in Ripperology has always been which two murders of the so-called canonical five are the ones most similar to one another. The discipline being what it is, Ripperology attracts all kinds of theorizers, and one branch has developed the idea that there was never any Ripper at all; the murders were unconnected and carried out by different perpetrators. Or so we are told.

There are those who are willing to partially commit to this school of thinking, and who sort two or three murders into the same man's tally, while ruling the remainder out. A less controversial take on things is that Elizabeth Stride does not belong, since she did not have her abdomen cut open and her organs taken out.

A view sometimes aired is that Polly Nichols and Annie Chapman are the two victims who most resemble each other. And yes, they shared the same age, the same victimology, the same part-time prostitution, and they were killed in the same area and had their abdomens cut open as well as their throats cut twice, the cutting reaching down to the bone. Nichols of course lost no organs, but the general reasoning is that she would have, had the

*Sir Melville MacNaghten was the originator of the idea that Jack
the Ripper had five victims only. Today they are
known as the canonical five.*

killer not been disturbed. So yes, they are very much alike and the suggestion
of a single killer is therefore an extremely good one.

I would, however, propose a very different answer to the question about
which two victims were most alike.

BRIDGE NUMBER ONE: TWIN SISTERS

On September 8, 1888, a prostitute named Annie Chapman was laid down
on her back in London. She had her throat cut with a knife. She also had her
abdomen opened up all the way from her groin to the sternum. The killer
went so far as to remove her abdominal wall in a number of large flaps with
subcutaneous tissue attaching to them. Through the opened-up abdomen,
the killer extracted Chapman's uterus. Annie Chapman was wearing two
rings as she was killed. These rings her killer wrenched from her finger.

On one of the very first days of June 1889, a prostitute named Elizabeth Jackson was laid down on her back in London. She had her throat cut with a knife. She also had her abdomen opened up all the way from her groin to the sternum. The killer went so far as to remove her abdominal wall in a number of large flaps with subcutaneous tissue attaching to them. Through the opened-up abdomen, the killer extracted Jackson's uterus. Elizabeth Jackson was wearing a ring as she was killed. This ring her killer wrenched from her finger.

In any sane world, there are so many and such rare similarities that they effectively rule out any possibility of two killers. But the world of Ripperology was never any truly sane world, and accordingly the traditional view has always been that these two Victorian murder victims could not have been claimed by the same man, since Jackson was a dismemberment victim from Battersea, while Chapman was an evisceration victim from Whitechapel.

Let's take a fresh look at these objections and see where we end up.

The location matter first: Elizabeth Jackson was known to frequent the Battersea area where she, at least occasionally, worked as a prostitute. Whether she was also picked up by her killer in Battersea is another question, and whether she was killed and dismembered there is a third one. All we can say is that dumped parts from her body appeared in Battersea, although some of them surfaced in Southwark, Nine Elms, and Limehouse, for example. The bottom line is that while there can be a lot of guessing about where the parts were originally dumped into the river, there can be no absolute certainty about it. Moreover, as we have seen in the Rainham case, the killer would actually at times choose to dump parts from the same body in different spots.

Trying to find the spot where the murder had taken place is by all accounts the hardest thing to do. It is often reasoned that the Thames Torso killer had a bolthole where he killed and cut up his victims. If we were to accept that this bolthole was located in Battersea, we will find ourselves in trouble when trying to explain the Pinchin Street dumping site. In that case, the torso had apparently been carried in a sack to the site where it was dumped; there were imprints from sack cloth on the skin of the torso. And in a railway arch adjacent to the one where the body was found, people who had been sleeping rough had not heard any sounds of a cart. Nor were there any wheel tracks from such a cart at the site, and the police concluded that the torso had probably been manually carried to the site. Arguably, the killer had not carried the load on his back all the way from Battersea.

The inference is instead that the suggested bolthole, if it existed, was located in the East End, and that the killer transported the body parts from his victims from there to the western parts of London to dump them. We will return to the possible implications of such a maneuver later on, but for now we must grant that the idea that the Thames Torso killer found and/or dispatched his victims in other areas than the Ripper could well be seriously flawed.

Now as to the dismemberment versus evisceration issue. Let's start out here by quoting Charles Hebbert, who was sure that the four torso murders of 1887–89 were by the same hand—and who was equally convinced that the Thames torso murders and the Ripper murders did not have the same originator. Hebbert also assisted Thomas Bond in the examination of and subsequent post-mortem on Mary Kelly in the Ripper series.

There is every reason to agree with Hebbert and his conclusion about the four torso murders being by the same hand. However, there is equally good reason to disagree with him on the idea that the Thames Torso murders and the Ripper murders were unconnected. And it all boils down to distinguishing his professional insights when it comes to comparing wounds and cutting techniques from his psychological insights when it comes to identifying various types of criminals. Once we take a look at what Hebbert had to say in his essay «Criminology,» published in *Canada Medical Record* of March 1903, we can easily see where he gets things wrong:

> During the years 1887–1889, a series of murders was committed in London, by unknown and unidentified assassins. The victims were thirteen women of the class of prostitutes. These outrages were done by more than one man, the post-mortem examination showing very clearly that in one series the motive was the destruction of the identity of the person, and concealment of the crime. In the second, savage and singularly purposeless mutilation. The examination also proved the difference in the skill and intention of the operator. In the first series, as I may put it, the women's bodies were skillfully divided into sections as might be done by a butcher or a hunter, evidently for the purpose of easy carriage and distribution, as the different parts were found in various districts, some in Regents Park, Chelsea, Battersea, Isle of Dogs, even, in one case, the vaults of new Scotland Yard. In the other series, the women were horribly and unmercifully mutilated. Even the internal organs had been removed and taken away. It was in the last series that the theory of satyriasis was strengthened by the post-mortem examinations.

What we find is that Hebbert, who himself had reported some fourteen years earlier that Elizabeth Jackson's uterus had been cut out from her body and packed up together with placenta and cord inside two panes of flesh sliced from her abdomen, now speaks of how «even the internal organs had been removed» in the Jack the Ripper cases. Very clearly, Hebbert forgets about how the two series actually both involved organ retrieval. The heart and lungs had also been removed from Jackson's thorax, as per Hebbert in «An Exercise in Forensic Medicine.» There were organs missing in other torso cases too, although we do not know whether they were extracted by the killer or lost in the waters of the Thames.

At any rate, we can see that Hebbert tries to segregate the series by a factor that was instead common to them.

Hebbert's take on things was actually echoed by Dr. George Bagster Phillips as he testified at the inquest after the Pinchin Street deed and was asked whether he could see any similarities between that deed and the Kelly murder. Phillips's answer is in line with Hebberts way of reasoning:

> I have not noticed any sufficient similarity to convince me it was the [same] person who committed both mutilations, but the division of the neck and attempt to disarticulate the bones of the spine are very similar to that which was effected in this case. The savagery shown by the mutilated remains in the Dorset-street case far exceeded that shown in this case. The mutilations in the Dorset-street case were most wanton, whereas in this case it strikes me that they were made for the purpose of disposing of the body.

What we need to know before we proceed is that to the Victorians, dismemberment murders were either about concealing the victim's identity or about getting rid of a body—or a combination of these two things. The concept of aggressive dismemberment—cutting a body up because of an urge to do so—was unknown to them. Therefore, Hebbert and Phillips would both conclude that practical concerns governed what the Thames Torso killer did, whereas the Ripper murders were «wanton,» «savage,» and «purposeless.»

Today's researchers into matters like these know full well, having been exposed to the deeds of killers such as Richard Cottingham, that dismemberment can be led on by an urge. Perhaps the best example would be the so-called «Mad Butcher of Kingsbury Run» from depression-era Cleveland, who decapitated and dismembered his victims while they were still alive. Neither of these two killers attempted to hide away their victims.

This, however, was not something the Victorian doctors understood. They were to a large degree caught up in the very peculiar «science» of the era that went by the name of «criminal anthropology.» It was, by and large, the order of the day back in the late 1880s. Although echoes of the ideas were on horrific display during the Nazi years in Germany, the late Victorian period represented the very peak of criminal anthropology.

Criminal anthropology seems dated and deranged to us today, but it very much ruled the period we are looking at, not least in the practically oriented spheres of society. Although many scientists were doubtful about the theory, those who worked on the ground, so to speak, were not. If we turn once more to Hebbert and his essay «Criminology» from 1903, we can pick out bits and pieces that are quite illuminating about where he stood in this respect:

> … the investigations of students establish the existence of a constant class disposed to crime in all civilized lands…
> The criminal class specifically consists of all those who from physical deformity, mental incapacity, or normal depravity, are either unable, or indisposed, to regulate their lives in conformity with the laws of the community. …
> The percentage of criminals is estimated at 2 per cent. The classification of criminals has been variously indicated. Probably the best and most satisfactory is:—
> I. Criminal madmen, 5–10 per cent.
> II. Instinctive criminals, 40–50 per cent.
> III. Habitual criminals, 40–50 per cent.
> IV. Single offenders.
> V. Presumptive criminals.
> …
> In the skulls of some of the primitive races that I have examined, there are abnormal developments in the ossifications of the skulls, such as the presence of wormian bones in unusual positions, and in unusual numbers, the anterior fontanelle for instance, and it is known that in the skulls of some criminals similar conditions have been described»

These are but a few examples of the kind of thinking Charles Hebbert engaged in when it came to matters of criminal psychology. And understandably so; just like us today, he was a captive of the time he lived in and accepted the science of his day as being correct.

Hebbert's stance would be echoed for many decades to come. For example, we may today visit the «Ripley's Believe It or Not Museum» in Wisconsin Dells, US, and take a look at the mummified head of serial killer Peter Kürten. Kürten was active in the late 1920s and early 1930s in Düsseldorf, Germany. He committed so many and so atrocious crimes that it was decided that his head, chopped off by way of guillotine in Cologne in 1932, was to be handed over to science to discover the deformations that everybody expected to find within the skull. Accordingly, the head was cleaved vertically, right over the nose, and opened up. A slight enlargement of the thymus gland was all that was found.

Let's now take a look at how Charles Hebbert described the murder of Mary Kelly in «Criminology»:

> A woman was killed in a room. After the most frightful mutilation and destruction of her body, she was placed in a bed in such a position as would indicate the overpowering fiendish sensual passion of the brute. There was nothing to suggest any knowledge of anatomy or surgical skill. In fact, he evidently had attempted to remove the heart by cutting the ribs, and failing to do this, he had dragged it down the midriff. As I saw the awful sight before any disturbances of the body, or interference with the room, I can vouch for the truth of the conditions and shall never forget my vivid impression of the scene.
>
> When one thinks of such a monster, the fierce invective against Macbeth recurs to one, and may be aptly quoted:
> «Not in the legions of horrid Hell, can come a devil more dammed in evil.»

So here we have a «monster» imported from Hell—as opposed to the clean-cutting, composed gentleman who killed the torso victims…?

We have strayed a long way from building a bridge between Anne Chapman and Elizabeth Jackson, but it has all been for the purpose of explaining why the Victorians themselves were unable to construct that bridge. We, however, are not only able to do so today; the question is whether we can avoid doing it, given the breathtaking set of similarities between the two victims:

—Both women were prostitutes.

—Both women lived in the same town and time.

—Both women had their abdomens cut open from sternum to groin.

—Both women had their uteri cut out from their bodies.

—Both women had large parts of their abdominal walls cut away in sections of flesh and subcutaneous tissue.

—Both women had rings wrenched from their fingers.

Furthermore, it is of course obvious that both women had their throats cut. It can be reasoned that since Jackson was decapitated, hers was another form of throat cutting. But there may well be reason to believe that both Jackson and Chapman had their throats cut in a similar manner and for a similar reason.

No actual cause of death could be given for Jackson as the head was never found, but we know from the Pinchin Street case that George Bagster Phillips suggested syncope as the case of death, likely from having the throat cut. This passage from the *Times* of September 25, 1889, reporting from the inquest into the Pinchin Street case, clarifies how Phillips reasoned:

> Dr Phillips: I believe that death arose from loss of blood. I believe the mutilation to have been subsequent to death, that the mutilations were effected by some one accustomed to cut up animals or to see them cut up, and that the incisions were effected by a strong knife 8in. or more long.
>
> The coroner: Is there anything to show where the loss of blood occurred?
>
> Dr Phillips: Not in the remains; but the supposition that presents itself to my mind is that there was a former incision of the neck, which had disappeared with the subsequent separation of the head.
>
> The coroner: The loss of blood could not have come from either the lungs of the stomach?
>
> Dr Phillips: Certainly not the stomach, and I could not trace any sign of its coming from the lungs. I have a strong opinion that it did not.
>
> The coroner: The woman did not die of phthisis?
>
> Dr Phillips: There was no tubercle, but the top part of the lung was diseased.
>
> The coroner: The draining of the blood from the body was such that it must have been a main artery that was severed?
>
> Dr Phillips: Undoubtedly; and was almost as thorough as it could be although not so great as I have seen in some cases of cut throats.

Taking in this list of similarities, some of them of a very rare nature, isn't it strange that the two murder victims who suffered the most similar types of damage are regarded as non-compatible, whereas those who have much fewer and less rare similarities to display are forever tied together in the so-called canonical five Ripper victims?

And is it not odd that the experts who laugh at suggestions that the canonical five may not have been slain by the same man are, in many cases,
the same experts who also laugh at the idea that the Ripper and the Thames
Torso killer were one and the same?

In the end, any comparison between murder victims must always come
down to issues of similarities and the degree of rarity these similarities rep-
resent. Two knife deeds are similar in the choice of weapon, but knives are
not rare. However, when a knife is used to cut away the abdominal wall from
victims in the same geographical area and time, we have a similarity that will
in all probability have originated with the same perpetrator.

Over the years, I have searched for any other two cases of coexisting eviscerating serial killers in the same geographical area, but I have drawn a blank.
The implications of the scarcity of these individuals must be clear. Once we
have two people killed and eviscerated in the same area and time, the logical
conclusion must always be that these victims have fallen prey to the same
killer.

In the debate about whether the Ripper and the Thames Torso killer were
the same man or not, it is sometimes suggested that it is ridiculous to claim
that «every case of murder in late Victorian London had the same killer.»
And of course, phrased like that, it does sound preposterous. But once we
rephrase it and say that every case of murder in late Victorian London that
involved mutilations and eviscerations would probably have had the same
originator, we are in fact opting for by far the most likely scenario. The more
eviscerators and mutilators we suggest, the less likely our solution will be.
And that is because these killers are very rare.

Killers as such are rare, luckily.

Serial killers are much more rare.

Serial killers who eviscerate their victims are rare in the extreme.

Two serial killers who eviscerate their victims in the same town or geographical area at the same time are—as far as I understand—unheard of.
Logic dictates that when and if they should ever surface, they would at least
not do the same things to their victims. But this was exactly what happened
in these two series.

Cutting the abdominal cavity open from sternum to groin is a very unusual practice.

Cutting out the uterus from a victim is also something that is truly rare.

Cutting away the abdominal wall in large panes is rarer than hens' teeth.

If we add to this that rings were taken from both women's fingers, a practice that either points to trophy taking or to a hope of financial gain, we have

a set of similarities between Annie Chapman and Elizabeth Jackson that makes them twin sisters. And that cannot simply be due to coincidence.

What happened afterwards was that Elizabeth Jackson was dismembered and dumped, whereas Annie Chapman was not. In Jackson's case, she was probably killed and cut up in a bolthole that was quite likely to be linked to the killer in some way. This meant that if the body was left in place, it could get the perpetrator hanged.

In Annie Chapman's case, that problem was non-existent: she was killed out in the open, and therefore did not offer any geographical link to help catch the killer. And although her killer carried a knife, he was not likely to bring a fine-toothed saw—used in all the torso murders—to the murder site in the backyard off Hanbury Street.

The dissimilarity in the manner of dismemberment is therefore a dissimilarity that does not in any way prevent a common killer. And the similarities of course outweigh this single dissimilarity in overwhelming fashion.

There was one more difference between Chapman and Jackson that should be mentioned. Elizabeth Jackson had her heart taken out and removed, whereas Annie Chapman didn't. However, once we know that Ripper victim Mary Kelly also had her heart taken out, the act does not seem not to distinguish the two series in any decisive way. Instead, we get a further reason to make a link between the series, since they both involved organ retrieval from the abdominal cavity as well as the thoracic cavity, and in both series reproductive organs as well as non-reproductive organs were taken out. Obviously, the abdominal cavity is quite easy to access whereas the thoracic cavity is protected by the ribcage and much harder to reach into, making this similarity in between the series quite remarkable.

The observant reader will have noticed that a number of odd inclusions have been mentioned as the bridge between Annie Chapman and Elizabeth Jackson was built. For example, Charles Hebbert claimed that Mary Kelly's killer had tried to cut the ribs so as to enable him to take her heart out through an opening there. Here, once again, Charles Hebbert misremembers things. Let's go back to Thomas Bond's post-mortem notations about Kelly's body and see what really happened to her ribcage: «Both breasts were more or less removed by circular incisions, the muscle down to the ribs being attached to the breasts. The intercostals between the fourth, fifth, and sixth ribs were cut through and the contents of the thorax visible through the openings.»

In reality, there were no cuts to the ribs recorded—but the intercostals between the fourth, fifth, and sixth ribs were cut through, making the contents of the thorax visible. The difference is significant. Instead of offering a way out for the heart, it produced a possibility to look into the thorax.

The next odd inclusion is evident: both Annie Chapman and Elizabeth Jackson had their abdominal walls cut away to a large extent, creating a large hole and offering the possibility of looking into the abdominal cavity, just as the cut-away intercostals offered the possibility of looking into the thorax. This is a very strange coincidence—or not. There was actually a third victim in the combined series who suffered a removed abdominal wall. Mary Kelly had her abdominal wall taken away in three large panes that were found in the room together with her corpse.

As odd inclusions go, many would probably feel that the removal of the abdominal wall must be the oddest of them all, but that is actually not the case. One of the murders involved an even stranger inclusion. This is where we head back to the 1873 torso victim, and this is also where we turn to the second bridge between the two murder series.

This time we will not deal in physical similarities between two victims—the twin sisters Annie Chapman and Elizabeth Jackson have already clinched that element beyond reasonable doubt—but instead in more intangible features, namely the inspiration sources behind the two murder series. Of course, we will have to speculate, but since the speculation allows us to finally understand what the murders were seemingly about, I believe it is as necessary an exercise as it is an absorbing one.

BRIDGE NUMBER TWO:
A HEART OF WAX

The Victorians were famously prudish. We all laugh at how they supposedly even covered the curved legs of their tables with long table cloths so as not to cause any over-intimate connotations inside their homes. There was, however, an institution in Victorian society that very much allowed for nudity and even put it on display: the wax museums.

In order to create an understanding of what the wax museums were, we must once more dive head first into the Victorian society of the second half of the nineteenth century. And we will begin by making the all-important acquaintance of Joseph Kahn.

Having traversed Germany and Holland during a three-year period, Joseph Kahn arrived in London in 1851 together with his pregnant wife and his mother-in-law. Kahn called himself a doctor, but had no certificate to show for his claim.

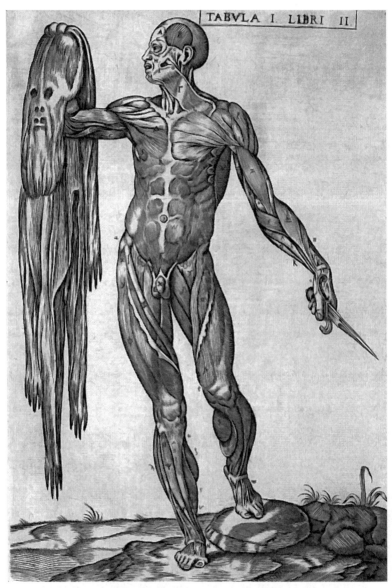

TABVLA I. LIBRI II

*An anatomical drawing by Andreas Vesalius (1514–1564), showing a man
holding his removed skin in one hand and the knife with which
it was cut away in the other. From «De Humane
Corporis Fabrica» (1543).*

It was, however, apparent that Joseph Kahn had studied anatomy and medicine, but those studies did not result in any academic honors. Instead, Kahn had started an anatomical museum in Germany in 1848.

As he traveled from Germany to England, he brought along his collection of anatomical exhibition objects. These were body parts contained in glass jars filled with alcohol, different kinds of cultures to behold with the aid of microscopes, and anatomical models in leather and—not least—wax.

The stated aim of the museum Kahn opened up in Oxford Street was to educate the people, to present the «wondrous» structure of the body, and to warn of various abuses that «distort or defile» its «beautiful structure.»

A reporter from *The Lancet* paid a visit to the museum and was much impressed by the collections as well as by how the various rooms were open to different categories of visitors. There were objects on display in the museum that Kahn did not think were suited for the general public, but instead only for those involved in the medical profession. Other parts of the exhibitions were adjusted to suit male or female audiences, respectively. Different categories of visitors were received on different days and were shown selected parts of the objects on display. The museum, it was said, accommodated families as well as schools.

As time passed, the collections grew to involve more than five hundred objects. Some of them were surrounded by an air of sensationalism, such as a male head, modeled in wax, and depicting the «[h]ead and face of a man who fell victim to the demoralizing and destructive habit of onanism.» To the Victorians, masturbation was a moral and physical evil. Medical manuals pointed it out as being responsible for all kinds of illnesses and even premature death.

Joseph Kahn's «Museum of Anatomy and Pathology,» as it was called, was in no way unique. There had been anatomical museums in England since the eighteenth century, and they had typically been regarded as useful institutions with pedagogical value. From the outset, they were very popular institutions, but in the beginning of the nineteenth century the interest in them began to wane.

What was to turn this development around was mainly two things. Part of it was the sensation caused by the Burke and Hare scandal, but there was also the fact that there was a growing interest in the possibilities of wax to produce incredibly realistic renditions of the human body with its contents and defects.

William Burke and William Hare were two Irishmen who in the 1820s eked out a living as laborers in Edinburgh. Finding out that various anatomical institutions were short on dead bodies to dissect for educational purposes, the two made a hasty change of business plans.

The first person to provide the two Irishmen with a handsome salary was an old man who died of natural causes at the boarding house where they were staying. Tempted to make even more money and frustrated by how people in their close vicinity didn't have the good sense to lie down and die, Burke and Hare decided to lend the Grim Reaper a helping hand. Before they were discovered, they had cut life short for some fifteen people.

The trial was a sordid affair. William Hare sold out his companion Burke in return for a promise to avoid getting a noose around his own neck. He then took off so completely that historians today cannot tell what became of him.

William Burke was marched to the gallows on January 28, 1829, fully aware of what was to become of his body once he had been deprived of his breath. The judge had informed him that it was to be delivered for dissection to the closest rival of the medico to whom Burke and Hare had delivered their murder victims. This was duly effected after the execution.

The story was one that captured the interest of the British, and everything that was connected to anatomy and the dissection of bodies had a huge boost after 1829. The surge was welcomed by museum owners, who made it a point to have both models of Burke and Hare (and numerous other killers, as time wore on) as well as intricate models of the anatomical construction of the human body. As a matter of fact, to a degree the anatomical wax models would put grave robbers like Burke and Hare out of work, owing to how the models partly enabled medical institutions to tutor students about the human body without having to use actual corpses.

Anatomical museums now emerged all over London. There was, for example, one such institution in the corner of Thomas Street and Whitechapel Road in the East End, in more or less direct proximity to the place where Polly Nichols was slain. The bulk of the audience visiting these establishments came from the working classes.

Victorian sexual morality did not tolerate any frivolous representations of nudity. Accordingly, a praxis came to exist whereby the anatomical wax figures on display were given an appearance reminiscent of classical Greek and Roman sculptures. This would sometimes result in rather strange representations, for example when wax models of women far advanced in pregnancy were presented as slim and fresh beauties with perfectly shaped limbs. The common accumulation of bodily fluids that follows with a pregnancy was conveniently skipped over.

Anybody who felt an urge to take a look at the «forbidden» exhibition

*Joseph Kahn's museum in London offered the opportunity
to learn about human anatomy from wax models.*

objects, namely those meant to be seen only by representatives of the medical sciences, were supposed to be denied the thrill. But at Joseph Kahn's museum, a custom of allowing anybody to see the objects who was willing to
pay for it developed over time, regardless of what medical qualifications you
had (or did not have) and which gender you were.

Protests against this were raised, and Kahn dealt with the issue by claiming that a careful selection was always made before any women were allowed
to take a peek. The truth of the matter was that Kahn, in spite of the many
visitors, was in dire need of money and prioritized income over morality
when it came to these questions.

When the previously benevolent *Lancet* demanded that some of the objects of exhibition be removed, Kahn consented to it. This put *The Lancet*
temporarily at ease, but it only lasted for a short period of time.

Economic problems continued to hound Joseph Kahn. He tried various
remedies to cure them. A national tour was made with the anatomical models, where the entrance fees were lowered to try and raise the number of visi-

tors. In spite of his efforts, the cash inflow remained too small. This prompted Kahn to look in another direction in order to resolve the problem once and for all.

At this time, there was a company called Perry and Co. in London. Its business idea was to sell various cures for venereal diseases. Advertisements were put up in public toilets and other well-frequented places, and the cures were sold by mail order.

A lecturer by the name of Mr. Sexton, hired by Joseph Kahn, openly criticized the activities Perry and Co. engaged in as unmitigated quackery. It was a criticism that was correct throughout. However, the company offered a solution to the economic problems the museum had: it financed a number of new anatomical models for the collections, thereby attracting more people and brightening up the economic figures. The museum was even able to move to new premises in Picadilly.

The aid provided by Perry and Co. came with a price. The museum had to start lecturing on venereal diseases. Visitors harboring dark fears of having been infected themselves could conveniently compare their own symptoms with the ones depicted by anatomical wax models. In addition to this, a book with the title *The Shoals and Quicksands of Youth* was discreetly sold at the institution. In it, Perry and Co. marketed their cures.

In a short period of time, the museum turned into London's most frequented clinic for treating venereal troubles. This did not go unnoticed by the medical science of the day. The operation was disclosed and that spelled disaster for Joseph Kahn.

The Lancet, which had from the outset been a keen promoter of the museum, now began to campaign against it, brandishing it as obscene and disgusting and «totally unfit for general exhibition.» In this context, *The Lancet* also disclosed in 1857 that Joseph Kahn, who not only claimed to have graduated as a doctor but had also actually worked in that profession after his arrival in England, had no license to practice medicine. The cat was out of the bag, and Kahn's reputation was sullied to such a degree that the magazine *Punch* suggested that he should change his name to Can't.

The problems did not end there for Joseph Kahn. 1857 was also the year when a bill named the Obscene Publications Act, presented by a politician named Lord John Campbell, was implemented in British law. Among other things, the law included a prohibition against public showings of anatomical models of the human body. *The Lancet* wasted no time in demanding that legal action be taken against Kahn's museum.

During this time, Joseph Kahn was still lecturing on matters of diet, hygiene, and sexual health, and he published various kinds of material relating to these topics. He applied to be included in the new medical register, but was denied. Instead, in 1864, a prosecution against him was being prepared, for unlicensed medical activities. The case was never tried, since it was found out that Kahn had left Britain.

In the absence of the escapee, Kahn's colleagues took over the museum and carried on the business, just as Perry and Co. carried on legitimizing their own business through the institution. Although the legislative institutions were satisfied that the cures on offer through the museum for venereal diseases were simple quackery, there was little they could do to stop the business. The law governing cases of improprieties in the medical sector only concerned itself with qualified practicing medicos and not with quacks. Ironically, this allowed Perry and Co. to proceed with its shady business. A foreign medical diploma had been purchased, and with its aid the company denied any accusations of falsely having claimed to have medical qualifications.

It was a tactic that allowed the museum and Perry and Co. to cruise lightheartedly past all legal reefs for quite some time, but the Obscene Publications Act would prove too formidable an opponent in the long run.

The wording of the law did not require that the material be of a pornographic nature to be ruled illegal. It was enough if, as it was put, it encouraged a «conduct inconsistent with public morals.» Consequently, it could be argued that information or a device that, for example, offered unmarried couples insights about how they could have their urges gratified without risking unwanted consequences like venereal diseases or pregnancy was in fact obscene. The lower classes and women were described as particularly impressionable in these contexts.

All of a sudden, the activity in Kahn's anatomical museum was in all sorts of trouble. *The Lancet* was now joined by the Society for the Suppression of Vice, an evangelical Protestant group specializing in pursuing legal cases against pornography. That was what broke the camel's back. In February 1873, a number of the anatomical models from the museum, at that stage housed in Tichborne Street, were seized by the police. And in December of that same year, the owners of the museum, Messrs. Roumanielle, Davidson, and Dennison, pleaded guilty to the accusations, whereupon the chairman of the court, Mr. Knox, ordered the destruction of the models.

The solicitor who had prosecuted the case, Mr. Collette, a representative of the aforementioned Society for Suppression of Vice, then asked permission from Mr. Knox to personally destroy the odious models. This request was granted, and a hammer was fetched so that Mr. Collette could go to work on the wax models. He was accompanied by Inspector Barnett and Sergeant Butcher of the police, who picked up the leftovers from the museum floor, handing them over to the owners.

Just a few days before Mr. Colette was let loose on the moral deficiencies of Kahn's museum, London had suffered a terrible smog, making the air very hard to breathe. In Islington, a number of prize-winning cows perished from suffocation, and mortality in London rose between the 8th and the 14th of February by around forty per cent. For the guardians of Victorian morality, Mr. Colette's hammering home of the consequences of the Obscene Publications Act must have felt like a very welcome breath of fresh air.

More trials linked to various anatomical museums and exhibitions followed all over the country, and a whole industry perished. All that remained were the wax models of Burke and Hare and their murderous soulmates. They were not regarded as obscene, something that saved, for example, Madame Tussaud's wax cabinet. The anatomical models, however, were not tolerated unless they were safely confined in medical institutions.

We will now take a closer look at what kind of objects there were on display in the anatomical museums, and establish in what way the wax models can be connected to the Ripper murders as well as the Thames Torso murders. It is an astonishing exercise, not least because it should have been undertaken by the Victorian police more than a hundred years ago. Instead, the police missed out on the obvious correlation between the series and squandered the option to take advantage of it in their investigations.

The most renowned object of the anatomical museums was a kind of wax model going by the name «The Anatomical Venus.» This was a wax representation of a female, normally in natural size, young and pretty and lying stretched out on her back on a bed. Her head typically rested comfortably on a pillow and she smiled sensually toward the audience.

There were numerous anatomical Venuses. Many of them were permanent attractions in the museums. Others were shown during tours made all over the country, together with other wax models and objects of anatomical interest. Joseph Kahn's museum was one of the many institutions that had an anatomical Venus on display.

The main object of the Anatomical Venus models was pedagogical. It was intended to be used to educate about and lecture on the inner anatomy of the female body. Accordingly, the abdominal wall could be lifted away from the model together with the exterior upper chest, the breasts included, and then the audience could see what was hidden underneath this lid.

Before the lecture was given, the lid was hidden under a nightgown that shielded the body of the anatomical Venus from sight. The upper border of the lid was, however, not hidden under the nightgown, since it passed straight over the throat. That problem was solved by putting a necklace over the cut in the Venus' throat.

After having removed the nightgown and taken off the lid, the different inner organs of the model could be plucked out one by one and shown to the audience, with a lecture on their names and their functions inside the body. As the lecture proceeded and more and more bits and pieces were plucked out, the wax organs were typically put on the bed beside the Venus. The more bulky abdominal lid with the breasts attached was instead sometimes put on the floor or on an adjacent table. The plucked-out organs subsequently framed the anatomical Venus, who smiled invitingly as her heart, liver, pancreas, lungs, intestines, stomach, and kidneys were placed by her side. The Venus in Kahn's anatomical museum had 85 movable parts, most of them being organs that could be lifted out of the body.

The anomaly of an anatomical Venus is obvious. It is a wax model that couples death, normally a stage of extensive physical deterioration owing to age and sickness, with great beauty and youth. She emulates a dead woman, but she is nevertheless seemingly vibrantly alive at the same time, erasing the dividing line between the two stages. And as a perfectly shaped young and naked woman, she is of course also very much linked to sexuality. A passive eroticism is an inherent part of the wax Venus, meekly reclining on her bed as the lecturer lifts her womb out and displays it to the audience.

This was the kind of act that was mirrored in the squalor of No. 13 Miller's Court on the morning of November 9, 1888, in the disassembled body of Mary Kelly. Let us return to Thomas Bond's report on what he had been forced to take part of at the crime scene:

The whole surface of the abdomen had been cut away in three large panes of flesh and subcutaneous tissue. The abdominal cavity had been emptied of its contents. The flesh had been cut away from the thighs, exposing the femur of Kelly's right leg. The breasts had been cut away from the body by means of circular incisions, and the tissues of the neck were severed all the way down to the spine.

The contents of the abdomen were found in various places: the uterus and the kidneys had been put under Kelly's head, together with a breast, forming a macabre makeshift pillow. The other breast was positioned by Kelly's right foot, her liver was placed between her feet, the intestines by her right side, and the spleen by her left side.

The panes of flesh from the abdomen were lying on a table beside the bed, together with the flesh from the thighs.

The murderer had fashioned his own anatomical Venus. It was all there, including the pillow and the removed abdominal lid on its table. Even the cut across the throat was in place. On her own bed and in her own blood, Mary Kelly exhibited a pedagogical summary of how the female body is constructed on the inside. And the lecturer in Miller's Court had been thorough: he had even created a possibility of looking into the thorax by cutting away the intercostals between the lower ribs with his knife.

It can of course be argued that the Venus of Miller's Court was in pretty bad shape. The sensual look on the face of her wax sisters was not evident; instead, the killer had cut her face to shreds. There was nevertheless a feature that was typical of the various anatomical models where the face had been lifted away, in the same manner as the abdominal wall: the eyes were miraculously left more or less untouched in the inferno of shredded flesh that surrounded them. In the exact same fashion, the eyes are always intact on the anatomical models with the face taken away, staring eerily from a base of uncovered tendons and muscles.

So close was the likeness between Kelly's face and the anatomical models that a reporter commented on it in his article in the *Pall Mall Gazette* from November 12, 1888:

> The face resembled one of those horrible wax anatomical specimens which may be seen in surgical shops. The eyes were the only vestiges of humanity, the rest was so scored and slashed that it was impossible to say where the flesh began and the cuts ended. And yet it was by no means a horrible sight. I have seen bodies in the Paris Morgue which looked far more repulsive.

The young detective constable Walter Dew also noted the eyes as he saw the remains of Kelly on her bed:

> Her face was terribly scarred and mutilated.
> All this was horrifying enough, but the mental picture of that sight which remains most vividly with me is the poor woman's eyes. They were wide open, and seemed to be staring straight at me with a look of terror.

If we take a look at a wax model from the Victorian museums with the face lifted off, we will understand what the *Pall Mall Gazette* reporter and Walter Dew spoke of.

The other damage done to the body is in line with this. The bared femur of Kelly's right leg also had pedagogical implications: it displayed how the innermost layers of the thigh were constructed. In this context, we can move 116 years forward to 2004 and take a look at another serial killer, Sean Vincent Gillis of Baton Rouge, Louisiana, US, who at his confession revealed one of the reasons he killed one of his eight victims by telling the interviewing police officer a baffling truth: «I wanted to see her femur.»

Anybody who is in any doubt about the overall link between Mary Kelly and the anatomical Venuses only has to compare a picture of Clemente Susini's «La Venerina,» a masterpiece anatomical Venus from the eighteenth century, to the infamous photo of Kelly on her bed, and whatever doubts there may have been will quickly dissolve.

Let's now return to Mitre Square, where the body of Catherine Eddowes was found on September 30, 1888. A section of her colon had been cut out of her abdomen. And Gordon Brown, a police surgeon with the City police, commented on it: «A piece of about two feet was quite detached from the body and placed between the body and the left arm, apparently by design.»

The colon section was not cut loose accidentally. One accidental cut through the colon may well occur, but it is a stretch to believe in two such accidental cuts, separated by two feet. And once we know that the section was not thrown in a heap somewhere but instead stretched out parallel to the body, we can see that something odd was going on. There is also the odd fact that both the Rainham torso victim from 1887 and Elizabeth Jackson from 1889 also lost parts of their colons.

As for Eddowes, there were other strange matters involved. Both of her eyelids had been purposefully nicked with the knife, but the underlying eyes seem not to have been damaged. There is at least no mention of any such damage in the very detailed post-mortem report.

So we have an exhibited body part stretched out alongside the victim, and what seems to be much care exerted not to damage the eyes.

Once again, we are reminded of the anatomical Venus.

Although the similarities between Mary Kelly and the anatomical Venuses are overwhelmingly clear, it can always be claimed that these similarities may have been purely coincidental—pillow, abdominal lid, and all. However, once we find another victim who is equally reminiscent of the models of the wax museums, the deal is sealed. And there is just such an example in the Thames Torso series, namely the 1873 victim—the faceless woman.

In the wax museums, there were two different types of models where part of the surface of the body could be lifted off like a lid to reveal the underly-

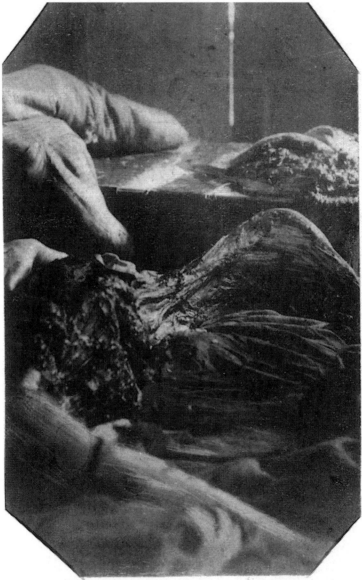

A photo from the Mary Kelly murder scene. Behind the body in the foreground, flesh from Kelly's thighs can be seen on the table in the background together with skin flaps taken from her abdominal wall. The inner organs were placed on the bed alongside the body as well as under Kelly's head.

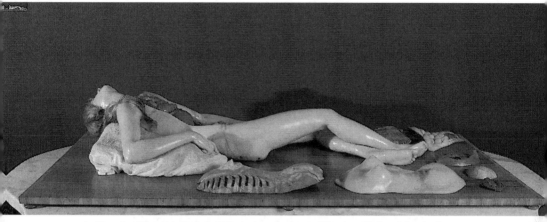

La Venerina, Clemente Susini's 18th century Anatomical Venus, with the abdominal wall and the inner organs taken out and placed alongside the body. Photo courtesy of Sistema Museale de Ateneo—Museo di Palazzo Poggi. © Università di Bologna. Fulvio Simoni.

ing structures. We have seen the first example: the abdominal wall could be lifted away from an anatomical Venus to show the underlying anatomy.

The other representation was where the face of numerous wax models also could be lifted away like a lid and for the very same reason: in order to exhibit and clarify the disposition of the underlying structures. And this was the exact thing that happened to the faceless woman. The killer made two cuts, one horizontal and one vertical, at the back of the skull of his victim; he then worked his blade in under the skin of the flaps produced so that he could loosen them and grab hold of them. Holding on to the skin, he then began to pull the skin forward toward the face, working more and more of it loose from the skull with the aid of his knife. Once he had loosened the scalp, he proceeded to loosen the face, all the while using his blade underneath the skin to work it loose from the underlying structures. The result was a macabre mask, with even the eyelashes intact.

It is easy to think that the killer's aim was to cut that mask away from the skull in as complete a fashion as possible, and that the mask was precious to him. However, we know that he threw it into the Thames afterwards, and so it would seem that all the work he invested was nevertheless something he was willing to rid himself of.

What one may fail to recognize is that there were two objects involved in the cutting process of the mask. And the second object was of course the underlying face, the real exhibition object of the anatomical museums. The face was just a lid, hiding the true prize—the bared muscles and tendons of the face, together with the staring eyeballs.

Are there any other indicators telling us that the 1873 torso victim was another mirror image of the wax museums? Yes, there are. Let's revisit the article in *The Lancet* about this victim and see what they wrote:

> Contrary to the popular opinion, the body had not been hacked, but dexterously cut up; the joints have been opened, and the bones neatly disarticulated, even the complicated joints at the ankle and the elbow, and it is only at the articulations of the hip-joint and shoulder that the bones have been sawn through.

First, we have the important information that we are once again dealing with a masterfully cut up body, a clean and neat piece of work, very unlike the ordinary sloppy dismemberment murder. And then we are informed that although the killer was knowledgeable about how to disarticulate the more difficult joints at the elbows and knees, he did not disarticulate the easier ones at the shoulders and hips. He instead sawed right through them, as you would saw off a tree branch.

Why?

Well, an answer that is in perfect line with the suggestion of the killer being inspired by the wax models is how these models were represented when they depicted armless and/or legless torsos. Not a single model showed a disarticulated limb, twisted out of its socket. Instead, when a severed limb was presented, it was always as a neatly sawn-through one, pedagogically displaying the layers of the leg or arm by way of a perfectly straight cut, right through the limb. The torso of the 1873 victim would have mirrored this exactly.

Moreover, we know that the 1873 victim was totally drained of blood, presumably by way of hanging the body upside down and slicing the neck open, allowing the blood to exit the body. Perhaps in order to provide the killer with a less slippery work when he sculpted his wax model replica with a real body?

Once we find not one but two murders that are closely reminiscent of what was on display in the wax museums, we can be more or less certain that we have identified the inspiration behind the deeds. The element is actually there in most victims to a greater or lesser degree.

The fascinating thing is when we realize that there will likely never have

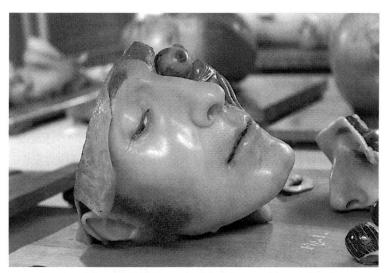

Another of Clemente Susini's wax models, this time with part of the face removed and lying by the side of the head. Photo © Università di Bologna.

been any fixed manual for what the killer would do to his victims. Instead, he had a large number of different elements to choose from when cutting up a victim. One day, he cut away a colon section, another day he carved the face from this victim, and a third day he took out a heart. And all the time, he effected various representations of the exact same script, depicting the many wax representations from the museums in different ways.

Cutting away the abdominal wall in large sections from a murder victim is an exceedingly rare thing to do. Cutting away a face and scalp from another one is even rarer. But both these things were on daily display all over London in the midst of the nineteenth century! And in Joseph Kahn's museum, it remained on display all the way up to 1873, when Mr. Colette prosecuted and won the case against the institution, ruling it obscene and closing it down. Interestingly, this happened in the exact same year as the first victim of the Thames Torso series fell prey to a hideous killer who did things to his victims that were—supposedly—beyond comprehension.

In fact, they were never any such thing. The models with removable abdominal lids and faces were quite common features in the wax museums, and it was the common working man's pastime to visit them. The wax models, and the wax models alone, supplied these features for educational purposes. And although Joseph Kahn's museum was the first one in the process of being shut down, it took many years for these institutions to disappear.

The important thing to note about the abdominal and facial lids of the wax figures is that there was no other context in society where these kinds of things were on display for a killer to see and learn from. Summing up why these nightmarish inclusions were present in our two murder series is therefore easy enough to do, once we know which book to read from. It's when we get hold of that book that we can see that the Ripper and Thames Torso murders always shared a common heart—a heart of wax.

Let's now turn to the third and final bridge I will outline. This time we will not compare victims from each series of murders to each other. Instead, we will take a look at a single victim from the Thames Torso series who was dumped in Ripper territory.

BRIDGE NUMBER THREE:
THE PINCHIN STREET JUNCTION

There are three main elements involved in the theory put forward in this book:

—The Ripper murders
—The Thames Torso murders
—Charles Lechmere

On September 10, 1889, these three elements fused together inside a railway arch in Pinchin Street to form the third bridge spanning the gap between the two Victorian murder series.

At around 5:15 on that morning, PC William Pennett felt a foul smell as he was walking his beat in Pinchin Street, St. Georges. He was doing this particular beat for the first time, and he had been around the exact same spot perhaps twenty minutes before. The smell had not been there at that stage—it was decidedly new. At the western end of the street, a series of railway arches built in the mid-1870s supported the passing trains of the Tilbury & Southend Railway Company. In one of these arches PC Pennet found the source of the smell. It was a decomposing female torso with the arms still attached to it but with no head or legs. The victim was lying belly down with the tattered remains of a cut-up nightgown thrown away alongside it. The garment had in all probability belonged to the victim. It was torn open all the way down the front. From the neck lining to the arm openings, it was sliced open by way of a knife. The inference was that the gown had been opened up to give full and unhindered access to the body of the victim when she was lying either dead or immobilized on her back.

Pennett summoned assistance by sending a man who passed by to the adjoining beat. When searching the arches adjacent to the one with the torso in it, the PC found three men sleeping rough. He put them under arrest, but they were released soon after. None of them had heard any passing cart at the relevant period in time. Since no tracks were found of such a vehicle, the police worked from the assumption that the torso had been carried manually to where William Pennett found it. According to newspaper reports, there were imprints of sack cloth on the skin of the body, which supported that idea. Both Pennet and his superior, Inspector Charles Pinhorn, suggested that a sack had been used for the purpose of carrying the body to the vault. The nearby area was accordingly promptly searched in a 250-yard radius.

There was an initial belief on many hands that the victim in Pinchin Street was a Ripper victim. She had a fifteen-inch cut to her abdomen, running from two inches below the ensiform cartilage at the sternum all the way down to the groin. The cut did not, however, open up the abdominal cavity, although it went deeper further down on the body, opening up the vagina.

In the *Walthamstow and Leyton Guardian* of September 14, it was said that «The abdominal injuries were an imitation of what have been recorded in previous Whitechapel murders, but scarcely so fiendish in their character.» This was also the stance of the police. They reasoned that the Pinchin Street victim was not a Ripper murder but instead a Thames Torso murder, where the killer had seemingly tried to mislead the police by crudely imitating the work of the Ripper. The choice of dumping site was of course in line with that suggestion; if one imitates the Ripper's work, the wisest spot to depose the remains must be in the midst of the Ripper territory.

This solution of the police was well suited to dissolve any fears that the Ripper had returned. And there may have been a precedent. When a prostitute by the name of Rose Mylett had been found dead with ligature marks around her neck on December 20, 1888, in Clarke's Yard, Poplar, a handful of medicos including Thomas Bond concluded that it was a case of murder; it was reasoned that Mylett had been strangled. One man disagreed, and that man was someone who was not keen on the idea that the Ripper was still on the prowl. It was Sir Robert Anderson, the assistant commissioner of the Met. He claimed that Mylett's death was an accident and sent Bond to make a second examination. After that examination, Bond changed his mind and it was suggested that Mylett had fallen over in a drunken state and choked on her own stiff collar. It was perhaps not the likeliest of explanations, but it served the purpose of getting the Ripper off the stage.

Now, the Pinchin Street case was also wrenched out of the Ripper's hands, and the fact that the two murder series merged in the railway arch was proclaimed a willful act of imitation on behalf of the Thames Torso killer. In modern terms, it was believed that the Thames Torso killer had chosen to copycat the Ripper. We will soon return to how great a likelihood there can be that this suggestion was true.

The police never found any likely murder spot within the 250-yard radius they searched. If they had added another 50 yards or so, it may have been another story. The search would in that case have encompassed 147 Cable Street, to the east of Pinchin Street.

On that address, an elderly man by the name of Joseph Forsdike resided together with his wife Maria Louisa—Charles Lechmere's mother. In the 1891 census, she was listed as a horseflesh dealer. Whether she was already in that occupation in 1889 is impossible to say, but the Lechmere family as represented by Charles Lechmere's sons went on to become engaged in the horseflesh business for many years, all the way up to the mid-twentieth century. And horseflesh dealers would be quite accustomed to cutting up large chunks of horseflesh, just as they would have access to fine-toothed saws and sharp knives—the very implements used to cut up the Thames Torso victims.

Could it be that Charles Lechmere killed and cut up the Pinchin Street victim at his mother's place in Cable Street? The possibility is certainly there. Moreover, in September 1889, Joseph Forsdike was seriously ill. He suffered badly from dementia and would pass away three months later. This opens up the possibility that 147 Cable Street could have been empty for certain periods of time, if Forsdike was in hospital care accompanied by his wife.

It is an obvious possibility, but more of a tantalizing suggestion than something that offers a factual link between Charles Lechmere and Pinchin Street. However, once we take a closer look at the details, we begin to find such links.

In 1861, when Charles Lechmere's first stepfather, Thomas Cross, signed his stepson as «Charles Cross» in the census listings, he also added the address where the family lived: 13 Thomas Street. A few years later, the name Thomas Street was changed for Pinchin Street.

This establishes that the Pinchin Street victim was dumped in the exact street where Charles Lechmere grew up and spent his formative years.

And there is more! Charles Lechmere's second stepfather, Joseph Forsdike, had married his mother in 1872, with Charles Lechmere and his wife as witnesses. The newlyweds moved on to take up lodgings at 6 Splidt's Street. Splidt's Street ran north off Pinchin Street, but Splidt's Street got in the way when the new railway for the Tilbury & Southend Railway Company was to be constructed. Therefore, some of the buildings along Splidt's Street were torn down to give way to the very railway arches in one of which the Pinchin Street victim was found some fifteen years later.

As the demolition work for the new railway progressed in the mid-1870s, the couple left Splidt's Street and moved to new lodgings in 23 Pinchin Street, where they stayed until the mid-1880s.

Apparently, Pinchin Street played a pivotal role for the Lechmeres. It is the one street that is most tightly linked to the family.

So there we have it: in this, the very last case of the combined murder series that we are looking at, all the threads converge. And once again, we end up at the doorstep of the East End carman. There is seemingly no end to how the coincidences pile up when we research him and his links to the murder series.

When the 2014 documentary *The Missing Evidence—Jack the Ripper* about Charles Lechmere was shot, only the Ripper murders were touched upon. At that stage, the barrister James Scobie commented on the likelihood of Charles Lechmere being Jack the Ripper after having looked at the material: «When the coincidences add up—mount up—against a defendant, and they mount up in his case, it becomes one coincidence too many.» He went on to state about Charles Lechmere that «He's got a prima facie case to answer, which means its a case good enough to put before the jury, that suggests that he was the killer.»

This verdict was passed by James Scobie before any real work had been done on the Thames Torso connection and the many astounding similarities when it comes to the damage done to the victims in the respective series.

It was also before it was known that the final victim in that series ended up dead on the doorstep of Charles Lechmere's childhood dwellings, in a railway arch that had caused the demolition of his mother's and second step-father's lodgings when built.

The Pinchin Street junction is without a doubt of tremendous interest when it comes to linking Charles Lechmere to the combined series of murders. Once again, we are faced with a number of coincidences that are very hard to overcome. Once again, all the paths involved lead us straight to the carman's doorstep. And we are not done with Pinchin Street yet; there is one more matter to mention before we leave the sordid passage, so closely linked to Charles Lechmere, his family, and his formative years, behind.

TWO BLOODSTAINED RAGS

I mentioned in the introduction to this book that I was not going to comment on the so-called Goulston Street graffito. However, the reason why that graffito has a place in the Ripper saga is because it was accompanied, by accident or design, by what has always been considered the only existing physical clue away from the murder spots to relate to the Ripper case: a bloodstained rag.

This rag was part of the apron worn by Catherine Eddowes on the night she was murdered. The killer had cut away part of Eddowes's apron and carried the rag with him before throwing it away in the doorway of 108–119 Wentworth Model Buildings in Goulston Street, some 300 yards as the crow flies from Mitre Square where Eddowes lay dead.

Why this was done has been the subject of various interpretations. The most commonly offered explanation is that the killer wiped his feces- and blood-stained hands on the rag before discarding it; it was found soiled with these two substances.

It can be argued that 300 yards is a long stretch for wiping your hands, and so the reason for taking the rag may have been another one. Perhaps the killer cut himself as he killed and mutilated Eddowes, and used the rag as a makeshift bandage. In such a case, it would make sense if the killer waited until the blood from his wound had ceased flowing before he threw the rag away.

Adding to the conundrum is how the man who found the bloodstained rag in the doorway, PC Alfred Long, testified to the effect that the rag had not been present as he passed the doorway on his beat at around 2:20 A.M. Long was adamant about this, and it makes the whole affair very strange. The dead body of Catherine Eddowes was found at 1:44 according to PC Watkins, who was the one who made the discovery. Presumably, the rag should therefore have been dumped in Goulston Street a few minutes afterwards if the killer walked there straightaway after the murder. Instead, it was not until PC Long passed the spot at around 2:55 that he found the rag.

This means that we either have a case where Long was simply mistaken about how the rag was not in place at his earlier round, or the killer did not go directly to Goulston Street after the murder.

Whichever solution applies to this riddle, it has always been accepted that there is a good possibility that the location of the rag offers a clue to where the killer lived. And that becomes very interesting when we look at it in relation to Charles Lechmere's lodgings at 22 Doveton Street. What we find is that if we draw a straight line on the map from Mitre Square to the carman's home address, the Goulston Street doorway where the bloodstained rag was found is situated close to that line.

There is a possibility that Lechmere brought the rag and the innards taken from Eddowes along to his work at Broad Street, and that he made his way

there to wash up and perhaps tend to any cuts he might have received, before setting out for 22 Doveton Street. If this was so, it applies that a straight
line drawn from the Pickford's Broad Street station to Doveton Street also
cuts close to the place where the rag was found in Goulston Street.

Let's now move one year forward in time, to September 12, 1889, and
read a small article from the *Echo* of that day. It goes like this:

> It was reported last evening that at noon yesterday, while Police-
> constable 449 H division was patrolling this beat in Oxford-street,
> Stepney, he was accosted by a man who said he was a mason, and that
> he had discovered a portion of a woman's attire saturated with blood.
> The officer immediately proceeded to St Phillips Church, now in
> course of erection, in the above street, and beneath a plank within the
> hoarding the constable discovered a coarse apron, such as is usually
> worn by the poorer classes of the East-end. The apron had apparently
> contained human remains, as it was coated with coagulated blood.
> After taking the name and address of the mason, the officer took the
> suspicious garment to Arbour Square Police-station. Superintendent
> Arnold carefully examined the stained apron, and it was subsequently
> sent to Dr. Clarke, the assistant divisional surgeon, and Dr. Gordon
> Brown, the City police surgeon. The police, in reply to inquiries last
> night, however, disclaim any knowledge of this matter.

What we have here is another bloodstained rag, much less known than its infamous counterpart of Goulston Street, linked to the Ripper murders. And
lo and behold, the rag is once again an apron, just like the ones worn by
women from «the poorer classes of the East-end.»

And it was found on the day after the discovery of the Pinchin Street victim.

Of course, this second apron cannot be conclusively linked to the Pinchin
Street victim the way Catherine Eddowes's apron was linked to her. In the
Eddowes case, it was an easy task of fitting the two apron pieces together,
the one found in Goulston Street and the one still remaining on Eddowes's
body. This clearly established that they were two parts of the same garment.

In the Pinchin Street case, we do not have just half of the apron, but instead seemingly the whole apron. And we don't have the identity of the victim, meaning that we do not know what she wore. The similarities are nevertheless tantalizing, and bloodstained aprons would normally not line the
streets of the East End.

The conclusion that the garment seemed to have been used to transport

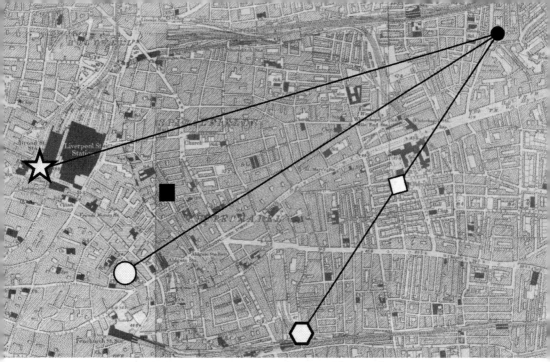

An illustration of how the two rags related to the routes as the bird flies from the murder spots to 22 Doveton Street. The circle marks the starting point in Mitre Square, the star marks an alternative starting point from the Pickford's station in Broad Street. Both the routes produced pass in close proximity to the rag in Goulston Street, the black square. The hexagon marks the starting point at the railway arch in Pinchin Street where the Pinchin Street torso was found. The route to 22 Doveton Street remarkably passes exactly through St Phillips' Church, marked by the white square, where the second rag was found on the day after the discovery of the torso in the arch.

body parts is more than anything else an unjustified effort on behalf of the reporter to make a scoop. The fact nevertheless remains that we have another bloodstained apron discarded not very far from a dumping site, and this time it may be linked not to the Ripper murders but to the Thames Torso series.

In this instance, the distance between the dumping spot and the rag is longer, around 500–600 yards. However, if we draw a straight line from the dumping site, straight over the rag discovery site, and stretch that line further into the northeast, we end up exactly where we always seem to end up—at the doorstep of Charles Lechmere's home in 22 Doveton Street. The three points are in astoundingly perfect line with one another.

And we are once again faced with the question of how many coincidences we are ready to accept before we decide that we have been served one coincidence too many.

TWO RECURRING QUESTIONS

In 2014, Blink Films made the documentary *The Missing Evidence—Jack the Ripper*, in which I presented the case for Charles Lechmere being the notorious Whitechapel killer, known as Jack the Ripper. The documentary was aired throughout much of the Western world. The reactions came thick and fast, spanning from those who said «Well, that's it, there's no further reason to research the case now that is has been solved» to disgruntled Ripperologists who made it their business to claim that the experts in the documentary had probably been fed misleading information, otherwise they would never reason that Lechmere was the likely killer.

As expected, the documentary found its way to the YouTube feed, and accordingly, thousands of comments have been passed on it. Reading through them, there are two recurring questions that need addressing.

The first question is of a general nature: If Charles Lechmere was really the killer, then why did the murders stop? Serial killers will never stop once they have started, it is claimed.

Answering this question must begin by pointing out that it is only when a serial killer is apprehended and truthfully confesses to his or her deeds that we can make a list of the murders involved. In Charles Lechmere's case this never happened, and so we cannot say that he really did stop. As long as we do not have a confession, we cannot tell when he started killing or when he stopped.

The reason for why it is generally believed that the Ripper stopped killing after Mary Kelly lies in the very specific character of the deeds. They were incredibly rare acts, involving eviscerations and far-reaching mutilation. Accordingly, when researchers look for possible Ripper murders beyond Mary Kelly, they do not take much interest in ordinary stabbings, shootings, strangulations, and so on. They are excluded from the list of possibilities, as are murders attributed to other killers.

And that is where the Thames Torso murders come into the picture.

The Victorian police decided that these murders were not the work of the Ripper but instead perpetrated by someone with a different mindset and a lot more calculation and composure. If we add to this that the Victorians knew nothing about the concept of aggressive dismemberment, we have our explanation for why they failed to make the connection. Now that the connection has been made, we can see that Lechmere's active period as a killer must be extended from a couple of months only to a large number of years. And once we realize that we are looking at a killer who was apparently able to kill in different enough manners to make the police accept that there were two sets of serial murders going on simultaneously in London, we must also accept that there may perhaps have been other murders of a different character that were the work of the same man.

Similarly, once we note that there were body parts from within the Thames Torso series that were found buried in the ground, we must open up for the possibility that other victims may have been disposed of in the same way and never found. There was no shortage of disappearances in Victorian London.

What this means is that it may well be that Charles Lechmere was killing his way throughout his life, and that numerous victims are unknown to us.

Apart from this chilling possibility, the fact of the matter is that there is no rule stating that serial killers will never stop killing. On the contrary, there is plentiful evidence to the contrary. In 2018, the FBI published a report in which seven serial killer myths were dismantled. The notion that serial killers will never stop was one of them. The report pointed out that changed circumstances in a serial killer's life are likely to also change the behavior of the killer. An increased participation in family life activities was mentioned, as well as sexual substitutions and other diversions. Two serial killers who had stopped killing were mentioned in the report, Dennis Rader, the so-called BTK killer, and Jeffrey Gorton. In Rader's case, engaging in auto-erotic activities kept him away from killing after having murdered ten people between 1974 and 1991. Jeffrey Gorton substituted his murderous activities for cross-dressing and masturbation as well as consensual sex with this wife.

It needs to be added that Gorton, although appearing in the report as a serial killer, was actually convicted for only two murders, and so he does not fill the requirement of three murders that is traditionally regarded as what makes a serial killer. But there are other examples of serial killers who stopped killing.

After the FBI report was published, another well-known case of serial murder was closed when Joseph James DeAngelo was arrested in Citrus Heights, Sacramento, US. DeAngelo was known under several monikers during his crime spree: the Visalia Ransacker, the East Area Rapist, and the Original Night Stalker. He was active in various parts of California and responsible for countless burglaries, more than fifty cases of rape, and thirteen cases of murder. His last murder was committed on May 4, 1986. After that, he seemingly disappeared from the face of the earth. Thirty-four years later he was arrested after having been found with the help of a DNA database where people could search for relatives. In June 2020, he confessed to the deeds. Aged seventy-four, he was sentenced to spend the remainder of his life in prison.

We do not expect to hear about a seventy-four-year old sexual serial killer. Not only would it be reasonable to assume that the sexuality in such a person

*The so-called BTK killer Dennis Rader, captured here with his
daughter at Christmas time, is an example of how a
serial killer can stop killing.*

had tapered off, but there would also be the issue of overall mobility and strength to consider. DeAngelo was an agile man when he terrorized California, able to fight his way out of a tight spot and to flee quickly when needed. A seventy-four-year-old sexual serial killer would find such demands a lot more challenging.

Presumably, numerous other sexual serial predators have gone through this transformation and are today living life without any murderous inclusions.

There are also examples of serial killers who have had inactive intervals of many years between victims. Although they have not actually stopped, they would have gone down in the statistics as if they had, if they were incarcerated or died before claiming their next victim. It is not uncommon that a novice serial killer has a long inactive time between the first victim and the second one. The Milwaukee cannibal Jeffrey Dahmer is one such example, killing his second victim nine years after his first. In such cases, it is as if the perpetrator harbors a hope of staying sane and lawful even after having killed someone. But when the pressure finally results in a second victim being claimed, the floodgates are opened.

Serial killers can stop. That stop can be one of many years, and it can be permanent. The myth that they cannot stop is exactly that—a myth.

The next question frequently asked after the broadcast of the Blink Films documentary was a much more case-specific one. It revolves around the Annie Chapman murder. Although many viewers had no problems accepting that Tabram, Nichols, and Kelly all could have died around the time when Lechmere may have passed en route to his work, there was witness testimony that seemingly pointed to a time of death on Chapman's behalf at around 5:30 A.M. That in its turn was one and a half hours after Lechmere would have started his work at the Broad Street branch of Pickford's.

There are two answers to this perceived enigma, one short and one long. The short answer is that although Lechmere may have begun his work at 4 A.M., he was nevertheless a carman, delivering goods all over large parts of London. There is absolutely no reason why he could not have been in Hanbury Street and committed the murder during a delivery tour at any time of the day, and so the suggested later timing does not in itself exonerate the carman.

The long answer works from the assumption that three witnesses may have been wrong, whereas the examining doctor is very unlikely to have been as wrong as has been suggested—and he had to be to make the witnesses right. As we shall see, the Victorian police seem to have worked from the assumption that the doctor was the one who got things right.

Annie Chapman was found dead in the backyard of 29 Hanbury Street by a carman named John Davis, who was residing on the third floor of the address. Davis had gotten up at 5:45 on the morning of September 8, 1888. He had had a cup of tea before going down the stairs and stepping out into the backyard. This was when he found the mutilated body of Annie Chapman lying in the recess between the stairs leading into the backyard and the fence dividing the premises from the backyard of 27 Hanbury Street. The time will have been somewhere in the vicinity of 6:00 in the morning.

Among the tenants of 27 Hanbury Street was a young carpenter by the name of Albert Cadosch. At the inquest into the death of Annie Chapman, he said that on the morning of the 8th, he had gotten out of bed at around 5:15, and some five minutes later, at 5:20, he made his way to the backyard to go to the toilet. Cadosch had recently had surgery and was a frequent visitor to the loo.

When he returned to the house, he heard a voice saying «No,» but he was not sure where the voice came from. It could have been from number 29, he said, but it could also have come from number 25. However, as soon as he had returned to the house he was forced to search out the toilet once more, a mere three or four minutes after his previous visit. And this time, instead of words being spoken, he heard what he described as «sort of a fall» against the fence dividing his backyard from that of number 29. It was, Cadosch said, «as if something touched the fence suddenly.» Asked by the coroner if he had heard anything else, the rustling of clothes for example, Albert Cadosch answered in the negative. He had heard nothing more. He had subsequently left his home to go to work, and as he did so, he had seen that the clock at Christ Church had reached exactly 5:32.

Testifying before Albert Cadosch but on the same inquest day was Elizabeth Long. She said that she had noticed a couple standing outside 29 Hanbury Street as she passed there on her way to Spitalfields Market. She supposedly overheard the man in the couple ask the woman «Will you?» whereupon she gave a «Yes» in reply. Elizabeth Long later identified the woman she had seen as Annie Chapman after having visited the morgue where Chapman lay on September 12. Long had earlier stated, though, that she did not take much notice of the couple, and so it seems the identification of Chapman in the morgue four days later rests on somewhat less than solid ground.

Just before Elizabeth Long turned into Hanbury Street on the murder morning, she had heard the brewer's clock strike 5:30, and so it would perhaps have been around 5:32 as she made her observation. If this was so, then Albert Cadosch should have seen Elizabeth Long and the couple as he left his house, but he did not do so.

Of course, adding or detracting a minute or two from Long's timing could well dissolve that particular problem. It nevertheless remains that Cadosh seems to have made his observations of what could have been the murder of Annie Chapman between ten and fifteen minutes before Elizabeth Long claimed to have seen Chapman outside the premises.

Something does not add up here. Both Cadosch and Long were adamant about their respective timings, and none of them were likely to have been wrong about them, since they would arguably have found out about that as they reached their respective destinations.

Traditionally, these two witnesses have been claimed to corroborate each other's stories. As we can see, the timings speak another language.

There may also have been another very interesting factor at play, but before we take a look at that, we need to scrutinize the story of John Richardson, the third witness involved.

Richardson did not claim to have either seen or heard Chapman. In fact, his testimony has traditionally been regarded as corroborating that of Long and Cadosch because of how Chapman was supposedly not present at the murder site when John Richardson said he was there.

John Richardson was the son of Amelia Richardson, who had a packing case business in 29 Hanbury Street. To that end, she kept tools in the basement of the premises. John Richardson lived in nearby John Street and was in the habit of checking the padlock on the door leading into the basement. Richardson had developed this habit after the basement was broken into by burglars who stole a few tools some time before the Chapman murder. After that, John Richardson visited the backyard on market mornings to check the lock.

On the murder morning, Richardson claimed to have opened the door into the backyard somewhere between 4:45 and 4:50 to do his check. The padlocked basement door was to his right as he opened the door, and the place where Chapman was found was to his left. The door was of a kind that swung back on its hinges once you let go of it, and it opened up to the left, into the yard. John Richardson said at the inquest that once he had opened the door he went on to sit down on the second of the three footsteps leading into the yard, resting his feet on the flagstones in it. He also said that if Annie Chapman had at that stage been lying to his left, only a yard or two from where he sat, he should have seen her. He added that it was still dark at the time, but starting to get light, and that he could see all over the yard.

If Chapman was not lying in the recess between the stairs and the fence at that stage, it would be in line with what Cadosch and Long implicated in their respective testimonies—that Chapman was killed after that stage, somewhere around 5:20–5:30 or thereabouts. Once we forget about the discrepancies in the timings of Cadosch and Long, it all makes for a logical sequence. But the medical expert witness, George Bagster Phillips, who examined Chapman in situ and who subsequently did the post-mortem on her, testified to quite another effect.

Phillips was alerted to the site at around 6:20 and arrived there at 6:30. The common practice back then was to feel the body for warmth in order to allow for an educated guess about the time of death. When Phillips undertook that task, he noted that apart from «a certain remaining heat» under the intestines of the body, the rest of it was cold to the touch. He also noted that rigor mortis was commencing in the limbs. Taken together with the general appearance of the body, Phillips opted for a time of death that was at the very least two hours removed from when he did the examination, but he pointed out at the inquest that the time elapsed was probably more than that. Perhaps the best description of the general appearance of the body can be found in the *Daily Telegraph* of September 14. In this report from the inquest it is pointed out that Phillips described the blood on the site as «well clotted.»

If we compare this to Catherine Eddowes, who was examined by Dr. Gordon Brown at around 2:20, we will find that there are major differences involved. Eddowes was found dead in Mitre Square at around 1:45 A.M. by PC Edward Watkins. She was in all probability observed by three men exiting a club in Duke Street around ten minutes before that time. If we work from the assumption that she died at 1:40 A.M., we have a period of forty minutes passing after her death and before Gordon Brown examined her. At that stage, the body was still «quite warm» and there was no rigor mortis to be seen. Part of the blood at the scene was clotted, while there was also fluid, blood-colored serum present at the spot. Brown's conclusion was that death had occurred within the half-hour.

It seems abundantly clear that Annie Chapman had been dead for a couple of hours when she was found. Every parameter points in that direction. No body grows cold in an hour or less; in fact, the temperature of the core normally stays unchanged during the first 30–60 minutes after death. Rigor mortis normally starts setting in after two hours, and the colder it is, the later rigor will appear. And Phillips's remark about «well clotted» blood is in line with a time of death well before the time suggested by Cadosch and Long.

How did the police look upon all this? Did they believe in Long and Cadosch? Did they trust Richardson? Let's go back in time and see what was written about it. In a report dated October 19, 1888, chief inspector Donald Swanson mentions how Long's observation is not in line with what Dr. Phillips said:

> *He was called and saw the body at 6:20 A.M. [sic] and he then gives it as his opinion that death occurred about two hours earlier, viz: 4:20 A.M. hence the evidence of Mrs. Long which appeared to be so important to the Coroner, must be looked upon with some amount of doubt, which is to be regretted.*

There is a flaw in this information: Phillips did not say that he thought that

Chapman died at 4:20. He said that she had been dead for at least two hours when he examined her at 6:30 A.M., not 6.20. This means that he was willing to accept—at a stretch—that Chapman died as late as 4:30, but his conviction was that it probably happened earlier.

Apparently, the police were none too impressed with Cadosch and Long. How about John Richardson, then? Well, the proceedings made it clear that he had told different stories. Richardson was initially interviewed by Inspector Joseph Chandler, who was the first policeman on the murder scene. Chandler was able to tell that in the initial interviews John Richardson had not claimed to have gone down the steps leading into the backyard of 29 Hanbury Street. Nor was it necessary to do so, since the padlock was visible from a stance on top of the stairs.

However, Richardson had said at the inquest that he had gone down the stairs and sat down on them, and that he had cut a piece of leather that irritated him from one of his boots. When the coroner asked Chandler about this, the inspector informed him that Richardson had said nothing about it to him.

The issue is a crucial one, since Chapman could well have been hidden from sight by the door blade, depending on where John Richardson actually was placed.

As for the cutting of the leather, when the coroner inquired into it and the knife with which the leather had been cut was fetched and displayed to the jury, it became evident that the blade would not have been sharp enough for the job. Richardson then changed his testimony and said that he had actually failed to cut the leather of the boot and had subsequently proceeded to the market where he had borrowed a knife and gotten the job done.

These discrepancies were not lost on the police. Nor did the press fail to pick up on it, and an article in the *Star* of September 13, the day after Richardson's testimony was given at the inquest, puts it into words:

> Considerable doubt is being thrown on the evidence of John Richardson, who stated that he was almost on the exact spot where the body was found at a quarter to five on Saturday morning, and no signs of the murder were then apparent. It is now beginning to be believed that the woman was brought to the backyard in Hanbury-street some time earlier.

In Swanson's previously mentioned report of October 19, we can see that the reporter for the *Star* knew what he was talking about:

If the evidence of Dr. Philips is correct as to time of death, it is difficult to understand how it was that Richardson did not see the body when he went into the yard at 4.45 A.M. but as his clothes were examined, the house searched and his statement taken in which there was not a shred of evidence, suspicion could not rest on him, although police specially directed their attention to him.

Apparently, far from believing in what Richardson told them, the police seem to have entertained suspicions against him. He was raked over the coals, and it seems obvious that this came about as a result of how his story was not compatible with the medical evidence, as presented by Dr. Phillips. And this is where we return, as promised, to the interesting factor hinted at in combination with the testimony of Albert Cadosch and Elizabeth Long.

High-profile murder cases have always attracted attention from people who want a place in the papers, and who are willing to tell untruthful stories to the police in order to achieve this. In the Ripper case, we have a large number of people who professed to being the killer, for example. Therefore, it is possible that some of the witnesses may have provided the police with false and misleading information. And there is a very good reason to believe that we actually have such a thing on record in the case of Albert Cadosch.

Let's return to what he said at the inquest, when he described the developments at around 5:20 on the morning when Annie Chapman was found dead in the backyard next to Cadosche's. We will use the wording of the *Daily Telegraph* of September 20, Cadosch having testified on the 19th:

> I live at 27, Hanbury-street, and am a carpenter. 27 is next door to 29, Hanbury-street. On Saturday, Sept. 8, I got up about a quarter past five in the morning, and went into the yard. It was then about twenty minutes past five, I should think. As I returned towards the back door I heard a voice say «No» just as I was going through the door. It was not in our yard, but I should think it came from the yard of No. 29. I, however, cannot say on which side it came from. I went indoors, but returned to the yard about three or four minutes afterwards. While coming back I heard a sort of a fall against the fence which divides my yard from that of 29. It seemed as if something touched the fence suddenly.
>
> The Coroner: Did you look to see what it was?—No.
>
> [Coroner] Had you heard any noise while you were at the end of your yard?—No.
>
> [Coroner] Any rustling of clothes?—No.

What we have is a rather vague wording. However, Albert Cadosch was much less vague on the evening of the murder day, when he gave the police his version of what had actually gone down. What he said at that stage is recorded in, for example, the *Morning Advertiser* of the 10th:

> Albert Cadosch, who lodges next door, had occasion to go into the adjoining yard at the back at 5.25, and states that he heard a conversation on the other side of the palings as if between two people. He caught the word «No,» and fancied he subsequently heard a slight scuffle, with the noise of a falling against the palings, but, thinking that his neighbours might probably be out in the yard, he took no further notice, and went to his work.

An even more explicit version was in *Lloyd's Weekly* on the 9th:

> On visiting the house next door to the tragedy, 27, our representative saw Mr. Albert Cadosen, a carpenter, who resides there and works in Shoe-lane, Fleet-street. He says: I was not very well in the night and I went out into the backyard about 25 minutes past five. It was just getting daylight, and as I passed to the back of the yard I heard a sound as of two people up in the corner of the next yard. On coming back I heard some words which I did not catch, but I heard a woman say «No.» Then I heard a kind of scuffle going on, and someone seemed to fall heavily on to the ground against the wooden partition which divided the yard, at the spot where the body was afterwards found. As I thought it was some of the people belonging to the house, I passed into my own room, and took no further notice.

Lo and behold, Cadosch had heard two people engaged in conversation, and he was in no doubt at all where they had been: in the backyard of 29 Hanbury Street. He heard somebody saying «No,» and then a scuffle ensued, indicating that Cadosch had heard Chapman fighting for her life. After the scuffle, a noise of somebody falling against the fence and landing heavily on the ground had been picked up on by Albert Cadosch, at the exact spot where Chapman was later found. Cadosch had reasoned that it would have been something to do with his neighbors and he had gone on his way.

Here it seems that Cadosch was very eager to convince the police that he had overheard the murder in great detail. Then, eleven days later and at the inquest, his story became totally diluted. Cadosch suddenly could not say from which yard the «No» came; he did not say that it was a woman who spoke it and he had nothing at all to say about any scuffle or heavy fall to the ground. The sound against the fence was merely one of someone or something «suddenly touching» it, and the events are no longer one unbroken sequence. Instead, Cadosch speaks of having made two visits to the loo, picking up the «No» on the first trip and hearing the sound against the fence on the second. And nothing more.

How shall we understand all this? And how does it imply that Cadosch may not have been truthful? Well, it all boils down to how Richardson's testimony was treated. As we have seen, Richardson was raked over the coals. The police obviously distrusted him, and the reason they would have had for doing so was, in all likelihood, Dr. Phillips's estimated time of death. The police reasoned, as per the *Star* of the 13th, that Richardson would seemingly not have been correct in stating that Chapman was not in the backyard at 4:45: «It is now beginning to be believed that the woman was brought to the backyard in Hanbury-street some time earlier.»

John Richardson testified on September 12. The day after his testimony was given, the papers reported on how the police did not believe him. We know from Swanson's reports that the outcome of the police's disbelief was that Richardson's house was searched and his clothes were examined. In short, he was looked upon with great suspicion and apparently investigated as a possible suspect. And all this seems to have been triggered by the fact that Dr. Phillips's estimated time of death for Chapman made Richardson's testimony questionable.

Albert Cadosch would have been able to take note of this development via the papers. And he had told the police a story that was much worse in terms of the timings. He had added a further 35 minutes to Richardson's 4:45 timing, and so it can easily be understood that Cadosch would risk getting in even more trouble than Richardson. If we make the presumption that Albert Cadosch's story was not true but instead the result of a craving for attention, as is so often the case in connection with high-profile murder cases, then he would at this stage need to trim the edges off his story. He needed to be open to the possibility that it was not Chapman and the killer he had heard, and so he suddenly didn't know where the «No» had come from; he had not heard any scuffle and there was never any unbroken chain of events with a conversation, a «No,» a scuffle, and a heavy fall against the fence and to the ground at the exact spot where Chapman was later found. The fall was diluted into what could have been a cat jumping at the fence.

This looks like a prime example of someone who wants to secure himself a role in the drama on false grounds, and who, on realizing that the police know that his story is untrue, changes his story when under oath.

We can now begin to see a very different picture from the one suggested by the three witnesses. The more probable scenario seems to be one that is perfectly in line with all the other Ripper murders, where the killer worked under the cover of darkness, striking in the early morning hours.

This was also a sentiment that found its way into the Home Office files, where we may read that «*doubtful evidence points to some thing between 5:30 and 6:—but medical evidence says about 4 o'cl.*»

And there we have it, the long answer to the question why the Annie Chapman murder was not in line with Charles Lechmere's early morning trek: it seems it was, after all.

TWO COINCIDING COPYCATS?

An explanation sometimes offered for why the damage done to the victims is so similar in many ways when comparing the Ripper series and the Thames Torso series is that there could have been copycatting involved.

When we examine the likelihood of such a thing, we must start by once again emphasizing that serial killers who eviscerate are extremely rare creatures. As I have stated before, I have been unable to find any example of two such characters working alongside each other geographically and chronologically—unless there were two such serialists active in late Victorian London.

This in itself is a very important point to make: the rarity of these killers makes it far more likely that there was just the one killer involved in the two series. This fact of course points away from any copycatting.

However, a murder series like the Ripper outrage was something that would have made a tremendous impact on Victorian society, and that will to an extent have paved the way for other killers than the Ripper trying their hand at evisceration murders, or something that looked like evisceration efforts. There is also a practical side to this: anybody in the area and time who had decided to do away with any woman for any reason could perhaps be able to get away scot-free by passing the deed off as a Ripper murder.

In fact, there are at least two murders that are of great interest to look at in this context. They are the murders of Jane Beadmore in Birtley on September 22, 1888, and of Ellen Bury in Dundee on February 4, 1889.

Let's begin with the former one.

Birtley was a small mining village in the northern part of England. On the morning of September 23, 1888, roughly a fortnight after the murder of Annie Chapman in the backyard of 29 Hanbury Street, a young woman by the name of Jane Beadmore was found dead in a ditch alongside a small road by a boilersmith on his way to work. Jane Beadmore's clothes were disarranged and her lower body exposed to the elements. She had suffered a number of knife wounds to the body; there was one wound on the right side of her face, one cut behind her left ear, and, not least, her abdomen had been cut in a fashion that made her intestines protrude from the wound.

It didn't take the press long to start speculating about how Jack the Ripper could be responsible for the murder. In fact, Dr. George Bagster Phillips was sent north together with a police inspector to see if there was any substance to the rumors. After having examined Jane Beadmore, it was concluded that there was not. Phillips pointed to how it was instead a case of clumsy butchery, distinguishing it from what he had observed in the Chapman murder two weeks earlier.

If there was anybody who was not satisfied that Phillips was correct, their misgivings were rebutted when the real killer was subsequently apprehended. The culprit was Beadmore's boyfriend, William Waddell. It turned out that the two had quarreled and Waddell had killed Beadmore in a drunken stupor. He confessed to the murder and was duly executed in Durham Gaol on December 19, 1888.

When asked about why he had killed Beadmore, he blamed it on how he had been so drunk that he lost his mind. Interestingly, he also said that he had read about the Ripper murders and that his mind must have been deranged. It seems entirely plausible that Waddell harbored a hope that what he had done would be attributed to the Ripper. As we have seen, he was not all that far off the mark.

The next murder we will look at in this respect is that of Ellen Bury, some four months after the Jane Beadmore case. When it comes to the Ellen Bury case, the man who professed to have killed her, her husband William Henry Bury, is actually himself a much-favored Ripper suspect today.

The marriage between William and Ellen Bury was filled with rows and abuse. Ellen was a former barmaid and prostitute and Henry was a sawdust collector working for a man called James Martin. In fact, Henry had found Ellen working in an East End brothel run by Martin. The couple were married in April 1888.

On January 19, 1889, the Burys moved to Dundee. Three weeks later, William Bury walked into a Dundee police station and said that he was Jack the Ripper. To substantiate his claim, he told the police that if they visited his house in Princes Street, they would find the cut-up body of a woman in a box there.

William Henry Bury, often regarded as a Ripper suspect,
was probably instead emulating the Ripper murders
when killing his wife in Dundee in 1889.

The woman was of course Ellen Bury, and when the police found her, they also found that she had been strangled to death and that there was a four-and-a-half-inch-long gash in her abdomen, through which much of her intestines were protruding. There were nine other knife wounds to Ellen Bury's body, and one of her legs had been broken and the other smashed to allow for her body to fit inside the packing-case in which it was found.

Nearly a week had passed after the murder of Ellen Bury before the body was found. It transpired that William Bury had spent some of that time drinking with a friend. During the drinking sessions, Jack the Ripper had been repeatedly discussed between the two.

Once again, the London detectives tried to ascertain whether the Ripper had at long last been found. Once again, they came away from their task believing this was not so.

Although William Bury had initially confessed to the murder of his wife, he later had a change of heart and claimed to be innocent, perhaps hoping to have the murder attributed to the Whitechapel killer. If so, the strategy failed. Bury was convicted of the murder of his wife and sentenced to death.

William Bury was hanged on April 24, 1889. It has been claimed that the hangman, James Berry, tried to coax a confession out of him on the scaffold, but no such confession was given. What remains is the impression of another murder where the Ripper was certainly involved—but not as the killer himself. When comparing William Bury's deed to those of the Ripper, we are effectively comparing the commonest murder type of them all, the domestic murder, to what is arguably the rarest murder type in existence—that of killing complete strangers.

What these murders tell us is that we cannot categorically rule out that either the Ripper or the Thames Torso killer imitated the other killer's work. We can, however, point out how it is unlikely in the extreme for two reasons:

To begin with, the Beadmore case as well as the Bury case were domestic cases and single murders, not parts of any murder series. In 2019, it was estimated that fewer than one per cent of the murders in US were part of serial murder strings. Serial killing involves taking the lives of three or more people. This of course means that although there may be the odd case of copycat murders involved in the statistics, it is infinitely more likely that such cases will be one-offs and not parts of serial murder strings.

There is another, even more decisive reason not to believe in any copycatting having been involved in our specific two murder series: If there had been such a factor at work, then there would have been copycatting going on in both directions!

The Rainham case of 1887 was the first case in the two series where the abdomen was cut all the way between the sternum and the groin. So when the Ripper did the same more than a year afterwards, he presumably copycatted the Thames Torso killer.

When Annie Chapman was killed in the backyard of 29 Hanbury Street in September 1888, this was the first time that the abdominal wall was cut away in large panes. Nine months later, the Thames Torso killer supposedly copycatted that particular element from the Ripper when he cut up Elizabeth Jackson's body.

This means that the suggestion of copycatting goes from mildly ridiculous to completely improbable.

Adding to these problems, it can be pointed out that the contemporary papers didn't even write in their articles that the Rainham victim had had her abdomen cut open from the sternum all the way down to the groin. Since the body was subsequently dismembered, this was not directly evident and commented upon. It is only when one reads the first part of Charles Hebbert's «An Exercise in Forensic Medicine» that it becomes clear. Hebbert describes how the torso was divided into three pieces, and then adds how «An

incision had evidently been made from the ensiform cartilage to the pubes,»
meaning that this cut preceded the division of the body into parts.

It is hard to believe that Jack the Ripper read essays meant for the education of medical students. Moreover, the essay was written only after the
Whitehall Torso case, meaning that it was not available for reading when
Polly Nichols and Annie Chapman had their abdomens cut open in a fashion similar to the Rainham victim.

All in all, we may with well-grounded confidence drop any idea of either
of these two serial killers copycatting the other one.

THE SUSPECTS

GETTING IT WRONG 2: FREDERICK ABBERLINE—
*«You've got Jack the Ripper
at last.»*

Frederick Abberline was the street-smart Metropolitan Police inspector on whose shoulders the main hope of getting the Ripper caught rested back in 1888. The phrase «You've got Jack the Ripper at last» was allegedly uttered by Abberline in a conversation with Inspector George Godley, when the latter secured the arrest of George Chapman in 1902. Whether Abberline actually did congratulate Godley in this manner or not is an open question, but since the wording has a useful bearing on the suspect discussion, I will assume that he did so.

George Chapman was born Severin Antoniovich Klosowski in Poland in 1865. He was a serial killer who disposed of three successive mistresses by poisoning them slowly. He was convicted of the murders and hanged in Wandsworth Prison in April 1903. We shall return to him later on in this chapter, but we will begin by taking a look at a number of other suspects in the Ripper case.

More than three hundred suspects have been named over the years, and the identifications have typically rested on the assumption that the Ripper murders were a series of five murders encompassing a period in time of a mere ten weeks. Once we find out that the Thames Torso murders were part of the series, we get a radical change in chronology. Moreover, we can put an end to the discussion whether the killer was organized or disorganized, an old distinction that has somehow survived into the present day. Very clearly, the combined killer suggested by the evidence was quite able to plan his deeds and to take precautions so as not to be caught. In other words, he was a highly organized killer who managed to stay clear of the police for a minimum of sixteen years of murderous activities, and quite possibly more than that.

Using this angle, let's see what happens to the suspects who have topped the popularity lists over the years. We will begin by looking at the two top contenders, Aaron Kosminski and Montague John Druitt.

Frederick Abberline was brought into the investigation with the hope that his experience from the streets would crack the case.

Over the last decades, Aaron Kosminski has undeniably been the suspect with the largest group of followers. He was seemingly pointed out by Sir Robert Anderson, the contemporary assistant commissioner of the Metropolitan Police. During the Ripper scare, Anderson claimed that the police did not know who the killer was, but along the road leading into the twentieth century, he had a change of heart. In his memoirs, *The Lighter Side of My Official Life* (1910), Anderson wrote that the police had found out that a Jew was the killer by having him pointed out by a witness. In a copy of the book given to Chief Inspector Donald Swanson—the man Anderson had appointed as the spider of the Ripper hunt web—Swanson named the accused man «Kosminski» in an annotation in the margin of the book. Only the surname was used.

From Anderson's successor, Sir Melville MacNaghten, we know that the name Kosminski was already connected to the Ripper murders as early as 1894. MacNaghten mentions him in his memoranda, as one out of three men deemed likelier to have been the Ripper than Thomas Cutbush. Cutbush had at the time been pointed out as a possible Ripper by the *Sun* newspaper. In the so-called MacNaghten memoranda, Kosminski is mentioned together with Montague John Druitt and Michael Ostrog as being higher up on the Met's, or at least MacNaghten's, list of possible suspects. Once again we get only the surname Kosminski, although the other two men pointed out by MacNaghten are presented by their full names.

The common conception has always been that the man Anderson, Swanson, and MacNaghten mentioned was Aaron Kosminski, a Polish Jew who ended up in a number of asylums as a result of having developed schizophrenia. His first incarceration took place in 1890, when he was committed to Mile End workhouse. After Mile End, he was sent on to Colney Hatch Lunatic Asylum, and from there to Leavesden Asylum, where he died in March 1919.

There were always a lot of problems with Anderson's identification. The name of the identifier was not given, but this witness was alleged to be a Jew, just like Aaron Kosminski. Anderson claimed that the shared religion was the reason why the witness declined to give evidence against the suspect in a court of law. The implication was that this evidence would see the suspect hanged, and that the witness did not want to accept responsibility for such a thing. The conclusion must be that what the witness had seen was enough for passing a death sentence.

Just as the name of the witness was not given, neither the time nor the place for his alleged observation was presented. Whatever it was the witness had supposedly seen or heard has never been found out. Although there has been a hunt for the information for many decades, it has turned up nothing conclusive at all. This alleged witness identification has nevertheless formed not only the foundation but also practically all the brickwork involved in building what is most likely a castle in the air.

The first signs of a police interest in Kosminski date back to 1892, meaning that the information on which Melville MacNaghten built his presentation of Kosminski as a candidate for the Ripper's role must have come from the investigation under the rule of Robert Anderson. What is baffling about this is that MacNaghten actually ranks Montague John Druitt as number one of the three suspects, writing that «He was sexually insane and from private information I have little doubt but that his own family believed him to have been the murderer.»

Accepting that Melville MacNaghten drew upon the investigation into Kosminski made under Anderson to present him as one of the three suspects in his memoranda, one can only conclude that MacNaghten did not think that the material pointing in Kosminski's direction was very damning. Furthermore, the allegations made against the three men in the MacNaghten memoranda seems in a number of instances to lack factual anchor points. In the memoranda, they are portrayed like this:

1) A Mr M. J. Druitt, said to be a doctor & of good family—who disappeared at the time of the Miller's Court murder, & whose body (which was said to have been upwards of a month in the water) was found in the Thames on 31st December—or about 7 weeks after that murder. He was sexually insane and from private information I have little doubt but that his own family believed him to have been the murderer.

(2) Kosminski—a Polish Jew—& resident in Whitechapel. This man became insane owing to many years indulgence in solitary vices. He had a great hatred of women, specially of the prostitute class, & had strong homicidal tendencies: he was removed to a lunatic asylum about March 1889. There were many circumstances connected with this man which made him a strong «suspect».

(3) Michael Ostrog, a Russian doctor, and a convict, who was subsequently detained in a lunatic asylum as a homicidal maniac. This man's antecedents were of the worst possible type, and his whereabouts at the time of the murders could never be ascertained.

To begin with, MacNaghten misidentifies the occupation of his own preferred suspect, Montague John Druitt. He is claimed to have been a doctor, while in fact he was a barrister. It is also claimed that Druitt was «sexually insane,» and there has never been any evidence to match that accusation. Montague John Druitt worked for some seven years as a schoolteacher in a boarding school in Blackheath, and was dismissed for unknown reasons in November 1888. It has been suggested that he could have been dismissed for having had homosexual affairs with the schoolboys, but there is not a shred of evidence to support the accusation. If this was so, however, it could well have given rise to the accusations of «sexual insanity.»

On December 31, 1888, Montague John Druitt was found floating in the Thames. He had drowned himself and left a note where he wrote: «Since Friday I felt that I was going to be like mother, and the best thing for me was to die.» Druitt's mother had been incarcerated in July 1888 at an asylum, suffering from severe depression.

One of the key points in the accusation against Montague Druitt is that his suicide coincides roughly with the murder of Mary Kelly. Melville Mac-Naghten reasoned that the killer's mind would have given way after the horrendous excesses linked to the Kelly murder.

In his pockets when he drowned himself, Druitt had a train ticket dated December 1, and so we may conclude that Druitt was still alive for at least three weeks after Kelly was murdered. And just as it can be argued that Druitt killed himself for having burned out mentally after the Kelly murder, it can of course likewise be reasoned that whatever the reason for his dismissal from the boarding school was, it was perhaps shameful enough for him to take his own life.

What cannot be reasoned, however, is that it would be likely for Montague John Druitt to have killed the 1873 Thames Torso victim. Druitt was born in 1857, and so he was a mere sixteen years at the time of this murder. And of course, when Elizabeth Jackson and the Pinchin Street victim were killed, Druitt was himself long dead.

How about Aaron Kosminski, then? He was still alive and free in 1889. Could he be the killer? And do we even know that he was Anderson's suspect? Some students of the case actually believe that since Kosminski was only mentioned by his surname by Anderson, Swanson, and MacNaghten, it may be that the killer was somebody else carrying the name Kosminski. However, no other Kosminski has ever surfaced to shoulder that responsibility.

Once we scrutinize Aaron Kosminski, we find that he presents a candidacy that fails to fill the shoes of a combined Ripper and Torso killer. He was only eight years old in 1873, and he was still in Poland at that time. That effectively puts an end to his candidacy.

Having ruled out Druitt and Kosminski, let's take a look at another suspect named by the contemporary police, the American quack doctor Francis Tumblety.

Tumblety was brought out of the shadows by Stewart Evans and Paul Gainey in 1995 in their book *The Lodger*. We know there was contemporary suspicion against him by way of the so-called Littlechild letter, where Chief Inspector John George Littlechild in 1913 responded to a letter from the journalist G. R. Sims. In Sims's letter, apparently a Dr. D was mentioned, and since Sims had written about how a «doctor» had been fished out of the Thames in late 1888, a reasonable conclusion must be that Sims was referring to Montague John Druitt. And just as MacNaghten did, Sims also made the mistake of believing Druitt was a doctor and not a barrister.

However, in his response to Sims, Littlechild claimed that he had never heard of any Dr. D, but instead of a Dr. T, a man Littlechild claims was a likely suspect in the Ripper case. Other inclusions in the Littlechild letter clarifies that Dr. T was Francis Tumblety. Let's look at his candidacy for the combined role of the Ripper and the Thames Torso killer.

Tumblety fled Britain never to return in connection with the Kelly murder, and so he cannot have been the combined killer since he was not in London when the Liz Jackson murder and the Pinchin Street murder occurred, both in 1889. Furthermore, when the 1873 torso murder occurred in London, Tumblety was living in America. He was fined $750 for having spread obscene circulars and books in Rochester, New York, in September of that year, the very month when the parts from the 1873 victim were fished out of the Thames. Furthermore, Tumblety was a homosexual, and homosexual serial killers typically tend to victimize people of their own gender.

The inference is exceedingly clear. Francis Tumblety is not the man we are looking for.

We are now running thin on contemporary suspects. Author Tom Wescott has suggested that a career criminal by the name of Charles Le Grand belonged to this group. He is the next name to check out on our list.

Charles Le Grand caught the eye of the London police mainly as a blackmailer. Incredibly, Le Grand posed as a private detective during the Ripper scare, and played a part in the Elizabeth Stride murder inquiry together with his associate J. W. Batchelor. The two took it upon themselves to interview witnesses in the case, and their «discoveries» were written about in the newspapers. Having been born approximately in 1853, Le Grand could be seen as a possible contender for the 1873 torso murder. But in June 1889, he was charged and convicted of blackmailing a Harley Street surgeon, and sentenced to a two-year prison term. That means that he was behind bars when the Pinchin Street victim was killed and dumped in the second week of September of that year. And there ends the aspirations to Ripper and Thames Torso killer fame on his behalf.

This leaves us with only one man who can be said to have attracted the attention of the contemporary police, although they seemingly ruled him out at the time: William Henry Bury.

Bury killed his wife and cut her abdomen open in Dundee in early 1889. He himself claimed that he was Jack the Ripper or «a Jack the Ripper» or something to that effect. That was enough for the London police to take interest in him, since he had a past in London's East End. After having looked into the matter, though, the police decided against him being Jack the Rip-

Poisoner and serial killer George Chapman with his mistress
Bessie Taylor, poisoned to death in 1901.

per, for reasons undisclosed. Bury was sentenced to death for the murder of his wife and was executed by hangman James Berry in Dundee on April 24, 1889. The date prevents him from having been the killer of Elizabeth Jackson and the Pinchin Street victim, and so he can be discarded together with the other contemporary suspects. Furthermore, at the time of the 1873 torso murder, he would have been a mere fourteen years old, as he was born in May 1859. Bury is therefore not our man.

These are the suspects to whom most hope of having identified the Ripper correctly has always clung. If, as clearly suggested by the evidence, the Ripper and the Torso killer were one and the same man, neither of them could possibly have been that man.

A staggering portion of the rest of the suspects suggested over the years cannot be proven to have been anywhere near London—or even Britain—at the relevant time. Many are outright ridiculous. A good many have been accused simply because they had criminal records involving violence. Their cases have been made the wrong way around, by looking for violent men and then pinning the murders on them, regardless of whether they can be tied to the actual murder cases in any shape or form.

A popular category was always the celebrities—they are quite likely to sell books, and so they have come thick and fast: Lewis Carroll, the Duke of Clarence, Michael Maybrick, Vincent Van Gogh, and Walter Sickert are some of the many proposed Ripper suspects in this group.

Better cases have been made for other suspects like Jacob Levy, James Kelly, Joseph Barnett, and a number of other contenders. The main problem is that the links that involve them in the actual Ripper case are generally very weak, and some, such as Kelly and Barnett, fall away when we include the torso murders into the Ripper's tally.

In a sense, Frederick Abberline was to be congratulated for making the guess that George Chapman was not only a poisoner but also Jack the Ripper. Chapman was actually a proven serial killer, and serial killers were rare back in 1888. Since Abberline was aware that Jack the Ripper was also a serial killer, it seemingly made sense to him that the two were one and the same. Abberline may—wisely—have reasoned that it would be very unexpected for two serial killers to be on the loose in the same general Whitechapel area at times that roughly corresponded with each other.

The reasoning is very good on a general level, but not on a more specific one. The gap between poisoning women and cutting them to shreds by way of a knife and retrieving organs from them is a very large one. The transformation would also have run in the wrong direction. Much as it can possibly be reasoned that a poisoner can grow demented and develop a taste for cuttings and eviscerations, it sounds less likely that it could be the other way around: reasoning that a killer with an obvious interest in taking apart women by way of a knife would instead opt for poisoning them sounds very far-fetched.

A possible exception to this rule could be a killer like Peter Kürten, a sadistic killer dubbed the Monster of Düsseldorf in the late 1920s. Kürten was very versatile in his ways of taking people's lives. He switched between a pair of scissors, a knife, a hammer, and strangulation, and he had according to his own confessions set out killing as a mere boy by drowning a friend during swimming. When caught, he told the police about various morbid fantasies he had, one of which was mass poisoning. Then again, he also fantasized about other ways of killing people in large numbers, but at the end of the day his own killings were all strictly physical one-on-one matters.

It is one thing to fantasize about mass killings and quite another one to really do it.

There has actually been a book written that suggests George Chapman as the combined Ripper and Thames Torso killer. In 2002, R. Michael Gordon released his *The Thames Torso Murders of Victorian London*. In it, he awards the sinister double role to Chapman. In order to be able to do so, Gordon trades the 1873 Thames Torso murder away for the Salamanca Place torso of 1902. This torso provided Gordon with the obvious advantage of being found on the southern side of the Thames at a time when Chapman had moved there, a mile or so from the dumping spot. But it soon becomes clear to anybody who reads about the remains that they were distinctly different from what was on display in the other murders of the series; they were crudely cut, with no skill at all. They had been dumped in a pile after having been cut up with what would have been a coarse carpenter's saw and thereafter boiled and roasted. There was no sign whatsoever of any anatomical insights.

This was not the work of the combined Ripper and Thames Torso killer. It was instead a prime example of what an ordinary dismemberment looks like: crude and sloppy.

The apparent flaw when it comes to George Chapman's viability as the Ripper lies in how he could not possibly have committed the 1873 torso murder, a murder that contrary to the Salamanca Place murder bore all the typical traits of the Thames Torso killer. In 1873, Chapman was only eight years old, and still living in Poland.

If we were to disregard this fact and allow for Chapman to stay on the suspect list, we may contemplate the remarkable fact that not only Abberline, but also scores of others have chosen Chapman as their main suspect for the Ripper murders. One example is author Philip Sugden, who wrote *The Complete History of Jack the Ripper*, otherwise the perhaps best fact book on the Whitechapel killer ever written.

In proposing George Chapman as the Ripper, these people have accepted the transition from an aggressive street eviscerator into a cold and calculating poisoner, while a transition from an aggressive street eviscerator to a dismemberment killer has always been regarded as much more unlikely. And this in spite of how we know that the dismemberer in question actually eviscerated at least one of his victims, while the eviscerator according to the investigating medicos seemingly tried to decapitate two or perhaps even three of his victims.

Very clearly, the idea that the Ripper and the Torso killer cannot have been one and the same is not based on the existing evidence. It is also abundantly clear that this misconception has been responsible for throwing extremely important and decisive evidence to the wind.

And it is just as obvious that one person and one person only has been identified who is head and shoulders above any other suspect: Charles Allen

Lechmere, who was twenty-three years old when the 1873 Thames Torso victim had her face meticulously cut from her skull, Anatomical Venus style, and who was thirty-nine when a copy of the same wax museum exhibition object was perfected out of a human body in Miller's Court on a cold November night fifteen years later.

There is one more thing that needs mentioning when discussing the matter of how suspects have been picked for the role of Jack the Ripper over the years. It concerns the varying levels of proven connections to the case and what that factor does to a chosen subject. Out of the three hundred suspects who have been named, the overwhelming majority have no connections to the case at all—or at least, they did not until somebody named them Ripper suspects.

A few years ago, one such suspect was named on the Internet discussion boards, namely the famous Dutch painter Vincent Van Gogh. There was never any real evidence pointing in his direction, and the suggestion didn't gain any traction. Accordingly, the debate about Van Gogh as the Ripper subsequently died out.

However, he is interesting in the sense that he represents a kind of suspect that is far from rare in the context we are dealing with. Van Gogh was born in 1853 and he died in 1890, and so he was alive at the time of the Ripper deeds. And once we know that, we can of course ask ourselves why he could not have been the killer.

Of course, we know that Van Gogh moved to Arles in early 1888, and we know that Paul Gauguin visited him there on September 17 and that he returned on October 23, staying with Van Gogh for some months, painting with him in October and visiting Montpellier with him in December.

But who's to say that Van Gogh didn't pop over the Channel in August and early September to bump off Polly Nichols and Annie Chapman? And that he did not return in late September to do the Double Event? And in November, he would perhaps have had the time to revisit the East End and do away with Mary Kelly?

It is often very hard to decisively and definitely refute these kinds of suggestions, outlandish though they of course are. The truth of the matter is that once we cannot prove where somebody was on the dates the Ripper victims died, we cannot prove that this somebody was not at the murder sites unless it would have been practically impossible to reach those sites for the suspect named. Of course, if the chosen suspect lived in or near the East End or if there were means to reach the East End from the suspect's lodgings, then the suggestion that he or she could be the killer becomes hard to disprove.

Much more serious suspects, such as Aaron Kosminski, Joseph Barnett, and Jacob Levy, have the added advantage of having been proven to have had easy access to the streets where the murders occurred; they could have walked there. And so they must be regarded as much better candidates. Those who suggest them can with more credibility ask the same question that was asked about Van Gogh: who's to say that they were not at the murder spots on the murder occasions?

Regardless of whether we look at the outlandish suspects or the ones higher up on the ranking list over the top contenders—and Kosminski, Barnett, and Levy are all on that list—the ones suggesting these suspects all have the advantage of not having to explain (or explain away) various details linked to their presence at the murder scenes. The reason for this is simple: none of them has ever been proven to have been anywhere near any of the murder scenes at the times of the murders, and so no probing questions can be asked about it.

Charles Lechmere is another matter altogether. He is proven to have been present at one of the murder scenes; his actions, his demeanor, and what he said about it at the ensuing inquest are recorded in quite some detail; and this all lends itself to scrutinizing him very closely. We can ask all the questions that should be asked, the questions the police refer to as questions asked in order to exonerate a person. That is how the police are supposed to work; they should not try and snare people they know have been present at a crime site. They should instead try and eliminate as many as possible from their investigations. It is only when somebody cannot be eliminated that they should contemplate elevating that somebody into a suspect.

Charles Lechmere is a clear example of somebody who cannot be ruled out. If we take, for instance, John Davis, Charles Lechmere's fellow carman who found the body of Annie Chapman, he differs from Lechmere in the sense that he found Chapman when she was already cold to the touch and long dead. At the time she died, Davis would still have been in bed, and so the police could rule him out.

But Lechmere was in place at a remove in time when Polly Nichols would go on to bleed for many a minute from her neck wound. He therefore cannot be eliminated from the investigation on that score. Nor can he be eliminated on any other score. He fits the geography, he seemingly fits the timings, he has been pointed out as having misinformed the police, and so on.

Researching him point by point, we find that there are many occasions where he actually could have been eliminated; if the blood had stopped flowing when he came upon Polly Nichols, if Robert Paul had seen or heard

Lechmere in front of himself when walking down Buck's Row, if the victims who died on what were working days had died well away from his logical morning routes, if Stride or Eddowes had been killed around 3:30–4:00 on working days, for example.

But far from eliminating him, all these factors instead lend themselves very well to making a case against Charles Lechmere. Once we look at the full picture, no realistic doubt can be entertained about him being the killer of Polly Nichols. Once we find this, and once we establish that the Ripper and the Thames Torso killer were one and the same, we have our man. He is not only a perfectly logical suspect, he is also the only realistic one ever identified.

THE PSYCHOLOGY

GETTING IT WRONG 3: SIR ROBERT ANDERSON—
*«A maniac revelling in
blood.»*

In 1892, Sir Robert Anderson was interviewed by *Cassell's Saturday Journal*. During the interview, Anderson produced the horrible photograph taken of Mary Kelly in her bed after the Ripper had killed her and cut her up. Anderson said to the reporter: «There, there is my answer to people who come with fads and theories about these murders. It is impossible to believe they were the acts of a sane man—they were those of a maniac, revelling in blood.»

Once we scrutinize these words, we can see how a schizophrenic lunatic like Aaron Kosminski would have fit Anderson's bill. The crux is, however, that a schizophrenic killer is totally unlikely to be able to have the stealth that the Ripper must have had to creep in and out of the murder sites at the correct time. Nor would a schizophrenic killer be likely to leave no traces behind whatsoever, for example by always taking the murder weapon away with himself. Murderers of this disposition tend to be killers of one person only, simply because they normally do not take any measures at all to stay uncaught.

Moreover, schizophrenics are not likely to be killers in the first place. And when and if they kill, they tend to kill people they know: family members, personal caretakers and so on.

There was always reason to believe that Jack the Ripper was in at least some ways an organized killer, to make use of the old distinction. And that reason becomes much more viable when we include the Torso murders into the tally. Here we seem to have murders committed in confined spaces, we have transports of the parts to safe dumping spots, and so on. In short, the Torso killer was always thought to be very composed and cunning, something that has distinguished him from the Ripper in many people's eyes.

The gaze of the Victorian police seems to have been fixed mainly on two categories of people: lunatics and foreigners. Preferably lunatic foreigners, providing the whole package in one and the same suspect. Queen Victoria herself supposedly claimed that the one thing that was certain about the killer was that he was not an Englishman. And the police took the advice offered frequently in the press to search the lunatic asylums for the killer.

Identifying the killer as Charles Lechmere pulls the rug from under Robert Anderson's feet. Lechmere was—on the surface of things—a useful and honest citizen, a family man with a steady job and a decent income. He did not answer to Robert Anderson's description at all. But if we turn our focus to one of the founders of the FBI profiling method, Robert Ressler, who died in 2013, he describes the typical serial killer in a wholly different manner. Ressler's description speaks of a white male in his mid- to late thirties with a stable home and family situation and a steady job. A man with a perfect façade to hide behind.

A century of committed research and insights gained into the human psyche separates Anderson and Ressler. When we study the Ripper murders in 2020, we are 132 years removed from the East End events. If we go back a further 132 years from 1888, we end up in 1756. In 1749, the Bow Street Runners saw the light of day; in 1750, the king of Dahomey had an income of 250,000 pounds from the overseas export of slaves; in 1751 the first game of cricket on American soil was played; in 1752 the first Canadian newspaper, the *Halifax Gazette*, was published; in 1753 the Jewish Naturalization Act was passed in Britain, allowing Jews to become naturalized citizens «without receiving the Sacrament of the Lord's supper»; in 1754 Anthony Henday became the first white man to reach the Canadian Rockies; in 1755 Joseph Black described his discovery of carbon dioxide and magnesium; and in 1756 the first chocolate-candy factory opened up in Germany. It was a time when bloodletting would still rule another hundred years as the universal cure for medical problems, a time when sorcery was still legally pursued in parts of Europe, when we still could not detect arsenic poisoning, and when the Spinning Jenny, the manned hot air balloon, and the steamboats were still awaiting being invented.

To some degree, this indicates to us how careful we must be about the level of insights we can expect from the 1888 police. That is not to offer criticism but instead to establish a fact without which we cannot understand what happened back then.

Even if Robert Anderson was wrong about how the killer must have been a maniac, surely the murder scenes make him right about how the killer revelled in blood? Actually, they do no such thing. If anything, it seems clear that the killer actually disliked blood. The 1873 victim had been hung up so as to drain the body of all blood before the killer cut into her flesh. The medicos testified about how every vessel was absolutely empty of blood, and

The man in charge of the Met during the Ripper hunt, Sir Robert Anderson.

that can only occur if the blood is actively removed. We also know that the killer cut the throats of the Ripper victims, and that it was suggested in the Thames Torso series that the throat was cut, leading to death by loss of blood. This could not be proven, since the heads were gone, but it was nevertheless suggested by Dr. Phillips at the inquest into the death of the Pinchin Street victim.

Of course, if you are going to cut up a body, then there will be a lot of blood unless it is drained, partially or fully, from the body beforehand. And blood is messy and adds dramatically to the risk of having your hands getting slippery in the process, so there is a practical reason to clear it away as best as you can.

There may be various reasons to get rid of the blood. In a number of cases, killers are known to have emptied their victims' bodies of blood and even washed the bodies afterwards, before displaying them to the world. One such example would be the infamous so-called Black Dahlia murder in Los Angeles back in 1947. In that case, a wannabe actor named Elizabeth Short was found in a vacant lot of the Leimert Park area of the city, bisected at the waist. The two body parts were laid out as parts of a macabre puzzle, a yard dividing them from each other. There were also mutilations to the face; the killer had cut from the angles of the mouth out toward the ears.

The body parts rested on the back, both of them, and it seems obvious that they were presented the way they were for shock value. The total lack of blood made the body look strangely mannequin-like. The neatness of the body being thoroughly washed in many ways took away the focus of a grisly and gory deed, instead representing the corpse as more or less a polished showpiece.

The killer was eager to showcase what he had done; there could be little doubt about that. But he did not revel in blood. Nor did the killer of the 1873 victim—he was instead willing to go through a lot of work to have the blood removed from the body of his victim.

Sooner or later, anyone who endorses a named suspect in the Ripper case or in the Thames Torso case—and not least if a common killer for both series is suggested—is going to be asked to explain the underlying psychology of his or her suspect. It is of course a very interesting matter, but the truth of things is that any discussion about it will never amount to anything more than speculation.

My personal view after having looked at these cases for many a decade is that no other aspect of the crimes is as hotly debated as the psychological part. I also believe that flawed psychological reasoning is what has stood in the way of clearing the case up, from the misconceptions of Victorian days all the way up to our own time. In this chapter, I will outline my own take on the psyche of the combined Ripper and Torso killer, but I will do so after having laid down that the bulk of my reasoning is simply another example of speculation.

Although entering a discussion about the psychology of a serial killer who lived 130 years ago is always going to be a minefield, there are a number of accepted truths that can be tested against the killer I am suggesting, Charles Lechmere, and what we know about him. This is an absorbing exercise when we look in detail at what he said and did on the murder morning of August 31, 1888, and at the ensuing inquest.

We will also take a look at whether we can find any possible parallels in the annals of crime history. Are there any other killers who may have been inspired by the wax museums and acted upon it?

The discussion will always work from an acceptance that Charles Lechmere was what the evidence points to him being: the combined Ripper and Thames Torso killer.

Once we reach the end of the discussion, I will reveal what I believe to be the single most important insight to keep in mind when discussing the psychology of serial killers. It is an insight that was articulated as early as four hundred years ago, although not specifically in connection with murder. But before we go there, we must begin by looking at the basics.

By far the most discussed matter when it comes to the phenomenon of serial killings is why some of us turn into serial killers. This is in many cases difficult enough to establish even if a killer has been identified, and it is of course even harder without such an identification. There are, though, many elements on a crime scene that can potentially help to visualize the perpetrator. This is what criminal profiling is about: by looking at the victim and the crime scene, deductions are drawn and the underlying psychology of the killer is suggested. Although the actual roots of criminal profiling goes back a long time, it is generally thought of as a methodology that was developed by the FBI from the early 1970s onwards. The practice is common and continuously growing, although there is very little research confirming that it does what it sets out to do: to paint an accurate picture of the man or woman behind a crime.

From the above, it should be clear that the psychological implications of a case are not something that we are always able to read and understand. Arguably, looking at two strings of murders more than 130 years old will not facilitate things. As has been discussed before, the view of the human psyche back then was very different from our own view today. Perhaps the easiest way to go about things would be to take a look at the data that have been collected about serial killers over the years, and work from that angle. Once we do this, we find that there is one thing that is overwhelmingly common within the ranks of sexual serial killers, and that is psychopathy. The renowned American psychiatrist, Professor Michael H. Stone, established in a study from 2001 that out of 89 male sexual serial killers, 87 per cent met the Hare criteria for psychopaths. This is in line with other studies of the same thing; generally around 90 per cent of these offenders are diagnosed as psychopaths.

The so-called Hare criteria is a list of traits designed by the Canadian psychologist Robert Hare, twenty of them in all, shaped to test whether a person is a psychopath or not. Each point on the list is given a score of zero points, one point, or two points, meaning that 40 points is the maximum score. A score of 30 or over is what qualifies a person as a psychopath. Typically, non-

criminals will score around 5 points, whereas non-psychopathic criminal offenders will score around 22 points.

These are the 20 points on the list:
—glib and superficial charm
—grandiose (exaggeratedly high) estimation of self
—need for stimulation
—pathological lying
—cunning and manipulativeness
—lack of remorse or guilt
—shallow affect (superficial emotional responsiveness)
—callousness and lack of empathy
—parasitic lifestyle
—poor behavioral controls
—sexual promiscuity
—early behavior problems
—lack of realistic long-term goals
—impulsivity
—irresponsibility
—failure to accept responsibility for own actions
—many short-term marital relationships
—juvenile delinquency
—revocation of conditional release
—criminal versatility

If we couple these points with a few other observations made about psychopaths, we can see how a very interesting pattern emerges as we look at the
actions of Charles Lechmere on the morning of the Nichols murder from an
angle of guilt. One of these points is how full-blown psychopaths will not get
nervous or panic the way non-psychopaths will. Another is how a number
of them lack what is called the startle reflex; in other words, they are not
startled by unexpected sudden occurrences the way normal people are.

To clarify the effect of this, let's imagine that we are walking along a jungle
path when suddenly a jaguar leaps out of the woods and roars at us. In normal people, such a thing will set off a reflex that prepares the muscles of our
legs to run. It is a reflex, not something we need to think about; the muscle
tension process goes from spine to legs, skipping over the brain.

Not so with a full-blown psychopath. He will notice the jaguar, hear the
roar—but no reflex will make him run. If he runs, he does so on account
of having processed the situation in his brain and arrived at the conclusion
that running is the most logical thing to do.

These are matters that distinguish psychopaths from the rest of us. They are not at all as likely to panic and run as we are. There are of course various levels involved, but the crux of the matter is that a psychopath is much more likely to stay cool and undeterred even in situations of imminent threat and pressure. Many psychopaths have walked out into a rain of bullets during an armed conflict and been regarded as war heroes for it. What these people have demonstrated is, however, not true courage but instead an inability to feel fear. Courage is to face fear, but psychopaths do not sense fear as we do.

The picture of a guilty Charles Lechmere that emerges involves this very element together with numerous others from Hare's list. The callousness is extreme in anybody who kills solely to get access to another person's body. To stay put at the murder site thereafter and con a passerby, inviting him to inspect the body while prohibiting him from propping it up since it would give away the murder, is a very composed thing to do. It involves elements of pathological lying as well as a manipulativeness that is astounding. It is quite possible that Lechmere regarded it as a bit of fun, just as he may have enjoyed participating and testifying at the inquest.

The same way that Professor Stone identified 87 per cent of the perpetrators he looked at as psychopaths, he also established that around 60 per cent of them were narcissists. This correlates with the second point on the Hare list: self-aggrandizing. Many sexual serial killers are quite proud of what they do, and they feel they are much more clever and skilled than others. If we combine this with fearlessness, we can understand how a serial killer who feels that he stands to gain something from it would not mind going to a murder inquest and pulling the wool over the eyes of the coroner and jury. It would instead meet a demand for stimulation, another point on the Hare list. Some killers would enjoy it, want it, thrive on it.

The one point on the list that does not apply to Charles Lechmere is the one suggesting many short-term marital relationships. Then again, it may well be that Lechmere was a frequent user of prostitutes as so many sexual serial killers have proven to be. There are numerous examples of such killers who have enjoyed long-term marriages that were regarded as stable and good, such as Dennis Rader, Peter Kürten, and Russel Williams, to name but a few.

Moving deeper into the jungle of criminal psychology, we find that serial killers are categorized into a small number of different boxes. Researchers R. M. Holmes and J. de Burger have typified serial killers into four categories:

1. The visionary type.
2. The mission-oriented type.
3. The hedonistic type.

4. The power/control type.

The visionary type is described as responding to hallucinations or psychological visions emanating from notions of good and evil. This is the category where we find killers who «hear voices,» commanding them to kill.

The mission-oriented type of serial killer is represented by those who kill because they believe it is their calling or mission in life to do so. Typically, these killers hold a grudge against specified groups of society, such as prostitutes, homosexuals, and so on.

The hedonistic killers are divided into two sub-categories: those who kill for creature comforts and lust murderers. The second group kills for sexual gratification, and many representatives of this group will mutilate their victims sexually. Both categories of the hedonistic killer type are regarded as thrill seekers, gaining a sense of pleasure from killing.

The fourth and final group listed by Holmes and de Burger is the power/control killer group. Here, sexual elements may be present in the murders, but the primary source of the pleasure these killers are looking for is not sexuality but instead the option to exert as much power and control over another human being as possible. And of course, taking another person's life is the ultimate control of a person. Typically, these killers enjoy inflicting physical as well as psychological pain: multiple power/control killers have testified about bringing their victims to the brink of death (for example, through strangulation), only to revive them and start the process all over again.

So how do we categorize the combined Ripper and Thames Torso killer in this context? We know precious little of the psychological disposition of Charles Lechmere. But once we accept that he was the killer, we can at least study to what degree he fits the psychological bill laid down by researchers of such things.

We can see that he shares some parameters with many identified serial killers: the absent father in his formative years, the rootless existence in a squalid neighborhood, moving from home to home, for example. But many people who are dealt this hand in life grow up to become good and productive citizens. Until we find out more about the inner landscape of the carman, we are of course unable to make any deep analysis.

That leaves us with the murders. What do they imply? Actually, we can see how there are traits in them that possibly tick boxes in all four categories mentioned by Holmes and de Burger. There is nothing to say that Charles Lechmere could not have killed because he heard voices inside his head, urging him to kill. Nor is there anything that tells us that he could not have been of the mission-oriented type. On the contrary, lots and lots of students of the case have suggested that the Ripper could have been on a mission to eliminate prostitutes from society.

Could he have killed for creature comforts? This is not the likeliest of suggestions—but he did take the rings from his victims' fingers in two cases, and none of the prostitutes he killed had any money in their pockets.

Could he have killed for sexual gratification? Considering the fact that this type of killer will oftentimes mutilate the victims, the answer becomes obvious.

Finally, could he have been a power/control type of killer? This seems to be the furthest reach of them all, not least since it is obvious that Lechmere did not subject his victims to any prolonged torture. Of course, he would have had ample time with the Thames Torso victims, but there was no evidence of typical torture on their respective bodies, just as there were no such signs on the Ripper victims either.

However, once we look at how he took his victims apart and took away organs from a number of them—such as how he cut a fetus out of the uterus in the Elizabeth Jackson case and how he created an anatomical Venus out of Mary Kelly's body—it should be pointed out that as far as controlling another person goes, it is hard to imagine a more far-reaching control than turning human beings into building kits to disassemble at will.

Another factor that plays a role when it comes to the power/control type is mentioned by criminologist Scott A. Bonn on the website *Psychology Today*. Bonn points out that these types of killers do not necessarily lose interest in their victims just because they are dead, the way killers from the other three groups normally do. Instead, many of them will return to their victims to have sex with them long after the murders, simply in order to perpetuate their control over them.

Of course, Lechmere in the killer's role seems not to have had that interest. He killed swiftly and apparently without any instances whatsoever of torture. It seems his sole intention was to procure a dead body, so that he could indulge in the cutting. He did not engage in necrophilia as far as we can tell.

He may or may not have taken organs as trophies—he may equally have discarded the organs taken in relatively direct connection to the murders. We know that he left all the organs he cut out from Mary Kelly in the room in Miller's Court, with the possible exception of the heart, so he was no anatomical hoarder. We also know that he discarded the meticulously cut-away scalp and face from the 1873 torso victim, although one may have thought that it would have made a prized trophy for a serial killer with an interest in such things.

Whichever way we look at the murders included in the two series, we can easily see that they would have required a lot of callousness. Although we do not know how the Thames Torso victims were killed, we do know a fair amount about how the Ripper victims were dispatched. In itself, this speaks volumes about how the killer was likely of a psychopathic nature.

There is also the issue of how Lechmere left the bodies. Some serial killers will hide away their victims, but many will instead put them on exhibition, taking pride in what they have done. This brings us back to the element of narcissism. Was it present in how the killer left the victims?

Let's begin by taking a look at the Ripper murders. From Martha Tabram onwards, we normally have a scene with a victim who seems to have been put on display—legs spread and body exposed in a sexually inviting manner. It can be argued that the position of the body was a logical consequence of what had been done to the victim, but we have the Kelly case to refute this. Here, a pillow had been fashioned for the victim and tucked under the head, and one of the arms was laid over the opened-up abdomen.

The general impression is one of a killer who takes pride in what he does and wants to put it on display.

There were two exceptions to the rule, Polly Nichols and Elizabeth Stride. In Stride's case, it was generally accepted at the time that the killer had been disturbed and fled the scene before he was able to cut the body open. If this was so, it explains why the scene is much less aggressive than the ordinary Ripper displays.

In Nichols's case, it is another story. Although there was a great gash in the abdomen and a slit throat to put on display, Nichols was found with the clothes pulled over the wounds and stretched out on her back in a placid position. It is the one and only victim where it can be argued that the killer intentionally hid what had happened. It is also the only victim where Charles Lechmere is proven to have been present on the scene, alone with the victim for an unestablished amount of time.

How about the Thames Torso victims? In those cases we have no crime sites, we only have dumping sites. But dumping sites may well be employed by narcissistic serial killers. One such example is the case of the Hillside Stranglers, Kenneth Bianchi and Angelo Buono. In the late 1970s, they kidnapped, raped, and tortured ten women before killing them and dumping them naked in explicit positions on the hillsides surrounding Los Angeles. Very clearly, the killers wanted recognition for their work.

In the Thames Torso cases, we have dismembered bodies with parts being dumped mainly in the Thames, but also in Regent's Canal and sometimes on dry land. Specifically, body parts were dumped in the cellar vaults of the New Scotland Yard building that was under construction in central London, as well as in the garden of Percy Shelley, the son of Mary Wollstonecraft Shelley, who had written a horror novel about a man put together from body parts. These two instances alone are enough to serve as a possible indication of a wish to evoke sensation on the killer's behalf.

The suggestion becomes even more tantalizing when we add the fact that just about all the parts dumped in the Thames were subsequently found. If we work from the assumption that the killer knew from the papers and the gossip that these parts washed ashore with great regularity, then we may also conclude that he either did not care enough about the matter to weigh the parts down in connection with his next murder, or he actually wanted the parts to float ashore and be found.

Is there anything to tell us which of these two possibilities to support? Yes, there is. And to understand why, we must once more return to Pinchin Street. Out of all the Thames Torso cases, there was only one occasion when the police worked from the assumption that a victim—or part of a victim, to be more precise—had been manually carried to the site where it was dumped. That was the Pinchin Street case. In this case, sack imprints on the victim, together with the absence of anybody having heard or seen any means of transport in the vicinity at the relevant time, made the police reason that the body was manually carried to the vault where it was found. They accordingly searched the streets up to 250 yards from the dumpsite. This of course implies that if the killer had access to a place where he could kill and cut up this victims, then that place was situated in the East End, not very far from Pinchin Street. And since we know from Charles Hebbert's work that the four 1887–89 Thames Torso victims were cut up by the same man, it stands to reason that all four victims may well have been cut up in the same bolthole in the East End.

If this is true, then the fact that the body parts were regularly dumped either in central London or in the western parts of the metropolis clearly points to how the killer would not have wanted them to float ashore in the poor districts lining the easternmost parts of the Thames waterway through London. Nor did he want them to end up in the largely rural areas beyond London, and that is where at least part of them would have washed up if they were dumped in the East End. Instead, it seems that he employed a cart to take them to the central or western parts of the city, and dumped them there. The result was that the parts washed ashore along the banks of the most powerful metropolis of the time, in close proximity to the Houses of Parliament,

Peter Sutcliffe, the Yorkshire Ripper, often compared to his pre-
decessor in Victorian London, may also have shared an inte-
rest in wax museums with the Whitechapel killer.

to Westminster, and to Fleet Street, the heart and home of the British press. Small wonder, then, that it caused a sensation!

To this assumption, it needs to be added that the tidal waters of the Thames are not easily read and understood. Anybody with a specific interest in floating bundles to various points along the river would need to study its streams and eddies carefully for a very long time. The ones who were most likely to understand these matters were in all probability the lightermen of the river. Lightermen used a lighter—a flat-bottomed small barge—to trans-port various commodities on the river, and they would have been acutely aware of the many faces of it, streams, tides and all. In this context it needs to be mentioned that Charles Lechmere's father-in-law, Thomas Bay Bostock, was a lighterman on the Thames. From him, Lechmere would have been able to inform himself on the matter.

This is as far as we get when trying to answer the question why Charles Lechmere did what he did. In my view, he was a psychopathic and narcissistic serial killer who hid behind a façade of normality, more or less fitting the description of a typical serial killer according to prominent FBI profiler Robert Ressler, as outlined above. I believe Lechmere drew inspiration from the many wax museums and wax cabinets of Victorian London and replicated what he had seen there in his murders. I think he had an ability to charm people and put them at ease, and a talent for fooling people. I think his formative years, with an absent father figure and a seemingly dominating mother (who changed jobs and husbands numerous times, and who had a daughter of Charles Lechmere living with her), together with a rootless living situation where he was forced to move many times together with his mother, was something that was responsible to some degree for turning him into a killer. I believe that working in or close to the butchery trade helped desensitize him, as this line of work has a tendency to do. I sense that Charles Lechmere being two generations only away from wealth and money may have made him despise living in the squalor of the East End, perhaps choosing the prostitutes as the worst parts of the life he had to endure. I think the fact that one Thames Torso victim was found in the exact street where he had grown up had something to do with him taking revenge. I believe that taking women apart was perhaps his way of exerting the ultimate control he felt he had been denied in life. And I believe he took pride in what he did and wanted to showcase it to the world. I suspect that this factor was ultimately what lay behind his taking the murders to the open streets. If Martha Tabram was his first street victim, then it seems that he did not come prepared to cut up and eviscerate. None of the knives he used were suited to that end. One of them was too small, a mere penknife, and the other too large and inflexible, a sturdy dagger. Regardless of whether it was a spur-of-the-moment deed or a sort of test run, the deed will have shown him that it was possible to take his activities to the streets. And once he did, from Tabram on, the media interest exploded, urging him on to commit more «public» murders and to reach further in the graphic violence that ensured news coverage.

A progression is hinted at by the choice of weapons. With Tabram, he carried weapons unsuited for eviscerations; in the Nichols case, he had moved on to a moderately sharp knife with a long blade; and when he killed Annie Chapman, he carried a very sharp, thin, flexible, and long-bladed knife, perfectly suited for making clean cuts and probing deep into the body to perform organ removal. At this stage, he lived in a sort of symbiosis with the press, and that will have fed his narcissism. The fact that he did not abandon the more secluded torso murders may be explained by how he knew that these murders would always allow him to perform his cutting exactly as he chose to, with good lighting, lots of time, and no risk of getting disturbed and having to abort. One series gave the full attention of the press and the other supplied superior possibilities to do exactly what he wanted to the victims; and he may have wanted both of these benefits.

On the surface of things, one series looks very opportunistic while the other seems to speak of meticulous planning. It may well be, however, that both series involved the exact same element of a totally opportunistic choice of victim. It could well have been a matter of feeling an urge to kill and taking to the streets to look for prey. Then, once that opportunistic phase was over, the different settings dictated what happened to the victims. You either ended up as part of an elaborate, time-consuming, and precise cutting process in secluded surroundings, or as a much more rushed affair out in the open streets. In that sense, the Ripper murders would have been the light version of the Torso ones.

That is how I see it—and I may be wrong on just about every point of it. In this context, it is interesting to look at what the forensic psychologist Eric Hickey says about the classifications of serial killers. He tells us that there is always the risk that «we erroneously assume that if we stare long and intently enough at a perceived motivation we will be able to comprehend the dynamics of its etiology.» What Hickey points to is how we often fail to weigh in all the variables that result in a murder—and those variables are specific to each killer and each murder.

One can only imagine how many elements there may be in Lechmere's life that we are unaware of. It is a humbling insight, and one that cannot be denied.

There is nothing in what Lechmere did that necessarily points away from guilt. Conversely, it is only if we accept that Lechmere was the killer that his interactions with Robert Paul and PC Mizen becomes a cat-and-mouse game. Generally speaking, there is nothing wrong with engaging people to help examine a woman lying motionless in the street, just as there is nothing wrong with seeking out a policeman to report about it.

This may seem to leave us at a crossroads with no particular reason to choose one way over the other. However, as we have seen, there are a number of facts that point in the direction of Charles Lechmere being the killer. The facts are there: the covering up of the wounds in Nichols's body; the disagreement with PC Mizen about what was said; the convenient arrival of Robert Paul, seemingly supplying an alibi; the absolute correlation between the carman's logical routes and the murder spots, and so on. And this is where I fulfill my promise to reveal what I think is the most important point when we are discussing matters of psychology in serial killer cases: the facts always trump personal convictions.

While facts can dissolve convictions, convictions can never dissolve facts. The identification of Charles Lechmere as the probable killer should have been made after the Polly Nichols murder, but faulty convictions put a stop to it. Back then, it was thought that a seemingly good citizen of British descent with a family and a steady job, and who even sought out the police— not once but twice—could not plausibly be the killer.

Add to this how it was believed that all dismemberment murders were led on by either a wish to hide what had been done or by a need to make it impossible for the police to identify the victim, effectively disallowing any

Sadist, masochist, cannibal and serial killer Albert Fish, also known as the Grey Man, here portrayed with William King, the detective who caught him.

idea that dismemberment can be carried out to satisfy an urge within the killer—and we have a recipe for disaster.

Let us now take a quick look at two other cases from criminal history where wax models played a role for a serial killer. The first example is a man who earned the same moniker as the Whitechapel killer: the Yorkshire Ripper, Peter Sutcliffe.

Sutcliffe was jailed in 1981 for the murders of thirteen women and vicious attacks on seven more. Most of the victims were prostitutes, and Sutcliffe was sentenced to life imprisonment with a special recommendation from the judge that he should never be freed under any circumstances.

There were a number of similarities between the original Ripper murders and the Yorkshire ones, just as there were a number of mistakes made by the police in the hunt for Sutcliffe. He was examined on a number of occasions before the police finally realized that he was the man they were looking for.

Just like Charles Lechmere, Peter Sutcliffe lived a family life and had a steady job.

When he was at long last revealed as the Yorkshire Ripper, friends of his testified about how Peter Sutcliffe had been totally absorbed by anatomical wax models in the House of Horrors Wax Museum of Blackpool, depicting venereal diseases. He often visited the museum in company with his friends, and he would always linger at this display.

If we want to take a look at another serial killer who actually took things a step further, replicating horrors he had seen in a wax museum, we need to take a look at «The Gray Man,» Albert Fish. Fish was born in 1870 and suspected of a large number of murders, although he was only ever sentenced for one of them. He told a story of how he was once taken by a male lover to a wax exhibition where a bisection of a penis was on display. This had a great impact on Albert Fish, and in 1910 he took a young man by the name of Thomas Kedden to an old farmhouse, locked him up, and subjected him to two weeks of horrifying torture. At the end of the two weeks, he cut away half of Kedden's penis, whereupon he poured peroxide over the wound. He then left Kedden with a ten dollar bill and fled.

Whether or not these two killers were of the same ilk and mindset as Charles Lechmere is written in the stars. As we have learnt, these are not matters that are easily established. All we can say is that the wax museums and exhibitions have seemingly not only served benign educational purposes over the years.

THE SKILL

GETTING IT WRONG 4: DOCTOR GEORGE BAGSTER PHILLIPS—
*«... I think in this case there has been greater know-
ledge shown in regard to the construction of
the parts composing the spine ...»*

Criminal psychology was in its very infancy in the period we are looking at, so that shortcomings based on a lack of insight in the field are easy enough to understand. To exemplify how things went wrong, we will now turn to George Bagster Phillips, the vastly experienced and skilled H division police surgeon. We will also take a look at an angle of a question that has been hotly debated since the days of the Ripper scare: Was the killer skilled in anatomical matters, and perhaps even a surgeon? To shed light on this issue, we must turn our attention to Pinchin Street once more, more specifically to the inquest into the torso deed carrying its name.

At the second day of the inquest into the Pinchin Street deed, on September 24, 1889, we find Dr. Phillips comparing the death of the Pinchin Street victim from the Thames Torso series to that of Mary Kelly in the Ripper series. It was a question of great importance back in 1889, and the coroner, Wynne Baxter, made sure that the possibility was looked into. At this stage, a year after the so-called canonical Ripper murders, the press was much more eager to make the connection than the police were; their failure to catch the killer was an embarrassment, and it stands to reason that they did not want it prolonged.

Interestingly, as Dr. Phillips provided his testimony at the inquest, he finished off, as per the *Times* of September 25, by stating about the Pinchin Street victim: «I have no reason for thinking that the person who cut up the body had any anatomical knowledge.»

Since the remark seems strangely uncalled for, we probably have a case of Coroner Baxter asking Phillips about this element and the *Times* skipping over his question in its article. Regardless of this, we can see how, at the end of the inquest, the coroner returns to Phillips and asks him a very odd question: «I should like to ask Dr. Phillips whether there is any similarity in

*Dr. George Bagster Phillips, police surgeon of the H division
of the Met, was a hugely experienced medico.*

the cutting off of the legs in this case and the one that was severed from the
woman in Dorset-street?»

Much as the Pinchin Street victim did have her legs cut off, both of Kelly's
legs were in place as she was found. Luckily, when Phillips gave his answer,
he expanded on another comparison:

*I have not noticed any sufficient similarity to convince me it was the person
who committed both mutilations, but the division of the neck and attempt
to disarticulate the bones of the spine are very similar to that which was
effected in this case. The savagery shown by the mutilated remains in the
Dorset-street case far exceeded that shown in this case. The mutilations in
the Dorset-street case were most wanton, whereas in this case it strikes me
that they were made for the purpose of disposing of the body. I wish to say
that these are mere points that strike me without any comparative study of
the other case, except those afforded by partial notes that I have with me. I
think in this case there has been greater knowledge shown in regard to the*

construction of the parts composing the spine, and on the whole there has
been a greater knowledge shown of how to separate a joint.

We may here note how Phillips, when effectively comparing the Pinchin
Street victim to Mary Kelly, emphasizes that there is greater knowledge on behalf of the Thames Torso killer when it comes to the construction of the spine
as well as greater knowledge about how to separate a joint. Clearly, Phillips
distinguishes the Thames Torso killer from the Ripper by way of pointing to
the supposedly larger anatomical insights on behalf of the former perpetrator.

The strange thing is that at the exact same inquest, Phillips first tells us
that there is no evidence of any anatomical insights on behalf of the Pinchin
Street killer. Then, when he is asked to compare the Pinchin Street murder
to the Kelly murder, he suddenly changes his mind and tells us that there is
significantly more anatomical knowledge on behalf of the Torso killer! And
to exemplify this, he specifically speaks of the parts composing the spine
and the knowledge about how to separate a joint.

Of course, we know that no effort was made by the man who killed Kelly
to separate any joint at all, so no comparison can be made from that perspective. However, we do know that Phillips thought that an attempt to decapitate Kelly had probably been made, although the killer had failed to ac-
complish it. Therefore, this is the only separation of a body part that Phillips
can actually use for making a comparison. And the verdict he gives is that
although the Ripper and the Thames Torso killer cut in a «very similar manner» when trying to decapitate their respective victims, we may distinguish
the Thames Torso killer from the Ripper since he actually knew how to decapitate by way of knife whereas the Ripper did not.

That is fair enough—until we look at what Phillips's colleague, Dr. Charles
Hebbert, had to say about the decapitation skills of the Thames Torso killer.

Hebbert pointed out that there was no doubt that the four 1887–89
Thames Torso murders were perpetrated by the same man, because the cutting was in all respects similar within the four cases. He then went on to say
that it was even possible to trace how the killer had evolved. This was something he was able to establish by looking at how the killer gradually learned
how to sever the spine by way of a knife.

Here's how Hebbert describes this progression within the Thames Torso
killer:

In the first two cases the vertebrae had been sawn through, in the third
the sixth cervical vertebra was sawn through, but the dorsal and lum-

bar vertebrae were separated by cutting through the intervertebral substance, and in the fourth the intervertebral substance in the neck was cut, showing that the man was aware of the projecting anterior lip on the under surface of the vertebra, and suggesting that he was becoming more expert in his work, at the same time indicating that he was not necessarily a good anatomist, but rather a man accustomed to cut up bodies in somewhat large pieces.

The inference is very clear: It was not until in September 1889, in connection with the Pinchin Street murder, that the Thames Torso killer had learned how to decapitate by way of a knife. And now we can see how this has a huge impact on Phillips's comparison: in November 1888, when Kelly was killed, both series were at a stage where the killer was still unable to decapitate with a knife. Therefore, the difference in skill that makes Phillips segregate the two killers is a mere mirage. If Kelly had been killed a year later, she would most likely have ended up without a head.

If we return to Hebbert, we know that he distinguished the two series by another element: the Ripper went so far as to pluck out organs from his victims, while the Thames Torso killer did no such thing. This, at least, is what we are told by Charles Hebbert in his essay «Criminology» from 1903. The astounding thing is that we know that Hebbert himself established back in 1889 that the Thames Torso killer had cut out the uterus, heart, and lungs from Elizabeth Jackson's body!

We also have Hebbert claiming in the same essay that the Thames Torso killer showed more skill in his cutting than the Ripper did, something that should perhaps be expected, given how the Ripper deeds were typically perpetrated under pressing time and lighting conditions. In spite of this, George Bagster Phillips was very impressed by how the Ripper managed to secure the reproductive organs with «one sweep of the knife» in Annie Chapman's case, just as Dr. Brown thought that the removal of Catherine Eddowes's kidney from the front pointed to anatomical insights and skill.

Once Phillips, at the same inquest, goes from telling us that there was no anatomical insight on behalf of the Pinchin Street killer to claiming that he knew about the construction of the spine and how to separate joints, and once we have Hebbert tripping over his own findings, we can see how much effort was put into trying to interpret the various elements of the murder series in light of the psychological thinking of the day. Sadly, in the process, the facts were either disregarded or even altered to allow for this. The inevitable result was that the investigations into the murder series were deprived of the crucial information that they were undoubtedly perpetrated by the same man.

The simple truth is that the skill there was in connection with the Ripper as well as the Thames Torso deeds was one of cutting abilities. The man who perpetrated these Victorian murders was very speedy and precise with the knife, as witnessed about by Dr. Galloway in the Rainham case. From the outset, Galloway was certain that the killer had surgical skills. At the inquest, he instead opted for stating that the killer knew the construction of the human frame, but was not necessarily any anatomist. It was a sound conclusion, since what was done to the Rainham victim—and the ensuing torso victims—had nothing at all to do with surgical work. It was much more reminiscent of what an accomplished hunter or butcher would produce.

To adjust to the accepted thinking of the day is a very common thing to do. In the seventeenth century, it was an accepted truth that the sun revolved around the earth. When Galileo Galilei claimed that the earth in fact revolved around the sun, he was forced to abandon his very accurate idea and was sentenced to house arrest for the remainder of his life.

Realizing the oppressive power of «truths» accepted in the societies we live in, it is easy to forgive Phillips and Hebbert for following procedure. What is much more baffling is how today's students of the cases are still caught up in the net weaved by the Victorians. They are still claiming two different characters and mindsets on behalf of what they perceive as two different originators of the Ripper and Thames Torso murder series, although the stance is in direct conflict with the evidence. They would do well to ponder another thesis put forward by Galileo four hundred years ago, saying the exact same thing as I have tried to point to: there can never be such a thing as two truths contradicting each other.

Finally, it must be said that Phillips was not wrong as such when he said that the Thames Torso killer had shown more knowledge about the construction of the spine in Pinchin Street than the Ripper had done in Miller's Court. The problem was that Dr. Phillips failed to allow for how a killer can evolve, and it seems he did so for the simple reason that he had already decided against the possibility of a common originator of the deeds.

As a consequence of how the possibility of a common originator of the two murder series was ruled out, the Pinchin Street deed presented the investigators with the conundrum of how a victim from the Thames Torso series had been found in the Ripper heartland, with a Ripper calling card carved into the abdomen to boot.

As has been pointed out, the Victorian police chose to suggest that the

Pinchin Street deed was perpetrated by the Torso killer in an effort to emulate the Ripper murders. Why he would want to lay his latest murder in the lap of the Ripper was something they offered no reasonable explanation for. It would of course be useless as an evasive tactic, given that the Torso killer already had given away his existence by racking up a fair number of murders.

However, if we use the knowledge we have today about how a majority of the sexual serial killers are narcissists, another explanation offers itself up. Narcissists are eager to tell the world about their accomplishments and they take great pride in what they do. Could it be that a frustrated Charles Lechmere wanted to have it recognized that there was no other serial killer at work in London than himself, and that he placed his victim in Pinchin Street to make the connection obvious? And did he cut the torso from sternum to groin, graphically reproducing the Ripper calling card, to seal the deal?

As always, no certainty can be had. But such an explanation is definitely more consistent with what we know about sexual serial killers than the one the police opted for back in 1889.

ENDGAME

When looking at the case against Charles Lechmere, it must be said that as far as absolute proof goes, it does not exist today. We do not have the murder weapon(s), we have no CCTV cameras revealing the carman killing away in the East End streets, there is no DNA available that could provide a link between Charles Lechmere and the many victims who fell prey to him all those years ago. And really, those are the kind of things that amount to absolute proof. A written confession would not do so, for example—many innocent people have confessed to the vilest of crimes over the years. Similarly, no testimony would achieve status as absolute proof for the simple reason that witnesses are often given to making mistakes or outright lying, especially in high-profile cases like the Ripper enigma.

The simple truth is, therefore, that if Charles Lechmere is to be convicted in retrospect, then it must be done on circumstantial evidence only. In itself, such a thing is no obstacle to a conviction. Many cases are decided on circumstantial evidence, although when it comes to capital cases, the quality of the circumstantial evidence must clear away any reasonable doubt.

In the documentary *The Missing Evidence—Jack the Ripper* based on the case against Charles Lechmere, Queen's counsel James Scobie defined the quality of the evidence against Charles Lechmere as «the most probative, powerful material for the court to use against individual suspects.» In the years that have followed that verdict, more work has been done on Charles Lechmere, not least in connection with the Thames Torso murder series.

As has been pointed out before, one thing that clearly stood out to James Scobie was the many coincidences it would take to clear Charles Lechmere. That number has grown considerably since the documentary was shot.

The problem with these coincidences is that not just one of them or a few of them need to be accepted as coincidences or flukes to exonerate Charles Lechmere. In actual fact, each and every one of them must be accepted as coincidences or flukes before such a thing can happen. Therefore, the question becomes whether or not a suspect can be as unlucky as Charles Lechmere must have been if he was really not the killer. And this is where we can list an astounding amount of flukes or coincidences that must have followed the carman in his steps as he traversed the late Victorian East End—if he was truly innocent.

Was it a coincidence that he was found standing alone and in close proximity to the freshly killed Polly Nichols?

Was it a coincidence that he happened to end up at that precise point at a point in time when Nichols would go on to bleed for around nine minutes or possibly even more, a period of time that two forensic experts concur is considerably longer than they would have expected her to bleed?

Was the fact that Lechmere was still in Buck's Row at a point in time when he should have passed the street many minutes before if he left home as claimed, at 3:30, merely a sign of how the Eastenders had no reliable timepieces to work from?

Was it a twist of fate that governed how Polly Nichols was found stretched out on her back with her clothes covering her abdominal wounds, whereas all the other Ripper victims who had their abdomens opened up were left in positions that could be argued were staged by the killer, with the abdominal damage on very obvious display?

Was it a fluke that Robert Paul happened to arrive at the precise point in time that would supply a convenient alibi for Charles Lechmere?

Was it a mere slip of attention on behalf of Robert Paul that lay behind the fact that Paul never said he either saw or heard Charles Lechmere walking down Buck's Row a short distance in front of himself?

Was it a fluke that whereas PC Jonas Mizen noted how blood had run from the pool under Nichols's neck to the gutter, the carmen did not notice any blood at all, although they knelt by the side of Polly Nichols?

Was it merely coincidental that Charles Lechmere, who had taken Robert Paul to the body to examine it, refused to help to prop Polly Nichols up when Robert Paul suggested it?

Was it nothing but an incredible fluke that the four Whitechapel murders of Tabram, Nichols, Chapman, and Kelly all were committed along the two treks that were the logical routes from Buck's Row to the Pickford's terminal at Broad Street—a fluke that amounts to one in five million?

Was it another fluke that only the *Star* managed to get the carman's home address at the inquest?

Was it a strange coincidence only that the Pickford's carman «Charles Cross» who ran over and killed a child in 1876 was not recorded to have mentioned his address at the following inquiry—just as it seems that the carman avoided giving his address at the Nichols inquest twelve years later?

If the 1876 carman was our carman, was there nothing at all odd with how Charles Lechmere used the name «Cross» in connection with not one but two violent deaths, whereas he on all other recorded occasions used the name Lechmere in his contacts with different authorities?

Was it merely an unlucky misunderstanding when PC Jonas Mizen believed that he had been told by Charles Lechmere that another policeman awaited him in Buck's Row?

Did Charles Lechmere simply forget to tell PC Mizen that he himself was the finder of the body of Polly Nichols?

Was it a twist of fate that caused Charles Lechmere to come forward only after Robert Paul had established his presence at the murder site in the article in *Lloyd's Weekly*?

Was it a fluke that out of all the unprofessional witnesses, it seems that Charles Lechmere was the only one to arrive at the Nichols inquest in his working clothes?

Was it a coincidence that Elizabeth Stride got herself killed in Dutfields Yard, a stone's throw away from where Charles Lechmere's mother lived together with one of his daughters, in 1 Mary Ann Street?

If, as was the common view back in 1888, the same man who killed Stride was also the killer of Catherine Eddowes, was it not an odd fluke that this killer seems to have walked Charles Lechmere's old route to work from James Street to Broad Street when seeking out his second victim of the night?

Was it a cruel game of the Gods that the only two Ripper murders that did not take place along Charles Lechmere's logical routes to work also happened to take place on a Saturday night—a night when Lechmere was likely off duty?

Was it coincidental that these two murders were perpetrated at considerably earlier hours than the murders that took place along Lechmere's logical routes to work?

Was it a strange coincidence that the last of the Thames Torso victims happened to have her torso dumped in Pinchin Street—a street very much linked to the Lechmere family and the formative years of Charles Lechmere's life?

Was it a massive fluke that the Thames Torso killer also cut a number of his victims' abdomens open from sternum to groin, just as the Ripper did?

Was it a remarkable coincidence only that the Torso killer took out the uterus from Elizabeth Jackson's body, just as the Ripper had taken out the uteri from Annie Chapman, Catherine Eddowes, and Mary Kelly?

Does the fluke account cover the fact that the killer also removed the heart from Jackson's body, meaning that she was put on par with Mary Kelly in that respect?

Was it coincidental that the only identified victim in the Thames Torso series prostituted herself, just as the Ripper victims did, as per the Victorian police?

Was it an incredible fluke that there were murders in both the Ripper and the Thames Torso series that involved features that are very reminiscent of what was on display in the wax museums of the age, with body sections being turned into «lids,» covering either the abdominal contents or the facial structures?

Was it sheer coincidence that these two eviscerating serial killers should surface in the same metropolis, both of them in overlapping times and in an era when these types of crimes were practically unheard of?

Was it a simple fluke that both series involved failed attempts to decapitate by way of a knife in 1888, and that it was only in September 1889 that this was achieved with the Pinchin Street victim?

Was it an incredible coincidence that the two bloodied rags that were found in connection with the Eddowes murder and the Pinchin Street torso case were aprons—that were both found along lines drawn from the murder/dumping sites to 22 Doveton Street?

Answer any of the first twenty points with a no, and it must be accepted that Charles Lechmere was Jack the Ripper.

Answer any of the following nine points with a no, and it must be accepted that the Ripper murders and the Thames Torso murders had the same originator.

It is of course not as if coincidences and flukes do not exist. In actual fact, the very reason I am able to make my case against Charles Lechmere boils down to what must be regarded as a lucky coincidence.

On the morning of Monday, September 3, 1888, Coroner Wynne Baxter opened the second day of the inquest proceedings into the death of Polly Nichols. It was on this day that Charles Lechmere turned up and accepted the role as the true finder of Nichols's body. Two days earlier, on Saturday the 1st, PC John Neil had testified to the effect that he was the original discoverer of the dead body in Buck's Row. And as long as this was the official line, Charles Lechmere seems to have been reluctant to come forward.

However, this version of the matter was gainsaid on September 2, when Robert Paul's interview in *Lloyd's Weekly* was published. In it, as we have seen, Paul stated that as he had trekked to work on the morning of Friday, August 31, he had seen an unnamed man standing where the body was, a man who persuaded Paul to take look at the body together with him and who had subsequently disappeared from the scene.

If somebody was to suggest that this was a prime reason for the police to take a great deal of interest in that anonymous man, the suggestion would probably seem like a very good one to anyone acquainted with how proper police work is carried out today. Obviously, the police would not let something like that pass them by without investigating!

This too would probably have been how Charles Lechmere looked upon things: Paul had outed him, the cat was out of the bag, and he needed to do something about it. And there was really only one thing he could do: seek out the police and serve them a version of events that made himself look innocent and helpful.

The irony of it all is that there was at this stage a plethora of rumors about the murder, and the police were at a loss to distinguish potentially truthful stories from more imaginative concoctions. The result was that Paul's claims were refuted by the police, together with all the other stories that were doing the rounds. On September 2, in what is best described as a sort of press conference, the police commented on the matter, using PC Neil as their spokesman.

What was said was published in, for example, the *Daily News* of September 3, the very same day that Charles Lechmere reported in to the inquest on the second day of its proceedings. However, the inquest had started well before the news about how Paul's story was refuted broke. In the *Daily News*, it was worded like this:

> It is not true, says Constable Neil, who is a man of nearly 20 years' service, that he was called to the body by two men. He came upon it as he walked, and, flashing his lanthorn to examine it he was answered by the lights from two other constables at either end of the street.

Once this information was distributed in papers all over London, Charles Lechmere had already gone to the inquest, in all likelihood to quench the fire he was thinking Paul's story would have started. This is why we know about Lechmere's existence and why we can identify a large amount of circumstantial evidence pointing in his direction.

As it happens, if Lechmere had stayed away, the fire he feared would be the result of Paul's interview would likely have petered out by itself. Consequentially, Lechmere could have stayed away from the inquest and nobody would have known about him today. He would have been somebody who was mentioned in a strange story the police seemingly had been able to refute, a faceless, traceless, and nameless man.

In researching Lechmere as the killer, this is undoubtedly the single most fortunate event in the whole business. Without it, the likelihood is that the Ripper murders would have stayed forever unsolved. With it, it is a very different story.

Of course, this is a prime example of how coincidence can rule the day. It is not, however, any reason to accept that there is no limit to how many coincidences can be stacked on top of one another before the camel's back breaks. And in Charles Lechmere's case, the staggering number of coincidences and flukes that must be accepted before he can be regarded as innocent puts the case well beyond reasonable doubt.

London of today is a very different metropolis from that of the late nineteenth century. The Ripper tours visit streets and squares that are not even remotely like the streets the Ripper and the Thames Torso killer walked. People look surprised when tour guides halt them outside house façades that are in no way reminiscent of the downtrodden buildings lining the streets where late Victorian prostitution was on sale more than a century ago. Then, when they are informed that they are standing right outside where the dilapidated dwellings on 29 Hanbury Street once stood, they calm down and start listening to the Ripper saga.

Few, if any, tours do the walk northeast up to Doveton Street, still in existence although the houses on it are not the same as in the autumn of terror. Nor are they standing in the same place as the old buildings did. But this was in all probability where the combined Ripper and Thames Torso killer once lived.

Over the years, an agenda has been formed, catering to people who want to recognize the things they have read about and seen in imaginative contemporary drawings. It is all about top hats and capes, it is London fog and a ghoulish killer on the loose. That is what the crowds come for and that is what they get. An industry is an industry, and it will always weigh in supply and demand before shaping its product. And in the end, that is how the general picture of the Jack the Ripper murders and their originator has taken shape.

When a story is told over a period of many generations, it will inevitably be remolded along the process. Interesting and—not least—alluring parts will be told over and over again. And they will inevitably become refined and remodeled along the way, whereas less interesting bits and pieces will be overlooked over time. Basically, any such story will pass from truth into myth to a greater or lesser degree.

The great Swedish author Fritiof Nilsson Piraten once said, «Truth does

A painting of French impressionist Claude Monet depicting the River Thames.

not come about in the blink of an eye.» Rarely has that been more true than in the case of the Ripper tale. Untangling it and finding its roots is not an easy thing to do. In the end, it will many times come down to interpretations, and interpretations will always differ.

There are no Thames Torso killer tours. That murder series, though in many ways even more ghoulish than the Ripper murders, never offered any real competition for interest. It is by and large understandable; looking at places along the Thames where body parts once floated ashore is not a very interesting thing to do. The impact this has had on our ability to see the whole picture has been enormous.

As has been previously pointed out, more than three hundred suspects have been named in the hunt for Jack the Ripper. That amounts to roughly three suspects per year if we start counting from the year 1888. However, most of these suspects have been named in the last half-century or so. It is a huge inflation that has had severe drawbacks. One such drawback is mirrored in a number of comments on the Internet about the «Missing Evidence» documentary, expressing more or less the same sentiment:

«We will never find out for sure who did it.»

«The fact that he was never caught allows these latter day sleuths to claim almost any man of the time, could be ‹the Ripper›! Please!!!»

«… and the story keeps going on and on. Anytime it airs, new evidence, new suspects etc etc.»

The perhaps best example of this disparaging attitude is worded like this:

«Most of this is made up now to sell books and make new documentaries. They have no idea who it was.»

That is a mighty opponent to stare in the face. And the thing is, there is an absolute overload of evidence that goes to prove that this commentator is spot on. A huge number of magazines, books, and motion picture movies have been much more interested in making money than in making a case. Small wonder, then, that every new suspect is reflexively mocked and disqualified.

This is the kind of thing that has to be overcome when presenting a new suspect, and it has grown increasingly difficult to clear that hurdle as the years and suspects have passed by. Clever crime writers, acclaimed academics, fabulist writers, and ruthless researchers have all contributed their very own «solutions» to the Ripper riddle, thereby further diluting the confidence capital of the readers. With every new book the odds of somebody actually finding the real killer have risen to more and more dizzy heights.

Will those interested in criminology and the two great mysteries of Victorian London be able to take in and process that Charles Lechmere is not just another suspect pulled out of a top hat? Having been let down countless times by authors claiming to have solved the Ripper case on grounds loftier than London fog, will they be able to see the unique traction Charles Lechmere has as a suspect?

His case is not one of looking at zodiac signs. It is not a case of transforming the first letters of the streets where the victims died into some sort of code that gives away the killer's identity. It has got nothing to do with looking at old Masonic rituals and their possible influence on the case. It does not deal in getting some acclaimed contemporary celebrity on the stage. It does not work from the unlikely premise that somebody who has ended the life of his spouse in a domestic argument is a viable candidate for killing strangers out in the open East End streets. It carefully avoids putting that top hat and cape on the suspect, turning him into a deranged doctor, and it does not discuss how the royals of a monarchy are likely to turn killers of prostitutes living in squalor in the lowliest parts of their kingdom.

The reason for this is simple enough: the theory does not need the fog, the physicians, the freemasons, and the phantoms of Ripperology to make a case. Instead, it relies on proper investigative work, based on the simple truth that the ones who are proven to have been at a crime site are also the ones who need to be thoroughly investigated. And this is where sound investigative work has been left high and dry by the Victorian police and subsequent scholars of the Ripperological discipline.

Charles Lechmere should rightfully always have been the very first suspect. Instead, he became the two or three hundredth-something one, following a discouraging line of predecessors. It is not an environment in which it is easy to add another suspect, hoping to override the misgivings of the public as well as the frequently prejudiced thinking in Ripperology, implemented over more than a hundred years.

I have tried to make as clear and logical a case as possible for Charles Lechmere being not only the Whitechapel killer but also the Thames Torso killer. As I stated in the introduction, the evidence is there. From an investigative angle, the case is as close to an open-and-shut one as could possibly be hoped for when working only with circumstantial evidence in a case from the late nineteenth century.

In a sense, the case against Charles Lechmere resembles paleontology. What has been dug up from the depths of history can be regarded as bones from a skeleton. While it is obvious that the whole skeleton has not been retrieved, the parts that have been brought up to the surface clearly all belong to the same creature. And they enable us to reproduce enough of the frame to allow us to identify the beast that once walked the East End streets.

I do not assume that everybody interested in these cases will agree that Charles Lechmere was always the solution. But I know one thing: If he is not accepted as the Ripper and the Thames Torso killer, then nobody will ever be accepted as either. Because based on the case material, there can never be a better bid.

THE END

TIMAIOS PRESS

We publish thought-provoking, modern and classic
literature for those who are interested in speculative fiction and
fantasy, in the history of science, philosophy and
ideas—books for the general public, as
well as students and teachers.

Visit
www.timaiospress.com

BOOKS BY AND ABOUT:
S.T. Joshi — G.K. Chesterton — Lady Cavendish — Epicure —
Lucretius — Atomism — Francis Bacon — H.P. Lovecraft
— Camille Flammarion — Diogenes Laërtius —
Emanuel Swedenborg — Erasmus Darwin
— E.T.A. Hoffmann — Plato —
Andrew Crosse — Edgar Allan
Poe — And others.

Printed in Poland
by Amazon Fulfillment
Poland Sp. z o.o., Wrocław
11 May 2023

9bf995fb-154e-4807-8cd5-1c07c818fd7cR01